GOD'S HEART O

BOOK ONE

The WAR SONGS of GOD

" ... that I may conquer by His song ..."

—Habakkuk 3:19 CAB

JAMES M. MASSA

The WAR SONGS of GOD

Printed in the USA

ISBN: 978-0-9898216-0-5

Library of Congress Control Number: 2013914367

Prepared for Publication By

Palm Tree Publications is a Division of Palm Tree Productions
www.palmtreeproductions.com
PO BOX 122 | KELLER, TX | 76244

There are more than 60 different translations of scripture used in this work. A complete listing of all translations used is located in Appendix A. Abbreviations follow each reference to give proper credit for each version(s) of the Bible used.

TO CONTACT THE AUTHOR:

Sons of the Branch Ministries
P.O. Box 9871 | Bowling Green, KY 42101
270-777-8377 | sonsofthebranch@yahoo.com

www.SonsoftheBranch.com

DEDICATION

This book is dedicated to
Kyle and Tari Newton.
Their faith, friendship and
financial support made
this book possible.

ACKNOWLEDGEMENTS

I want to acknowledge the assistance
of four people in this work:

Mike Massa, my brother—
Thank you for your advice, encouragement,
and constant efforts to keep this work
moving along in a timely manner.

Sally Fuller, my editor—
Thank you for your skill and great suggestions
for honing and improving this book.
All mistakes are mine.

Wendy Walters, my publishing coach—
Thank you for your hard work and long hours in
order to reach our deadline ... and your gracious
patience when I kept changing things.

Sharon, my wife—
Thank you for your review of each chapter
and your invaluable prayers and ideas
for each one. I love you, Honey.

CONTENTS

PREFACE

God has an arsenal, a spiritual armory full of His spiritual weapons. These weapons of God release His glorious wrath upon the demonic hosts of hell. We are in a spiritual battle and only God's spiritual weapons will defeat our adversary. We are not at war against people. Our fight is not against flesh and blood, but against the demonic principalities and powers in high places. Only the spiritual weapons of God can be used—they *must be* used—to stop the devilish assault against the Lord, His Anointed One, and His children.

> *"The Lord has opened His armory and brought out* ***weapons to explode His wrath upon His enemies,*** *for the Lord God of Hosts has a work to do in the land of Babylon"* (Jer. 50:25 TLB/Amp emphasis mine).

> *"The Lord of Hosts is mustering the troops for battle, they come from a far country, from the end of heaven, even the Lord with the weapons of His wrath coming to lay the whole land waste"* (Isa. 13:5 NEB/JB/KJV).

Some of God's Spiritual Weapons are:

- God's War Cries
- God's War Horns
- God's War Flags
- God's War Bows
- God's War Swords
- God's War Songs
- God's War Clubs
- God's War Dances
- God's War Slingshots
- God's War Harps (Guitars & Pianos)
- God's War Drums and Cymbals
- God's War Horses

All of these weapons are found in the word of God and are at our disposal. God is handing them out to any and all who will take them.

Hear what the Lord is saying today: ***"My people listen to Me****. My nation, pay attention to Me. I will give the people My teachings, and My decisions will be like a light to all people. I will soon show what I do is right. I will soon save you. I will use My power and judge all nations.* ***All the faraway places are waiting for Me; they wait for My power to help them"*** (Isa. 51:4-5 NCV emphasis mine).

By these weapons of God we release the power of God to set people free. The nations are waiting for His power to help them. God has a plan, and He is *"on the move with the weapons of His wrath"* (Isa. 13:5 MSG).

Dive into God's war chest (that would be your Bible), pull out the riches of His glorious weapons waiting for us there. The word tells us, *"It is the glory of God to conceal a matter; but the glory of kings is to search out a matter"* (Prov. 25:2 NASB). The Message Bible translates this proverb: *"God delights in concealing things; scientists delight in discovering* things." As God's Holy Ghost scientists, we need to search out and discover His beautiful truths about His heart of war. I challenge you, "kings" search for these word weapons. Go for it!

AUTHOR'S NOTES

WARNING

DO NOT PROCEED UNTIL YOU HAVE READ THE FOLLOWING:

There are several things that are imperative for the reader to understand before delving into this study of God's holy word. I've briefly outlined them below. Please do not skip these few important words.

1. The title *God's Heart of War* series is not meant to imply that God loves war (although we all rejoice when Jesus destroys the works of the devil). What God does love are His children, and because of sin, war is necessary to set them free. The simplest definition of God's heart of war is that His heart is like the heart of an angry she-bear who has been robbed of her cubs (2 Sam.17:8 Voice). With that same heart of steadfast love, fearless compassion, and single-minded resolution, God has gone to war to win us back. This Bible series is a call to those who will join Him and equip themselves with God's arsenal in this fight.
2. This book is about spiritual warfare. Before we go into battle, we only go as the Lord leads us. One practical

truth is that a small group of believers does not take on a demonic stronghold over a nation. That level of warfare requires a larger group of believers. We match our army to the force we are coming against. Parents can intercede for their children, and churches can pray for their city, but when we move against principalities and powers on a state or national level our army needs to be larger. Just as we match our weapons to our warfare; it is wise to match the size of our army to the size and level of the adversary force we are coming against.

3. Everything in the Bible is the word of God, both the Old and the New Testaments. We need both to understand the whole counsel of God. Most of *The War Songs of God* come from the Old Testament prophecies, but there is a warning for us all to heed whenever we read the Old Testament. Paul tells us, concerning Israel: *"Their minds were made hard, stone-like; their senses were made dull. For to this day the same veil remains over them when they read the Old Covenant; so they cannot understand the truth. And this veil can be removed only by believing in Christ. But when Israel shall be converted and the heart of the nation return to the Lord, the veil is taken away"* (2 Cor.3:14 NIRV/NKJV/BBE/CJB/Dar/NLT/WYC/YLT). The warning is this: Whenever we read the Old Testament there is the same danger of a religious veil coming over our hearts and minds, just as it comes over the hearts and minds of the children of Israel. We are no better than they. We must always look at the Old Covenant with the New Covenant eyes of Jesus. We must allow Him to remove any veil of religion or works of the law as we study His word, especially the instructions and the guidance given by God in the Old Testament.

4. This is a book about songs. That is a challenge to the reader. It's like reading a book on how to play the guitar without being able to hear the guitar. It would just be a book full of musical chords. I would encourage you, as you read, to play some powerful worship music in the background. Ask the Holy Spirit to help you hear not just the words but the sounds of His war songs.
5. In this book I utilize what I call "The Combined Translations Bible" (CTB work in progress) method. Whenever I quote from the Bible, I may combine and repeat sections of a verse or verses from several different Bible translations in order to impart a more complete understanding of the scripture. For example, with Isaiah 13:3-4, we have:

   > *"I have commanded My sanctified ones, My holy ones, My sacred warriors, My special forces; I have called My mighty ones for Mine anger, (the Lord has called) His proud and confident soldiers to fight a holy war and punish those He is angry with; (God says His warriors will) rejoice in My highness, They will rejoice when I am exalted. They are eager for My triumph. They're busting with pride and passion to carry out My angry judgment. Hear the noise on the mountains! Listen, as the armies march! The Lord has brought them here to form an army for war"* (KJV/JB/MSG/GNB/NLT/NEB; words in parentheses mine).

   This rendition of these two verses comes from combining words or phrases from the King James Version (KJV), the Jerusalem Bible (JB), the Message Bible (MSG), the Good News Bible (GNB), the New Living Translation (NLT) and the New English Bible (NEB). Whenever this method is employed, the abbreviations for the specific translations will be noted parenthetically as above. Appendix A at the back of this book contains a list of all Bible translations used and their abbreviations.

6. It can be confusing to study words in the Hebrew language because when they are translated into English, many different words are used for the same Hebrew word. It is helpful to utilize a Bible study tool such as the Blue Letter Bible online at http://www.blueletterbible.org/search.cfm to assist in your studies. There are many other great sources out there. I would highly encourage you to find one.
7. I want to encourage and challenge the pastors and the worship leaders to search the Word of God for more of His Word Weapons to use against our demonic oppressors. We have only scratched the surface of the wealth of God's word.
8. When I quote from the Word of God, I take the liberty to capitalize the pronouns referring to the Godhead and I refuse to capitalize satan or lucifer. I desire to give honor only where honor is due.
9. This is a Bible Study not an exciting novel. It is about the word of God, and how we are changed as we allow the word to be made flesh in our lives. I do not write to entertain, but I hope that I encourage.

FOREWORD
BY MICHAEL MASSA

You are about to read an unusual book, as evidenced by its title. The author is my brother, and he is the real deal. He lives out in his private life with his family what he so enthusiastically writes in these pages. He loves the Lord and His word, something you will quickly recognize. Mark studies from more than 120 different translations of the Bible, and his "CTB" format is full of insights, if you will not be in a hurry.

The book's topic is unusual since most of us have never considered God singing war songs, but if you will invest a listening ear and a brave heart, your fellowship with the Lord and understanding His weapons will move into a new freedom. Mark's enthusiasm is real, but his theological conclusions are not the silly extrapolations that come from sloppy exegesis. He has diligently researched and invested years of labor and prayer to draw out these riches. If you disagree, well you may, but you cannot reject his view offhand as if it was the work of an undisciplined study. His effort is worthy of the honor of being heard.

As you read 1) Do not skip over the Bible verses, or you will miss much of the treasure the Lord has given. If this book is anything, it is first and foremost a tribute to the word of God. 2) Take your time. There is gold to gain from the Lord's heart in this project.

Our current church culture does not speak much of spiritual warfare, and we are weakened by that gap in our efforts to "make disciples." In the book you are about to read, Mark unveils many chapters in the prophetic scriptures that have been ignored or not understood for centuries. This book is a "game-changer" regarding our understanding of battle and God's weaponry. Entire sections of Isaiah and the Minor Prophets will come to life as you have never imagined. This is a trailblazer revelation, and you will be changed when you see it.

Pray before you read and ask the Lord to open the eyes and ears of your heart. You will not be disappointed. Finding gold requires diligent effort to mine it. Mark's years of mining these deep treasures in the word will reward you with new faith. Once you see his point, you will never forget it!

Mark, it is my honor to compose this simple foreword. You have labored in private for years with a burning heart to see our Master raise up His army. I KNOW He is pleased with you. You are an inspiration to me. May we both be favored like Caleb and go into the land to overcome the giants with those who will not be victims to the demonic threats in the future.

Until His enemies are made His footstool …

Michael *(your favorite brother)*

INTRODUCTION

GOD'S HEART OF WAR

When God delivered His people out of the bondage of Egypt, and Pharaoh and his army was destroyed, Moses led Israel in song and rejoicing. He declared, *"The Lord is a Warrior, a fighter; His name is Yahweh, The Almighty!"* (Ex.15:3 NRSV/WYC). The Lord God is our Divine Warrior, He is a fighter. God's heart of war is like the heart of an angry she-bear robbed of her cubs (2 Sam.17:8). God has come to win His "cubs" back. He is calling out today to all that have ears to hear, a call to become His warriors and go to war. God is delivering His people, and He is calling you to join His spiritual Army of deliverers—now.

In the natural realm a little over one percent of the population of the United States of America is involved in the military. They are the service members of the Army, Air Force, Coast Guard, Navy, Marines, the National Guard, and the Reserve armed forces. That means that nearly ninety-nine percent of the USA citizenry has no clue what it means to be a part of a combat-trained, battle-ready fighting force; no clue what it is like to leave family and friends and travel to a strange and unfriendly land; no clue what it is like to take up arms and fight, in a foreign land if necessary, to the death if necessary, for their country. Time and again throughout history, men and women have put their lives in harm's way and lived each day in danger and without the comfort and encouragement of friends, family, and home.

Ninety-nine percent of those who call themselves Americans have no concept of what the one percent endures on a daily basis so they can rest their heads in peace and comfort, surrounded by friends and family, and pursue their piece of the American dream. What if the same is true for God's Kingdom and only one percent in the church understands spiritual warfare and what it takes to stand in the gap for their family, friends, and neighbors, while the other ninety-nine percent is clueless?

Is 99% of the church clueless about spiritual warfare?

This book is a call and an encouragement to those who make up that one percent. This book is for those of you who have put your heart, soul, mind, and spirit into the fight to see the Kingdom of God's Son become fully manifested on the earth. This book is dedicated to you, in hopes that the other ninety-nine percent will soon join you, jumping with both feet into the battle; that we'll lock hearts, as well as arms, as we go forth into the conflict, into the warfare raging all around us, and that God's grace will grant us all the victory in Jesus.

We Are in a War

We are in a war: Whether we like it or not, we're at war; whether we believe that a war is going on or not, a battle is raging and we are smack-dab in the middle of it. Jesus said, *"This is war, and there is no neutral ground"* (Luke 11:23 MSG). This is not a war in the natural, physical world but one in the spiritual realm. It is not seen, yet seen. It is seen in the effects the forces of darkness have on the hearts and minds of God's creation, as well as the effects the Kingdom of Light has on the children of God.

There are two camps concerning spiritual warfare. In one camp you have those who don't believe there is a war, while in the other you have those who know there is a war, but they believe that the war is too overwhelming.

There Is No War

Those who believe there is no war typically will cite one of two reasons for their belief. First, they believe Jesus has won the victory and the believer's responsibility is simply to walk in His victory. Their philosophy is expressed something like this: "Don't give the devil any attention; he's defeated and that is it. If you give him any attention, it empowers him. Walk in total faith and you won't have any troubles or difficulties."

There is some validity to this school of thought, because it is true that Jesus has won the victory for us. However, for each of us there is still a path to walk, a race to win, and a battle to fight. Faith is a great thing, a fundamental thing, but this type of "hyper-faith" is unrealistic. This hyper-faith says you will never have a bad day and never feel any pain or sorrow as long as you can maintain this heightened level of super faith. If troubles do find you, it is then the logical conclusion that it's because you lack faith. While it is impossible to please God without faith (Heb. 11:6), nowhere in God's word has He said that you will never have any problems. All you have to do is read the Bible to realize quite the opposite is true. We are not only warned of troubles, we are promised them (John 16:33).

In the great "Hall of Faith" chapter in the book of Hebrews, the author tells of the men and women of faith who *"were laughed at and beaten. Others were put in chains and thrown into prison. They were stoned to death, they were cut in half, and they were killed with swords... They were too good for this world"* (Heb. 11:36-38a NCV/NEB). True, these are Old Testament saints who were under the law and not believers under grace, but in the New Testament we have the beheading of John the Baptist, the beatings of Paul and the martyrdoms of the ten apostles.

Faith is essential, it is powerful, and it is a keystone of Christianity, but the faith we must have is God's kind of faith. *"Jesus answered and said to them, 'You have* ***the faith of God in you'"*** (Mark 11:22 ARTB emphasis mine). We need the kind of faith God has: Biblical faith, word faith, not fantasy faith; faith based on the word and power of God, not based on the wisdom of the world and certainly not based on our emotional ups and downs. God's kind of faith, is a faith that speaks His word.

If this super, hyper, fantasy faith was legitimate and the believer did not face obstacles, turmoil, and persecution, why would the Lord then refer to His called ones as "overcomers?" In the Old Testament, the Israelites had to battle the *"seven nations greater and stronger"* (Deut. 7:1-8 Mof) that dwelt in their Promised Land and drive them out. The whole of the Old Testament is a portrayal of the conflict of God's people to keep and protect the promises given them by the Lord. In the New Testament, in the book of Revelation, Jesus promised a reward to the believers in each of the seven churches who became overcomers. Each church had a specific foe to defeat, and as they overcame this foe, they were rewarded for being a faithful servant (Rev. 2:1-3:22).[1] We can't be overcomers unless we have someone or something to overcome.

The second argument put forth by those in the "there is no war" camp is that there simply is no enemy, no devil, no demons. If there are no demons then there is no war. I was told a story about a church in Tennessee who would invite a preacher from England to come and preach at their church every year. He was a good preacher, and those southern people just loved listening to his British accent. One Sunday night before the service he held a question and answer session with the members.

We can't be overcomers if we don't have something to overcome.

"How do you minister to a person harassed by a demon?" someone in the group asked. "Well," the preacher slowly answered, "I minister to him by helping him understand his mental illness, because there is no such thing as demons."

The congregation became agitated. "Jesus cast out demons all the time in the Gospels!" someone yelled. The British pastor calmly replied, "Demons don't exist. It is only a mental illness."

"But Jesus would talk to the demons and they would talk to Him!" another angry church member shouted. The preacher remained calm and answered, "Jesus knew it was a mental illness. He realized that it would take some time before the people received this truth."

"But Jesus talked with one demon, and he even said his name was 'Legion for we are many'" (Mark 5:9 and Luke 8:30 NASB) another man argued.

Once again the preacher calmly condescended, "Jesus went along with them in their misunderstanding. Remember when Jesus told them, *'I have many things to say to you but you cannot bear them now'*" (John 16:12 KJV)? Well, this was one of those 'things' Jesus could not tell them yet. They weren't ready. So Jesus went along with the person who 'thought' he had the legion of demons. The man was delusional and believed he had a demon, so he acted like he was demonized. Jesus knew it was just his mental illness talking and acting out, not a demon."

The room fell silent. Many were clearly angry. A young man in the very back of the room raised his hand. "Yes, son," the preacher patronized. The young man stood. "If there is no such thing as demons, then what forced the 2,000 pigs to rush down the steep hill and drown themselves in the sea? Were they mentally ill, too?" (Mark 5:13 KJV).

If demons do not exist, what forced 2,000 pigs to rush down the hill and drown themselves in the sea?

The room exploded with laughter. Now it was the preacher who fell silent. Needless to say, he was never invited back.

Fellow followers of Christ, if there is no conflict in the spiritual realm over our heart and our life, if there is no enemy to battle, then there is no need for us to put on God's spiritual armor (Eph. 6:10-18). Clearly, the apostle Paul knew there is a battle raging between the forces of light and those of darkness, and that we desperately need spiritual covering and weapons to stand, fight, and be victorious.

The War is Overwhelming

In the other camp, at the other end of the spectrum you have those who believe in demons to the extreme. These are they who see a demon in every mishap of life, and in so doing inadvertently give the enemy far more power than he is due. You will recognize them by their constant requests for your prayers: "Pray for me. I had a flat tire on the way to work this morning. The devil is really harassing me today." In actuality, they probably ran over a nail or it's time they invested in a new set of tires.

The believers in this camp attribute everything bad, every disappointment, every mistake or failure that happens to them to the devil or some demon. "He's everywhere! He's everywhere!" they cry. If they would open their eyes they'd see that there is not a demon behind every rock and every tree, only God. Do not mistake that statement for an endorsement for any pantheistic belief that would contend that nature is God. Our God is omnipresent. It is Him, not satan that is everywhere.

These "he's everywhere" believers are more focused on the rise of the antichrist, his power, and his kingdom of darkness than on the power of Jesus and the growth of His Kingdom of Light. They believe this conflict will become so intense, so overwhelming that our only victory will be a retreat (i.e., rapture) from this world. If that last statement took you aback, what do you do with the word of God that says, *"The Lord says to my Lord: '**Sit** at My right hand **until I make Your enemies a footstool for Your feet**'"* (Ps. 110:1 NIV; emphasis mine)?

There is not a demon behind every rock and tree, only God is omnipresent.

Here, God the Father tells Jesus the Son to, *"Sit at My right, while I put Your enemies under your control. You will rest your feet on their backs"* (ERV/Voice). Peter tells us that Jesus *"must remain in heaven until the time comes for God to restore everything, as He promised long ago through His holy prophets"* (Acts 3:21 NIV). *"For **heaven must hold Him**, till the time when all things are made new"* (NTPE; emphasis mine).

Heaven must "hold" Jesus. Jesus ***"must stay in heaven** until the time when all things are made right"* (NLV; emphasis mine). Jesus is coming back, not when the antichrist is defeating His people, but when the church is defeating the antichrist. All enemies must be subdued and all things must be made right before the Lord returns. We've got a job to do, and it does not include retreating.

The Middle Ground of Meeting

Somewhere halfway between these two diametrically opposed camps there is a middle ground. It is in this middle ground where we must meet with those who need God's salvation; to go into the trenches with them as they accept God's wonderful gift and then begin the process of God's full deliverance from their past worldly lifestyle and from any possible demonic oppression or familiar spirits.[2]

All who come to the Lord for salvation bring with them excess baggage—old habits, beliefs, lifestyles, and life systems. All need someone to stand in the gap, to walk with them, and if necessary, to fight side by side with them for their total salvation and deliverance in Jesus. Yes, there is a battle, and that battle rages fiercely for control of God's children. Whenever Jesus faced off with a demonic spirit, He had to forcibly remove them—their presence, their control, and their ownership—from the possessed. Demons did not then nor do they now go quietly. It was a battle then; it is a battle now.

One day, as Jesus was teaching, a man with a demon tried to interrupt His class. The demon cried out,

> *"'Leave us alone, Jesus the Nazarene! Have You come to destroy us?' 'Be quiet!' said Jesus sternly. 'Come out of him.' At that, the evil spirit screamed and threw the man into a convulsion, but then left him"* (Mark 1:25-26 NIV/NLT).

It's no picnic when the forces of light meet the forces of darkness. People need the salvation and deliverance of Jesus and that requires a battle. Jesus said, *"The kingdom of heaven suffers violence"* (Matthew 11:12 NASB). One translation reads: *"The Kingdom of Heaven has been forcefully advancing, and violent people attack it"* (NLT). Either way you translate this verse, violence is involved whenever the Kingdom of Light and the kingdom of darkness meet.

War is raging all around us. Whether you like it or not, we were all born, live, and function every day in the midst of an invisible battlefield. We have an enemy who hates us with a passion. He hates every attribute, every expression, and every characteristic of who we are: Our spirit, our soul, and our body. Jesus said the evil one's driving desire is to "steal, kill, and destroy" (John 10:10 NASB). The enemy wants to "steal" from our body by taking away our health. He desires to "kill" our soul by assaulting us with his lies and false accusations, wounding and attacking both our heart (emotions) and our mind (thoughts). He wants to "destroy" our spirit forever by trying to draw us away and seduce us from the presence of the Father. You see, the devil is going to hell, and he wants to take as many of us with him as he can, but God has given us the power to stop him. The sooner you come to grips with this reality and acknowledge this truth, the sooner you'll begin to experience the joy of the victory Jesus has in store for you.

INCREASED WARFARE

Today we are entering into a level of spiritual warfare that we have never faced before. The intensity of the conflict has increased dramatically. We need more weapons. We need specialized weapons. Many times the natural realm reflects the spiritual realm.

Just as the United States of America is under a different type of warfare, where our enemy in the natural realm can strike at us without warning using nonconventional weapons (such as flying commercial airplanes into buildings, using the U.S. mail to send Anthrax filled envelopes, and putting explosives into cars, trucks, on people, and even in shoes), so has the landscape of our spiritual warfare changed. Our spiritual enemies are coming at us through different avenues of attack. We must adapt and overcome this new type of warfare. Satan knows his time is short. He is pouring out a flood of wickedness against God's children (Rev. 12:13-17), but the devil is going to lose this war.

Breaking Open God's Spiritual Arsenal

The word tells us the Lord is breaking open His spiritual arsenal. He's bringing out the spiritual weapons of His wrath against evil and wickedness (Isa. 13:5 NEB/KJV). These weapons are not new. They have always been available. Now is the time to use them.

The prophet Jeremiah tells us that *"The Lord has opened His armory and brought forth* ***the weapons of His indignation, the weapons to explode His wrath upon His enemies,*** *for I have a work to do in Babylon!"* (Jer. 50:25 TLB/NASB/GNT; emphasis mine). The prophet Isaiah repeats this call and tells us that the Lord is coming with *"the* ***weapons of His wrath****"* (Isa. 13:5 NIV; emphasis mine).

The devil and the demons hate God. But no matter—God doesn't like them either. He knows they are incapable of and uninterested in changing or repenting. His righteous indignation burns against them for what they are doing to His children. The Hebrew word for indignation is *za-am* and literally means "the weapon that sees chaos."[3] God sees the devastation of chaos, and He is opening up His arsenal to put a stop to it.

The devil and his demons hate God—no matter: God doesn't like them either!

WMDs, weapons of mass destruction, are capable of producing horrific, widespread destruction on a population. Sadly, in today's world, we are far too familiar with the ominous proposition of weapons such as "dirty bombs" that can release radiation over a city, or a crop duster plane that could drop a cloud of Anthrax over a packed football stadium. In spiritual warfare, the arsenal of the Lord is stockpiled with His WDWs—"weapons of divine wrath." God is calling His army to take up His weapons of divine wrath against the enemy:

> *"Be prepared. You're up against far more than you can handle on your own. Take all the help you can get, every weapon God has issued, so that when it's all over but the shouting you'll still be on your feet"* (Eph. 6:13 MSG).

We want those weapons that "explode God's wrath" on the demonic strongholds in the land. We know about the armor of God and His foundational weapons, but in the times we face today, we also need the weapons of His wrath. God's WDWs have an effect of widespread destruction on the hordes of hades. God's arsenal is filled, wall-to-wall, with His weapons of divine wrath. It's filled with His war horns, His war cry, His war flags, His war dance, His war songs, His war bow, and a plethora of other godly artillery, each designed to destroy specific demonic strongholds and forces set against us, God's children.

We are in a heated spiritual battle. *"We wrestle not against flesh and blood, but against principalities, against powers, against the rulers of the darkness of this world, against spiritual wickedness in high places"* (Eph. 6:12 KJV). To walk out the victory Jesus has won for us, we must use these weapons of God's divine wrath.

Peace Through Victory

The Biblical picture of peace is not the absence of problems and adversaries. The Hebrew word for peace is *shalom* and literally means "to destroy the authority that establishes chaos."[4] Peace is victory over the power of chaos and turmoil in the world around us. God through Jesus has supplied us with His victory.

So what are these spiritual weapons of God's wrath? What do they do and how do we use them? That is what the *God's Heart of War* series is all about. One of these WDWs the Lord is handing out today is the war songs of God. This book is divided into two parts. The first part defines and explains the war songs of God and how they are applied in spiritual warfare. The second part goes over a few of the many war songs in the Old Testament prophetic books and shows how each war song is a specific weapon from the Lord to be used against a specific attack of our adversary.

Go into God's armory. Grab a weapon. Take one. Take two. Bless God, take them all! Learn to use them. Then charge boldly into the battle, knowing no weapon formed against you can succeed because your King of Kings has already declared you triumphant.

Lord, teach our hands to war. Show us the victory in Jesus. Fill us with Your love and grace. Lead us forward in Your songs of triumph, until Your glory fills this world like the waters cover the sea.

Go into the armory of God,
grab a weapon, grab them all!

ENDNOTES:

1. In Revelation 2-3, the Lord Jesus addresses seven churches in Asia Minor and promises them a prize if they overcome their adversaries. Some of their adversaries were internal, while others were external such as unclean spirits operating through people and their false teachings. It is the same for the church today. We have spiritual opponents standing against us that we must overcome. Here is a short review of the opponents those seven churches were called to overcome.
    1. In Ephesus (2:1-7): wicked, evil men; false apostles; the loss of its first love; the deeds of the Nicolaitians
    2. In Smyrna (2:8-11): false Jews who belong to satan's synagogue; the believers were being thrown in jail and tested.
    3. In Pergamum (2:12-17): satan had his throne and his home there; the teachings of Balaam; the teachings of the Nicolaitians
    4. In Thyatira (2:18-29): they tolerated Jezebel's false teachings; Jezebel's spiritual and physical seduction; the so-called deep secrets of satan.
    5. In Sardis (3:1-6): the church said it was alive but it was dead; their works were not complete before God; they needed to wake up and repent.
    6. In Philadelphia (3:7-13): members of the synagogue of satan; false Jews; the believers were to hold fast what they had.
    7. In Laodicea (3:14-22): they were lukewarm, not hot or cold; they were deceived. They thought they were rich and needed nothing, but in reality they were poor, miserable, blind, and naked. (Answer the door, Jesus is knocking. Buy from Him gold, white garments, and eye salve).
2. A familiar spirit is a spirit passed from one generation to the next. The word familiar comes from the word for "family" or "household." Therefore, a familiar spirit is a family spirit. Just as natural traits, like hair, skin, and eye color are passed on from one generation to the next, spiritual traits also can be passed on.
3. Seekins, Frank T., *Hebrew Word Picture: How Does the Hebrew Alphabet Reveal Prophetic Truths?* (Scottsdale, AZ: Hebrew Media 1, 2012),164.
4. Seekins, pp. 193, 114.

PART I
WHAT ARE THE WAR SONGS OF GOD?

" ... that I may conquer by His song ..."

—Habakkuk 3:19 CAB

CHAPTER ONE

Three Lessons on Spiritual Warfare

For the past 25 years, I have been studying the war songs of God. Now is the Lord's time to reveal and release these war songs to the people of God. In order to ensure a clear understanding of where the Lord is taking us, I need to first lay a foundation based on military tactics and history. After I graduated high school, I joined the U.S. Marine Corps. From 1970 to 1976, I served in the USMC during the Vietnam War, and while there I learned many valuable lessons. Three vital lessons I learned as a Marine apply to the spiritual warfare we face today.

Lesson 1: Know Your Weapon and Be Effective with It

In the Marine Corps everyone is first and foremost a grunt— a man or a woman with a rifle. It doesn't matter if you are going to be a commander or a cook, you are first and foremost a grunt. We grunts learned about our M-14 or M-16 rifle backwards and forwards. We were constantly breaking it down and putting it back together. We'd practice putting it back together in pitch-black darkness, because you don't always get to fight in the daylight. You had to know your weapon and be able to use it, whether you were fighting in the light or fighting in the darkness. Most of our spiritual battles are not fought in the beautiful light of God's day, but in the dead of night when the darkness seems so strong and oppressive.

Everyone was assigned to a rifle team and they would learn to fight together. During our war games we would dig lovely things called foxholes for protection. When I was in that foxhole with my team, I only had two questions for those men and women around me. I didn't care if they were a Protestant, Catholic, Charismatic, Church of Christ, or even a Charismatic Catholic. All I wanted to know was: First, do you know how to use that rifle? Second, are you any good with it? That's it. That's all I wanted to know. If you didn't know how to use your rifle, we were going to be in a world of hurt. If you weren't any good with it, that wasn't going to do any of us much good either. If you needed help with your weapons skills, we were all going to spend extra time on the rifle range, because in a real firefight, my life was in your hands. I needed to know you knew what you were doing and that you did it well.

In a foxhole during a firefight, the only thing I want to know is, "Do you know how to use your weapon?"

The army of God must have this same attitude. We don't need to agree on every single jot and tittle in our doctrine. We don't need to get caught up in what religious label our fellow soldiers are wearing. In a spiritual firefight, all I want are men and women around me who are ready to fight, ready to obey their Holy Commander, and who know their spiritual weapons and are very effective with them.

Lesson 2: Match the Weapon to the Warfare

In a battle, if infantry are fighting infantry, the match is fairly even and the army with the best leaders and soldiers will usually win. But as soon as an enemy tank shows up and starts blasting away at your position, things change drastically. At this point, you must make an adjustment or things are going to go very bad, very fast. You don't keep on fighting as if there was no tank on the scene. You change your tactics. You don't keep shooting at the tank with your M-16. You might as well be using a peashooter and spit wads for all the effect you'll have. You call for someone who has a bazooka, or what's now called an RPG (rocket propelled grenade) launcher. You match your weapon to your warfare. That RPG is specifically designed to take out tanks. You use that specific weapon and let it do its job.

In the Marines we learned how to use all kinds of weapons. We trained in hand-to-hand combat using everything from a bayonet, to clubs, to rocks, to our bare hands. We also learned how to throw grenades, shoot a bazooka and a LAW (light anti-tank weapon). Other soldiers would go into their specialties as a gunner on a tank or helicopter or fly planes. We learned to do it all. It's the same with the Army of God. There are many weapons the Lord has given us to fight on the spiritual realm, and we'd be wise to learn to use them all.

Too many times we have "brought a knife to a gunfight," to coin a phrase. There's a scene from the first *Indiana Jones* movie where a bad guy is coming at Indiana Jones waving this huge sword. Indiana gives him a quizzical look, calmly takes out his pistol, and takes the bad guy down with a single shot. Recently, I thought about that scene, laughing to myself, when the Lord spoke: "Many times My people are like the man with the sword." We have stood in the gap and fought in spiritual warfare with little or no results. Too often we have brandished a sword at the enemy, only to have him open up on us with a RPG launcher. We walk away confused, hurt, and wounded. God's warriors need to know not only what the spiritual weapons of divine wrath are and how to use them effectively, but also how to strategically match the weapon to the warfare.[1]

Too often God's people come to a spiritual gunfight with a knife.

Examples of the importance of this principle fill the scriptures. One that is well known is the story of David playing his harp for King Saul in order to drive away the demons that tormented the king. Most of the time when David played, King Saul was refreshed and the demons left him (1 Sam. 16:23), but on two occasions it didn't go so well (1 Sam. 18:10-11 and 19:8-10). In both of those situations Saul threw a spear at David and tried to nail him to the wall. The last time I checked, a harp makes for a lousy shield against a spear. Both times David had to flee. So while there were times when David's harp/M-16 got the job done, there were others when he needed to pull out an RPG and blast away.

The second example is one of a much larger scale, where thousands were fighting against thousands. The story is found in 2 Kings 3:4-27. It's a long story so we'll do a quick recap just to get the point across. There were three kings (king of Israel, Judah, and Edom) engaged in a war against the king of Moab. The story starts with the three kings getting a "word" from the Lord through the prophet Elisha guaranteeing them victory over the Moabite king (2 Kings 3:15-19). Next this victory was declared to be *"a* ***little thing in the sight of Yahweh****, for He will put Moab itself into your power"* (2 Kings 3:18 JB, emphasis mine).

So these three kings go off to fight a foe that in their mind is already fallen since they've been assured that the victory will be no big deal for God to accomplish. At first everything goes as planned and city after city falls before the armies of these three kings. Then they reach Kir-hareseth, the capital of Moab, where they suffer a demoralizing defeat and have to return to their homeland.

To understand the reason for this loss, we first need to look at the meaning of the city's name. Kir-hareseth is a combination of two Hebrew words. One means "fortress or stronghold" and the other word means "magic."[2] The three kings had come against Moab's "stronghold of magic," the throne of Moab's false god Chemosh. When the Israelites attacked, the king of Moab took his first born son and offered him as a burnt offering to their demon Chemosh on the city wall. As a result of this ghastly ritual, "there was great wrath against Israel, the fury that came upon the Israelites was so great, they gave up the siege and returned to their own land" (2 Kings 3:27 Amp/CCB/NAB).

This fortress of magic was not going to fall under the swords and spears of Israel because the Israelites were not fighting against the people of the city but against a dark, demonic spirit. It was going to take some serious spiritual firepower to take this stronghold, and apparently they didn't know any war songs and had left their war horns back at the house. They had only brought a knife to this gunfight.

The last example to drive home the importance of this principle we find is when Jesus battled the devil in the wilderness for forty days. Our Lord knew how to match His weapon to the specific attack of the evil one. Looking at the account of that battle in Matthew 4:1-11 and Luke 4:1-13, we note two vital doctrines of spiritual warfare. First, Jesus' weapon of choice was always the word of God. It was always the, "It is written!" Second, Jesus matched the specific word weapon to the devil's specific attack. For the attack on His physical need for food, Jesus proclaimed His need for the spiritual bread of God. For the attack to tempt Jesus to test God, Jesus spoke the exact word weapon to silence that temptation. And with satan's inducement to take the shortcut in order to gain the whole world, Jesus stood on the word to worship the Lord God and Him alone. Each time Jesus used the word weapon that fit His conflict. We will do well if we follow His example.

TWO SPIRITUAL WEAPONS

The history of God's people has been a history of warfare. The battle of Jericho as told in Joshua Chapter 6 is the first battle the children of Israel had to fight to begin to take their Promised Land, and it is a clear exposition on God's principles of spiritual warfare. Jericho was a formidable stronghold that had to be annihilated before the Israelites could move forward into the land God had promised them.

> *"The Lord said to Joshua, 'I am putting into your hands Jericho, with its king and all its brave soldiers. You and your*

> *fighting forces are to march around the city once a day for six days. Seven priests, each carrying a ram's horn are to go in front of the Covenant Box. On the seventh day you and your soldiers are to march around the city seven times while the priests* ***blow the ram's horn****. Then they are to sound one long note. As soon as you hear it, all the people are to give a shout, and the city walls will collapse. Then the whole army will go straight into the city. Joshua had given the people the following order: 'Do not shout, do not utter even a word; let nothing be heard from you till the day when I say:* ***Raise the war cry.*** *Then you are to shout'"* (Josh. 6:2-5, 10 TLB/JB, emphasis mine).

Just look at the weapons God gave them to use. There were no swords, no spears, but instead His spiritual weapons: To sound His war horn (*shofar*) and to shout His war cry. Can you imagine what the Israelites might have said in response? "Lord, are You out of Your mind? What kind of fighting is this?" Very similar to what we would say today if given such an instruction. When the realization came that their swords and spears would have no effect on the huge walls of Jericho, they began to see the wisdom of God's instruction. The Israelites could have beaten on the walls of Jericho with their swords all day long and all they would have gotten would be tired arms and bent and dull swords. No doubt many would have been wounded or killed in the process. To be victorious, they had to use the weapons that God designed for that specific obstacle, that specific stronghold.

> To be victorious, we must use the specific weapons God has designed for that specific stronghold.

The Israelites heeded the word of the Lord, and by faith did what He told them. They blew God's war horns and shouted God's war cry, and by their "faith the walls of Jericho fell down" (Heb. 11:30 NKJV). Once the walls of the stronghold fell, they could freely move in and take the city with their swords and spears.

The Israelites weren't standing on blind faith but on word faith in their obedience to God's instruction. Not only did they have His specific instruction given in Joshua 6, but they also knew of the promise He had made to them in Numbers 10:9:

> *"When you go into battle against an enemy who oppresses you and you are hard pressed by him, you shall raise a cheer when the trumpets sound,* ***you must sound the trumpet with a battle cry,*** *the Lord your God will take note of your situation and you will be delivered from your enemies"* (Num. 10:9 NEB/JB/MLB; emphasis mine).

They stood on these words from God. They were confident that when they sounded His war horns and shouted His battle cry, He would respond. He would remember them. He would deliver them and give them victory over their enemies.

There are people in homes, churches, and cities around the world who are bound by demonic strongholds and our prayers and petitions don't seem to have any effect in setting them free. It's because there's a wall of demonic stronghold around these people and the wall must fall first. This wall keeps our spiritual swords, the word of God, from reaching them,

People (like Rahab) bound in a stronghold need more than the Sword to set them free.

from cutting them free from their bonds to sin. When we learn to crumble that wall of resistance, just as the children of Israel crumbled the walls of Jericho; then the word can charge forth and set the people like Rahab free (Joshua 6:22-23).

Lesson 3: Sing and Shout Your Way to Victory

If someone had told me before I went into the Marines that I would be running 10-plus miles a day before boot camp was over, I'd have said they were crazy. I had asthma and I could scarcely run 10 yards—much less 10 miles—without running out of breath or having an asthma attack. But I did.

The Marine Corps knows how to accomplish this. Our runs started slowly. Day by day we would run farther and farther. We ran wherever we went. The only time we didn't run was when we were eating, sleeping, marching, or in the bathroom. There was a trick the drill instructors used to help us make it through those runs. It was the cadences they had us shout and sing.

We would be screaming our heads off, singing a cadence at the top of our voices as we ran. We'd become so caught up in what we were singing and shouting that we'd forget we were running forever and a day. We didn't think about how far we'd come or how far we had to go, we just sang and shouted. Then suddenly, it would be time to stop. I can't help but think about the children of Israel marching around the city of Jericho, singing and shouting until the walls fell down. There's something about singing and shouting that brings forth God's victory.

GOD'S ARMY OF DIVINE DESTROYERS

God is calling forth His army of divine destroyers. The prophet Isaiah tells us that God declares:

> *"I have commanded My sanctified ones, My holy ones,* ***My sacred warriors, My special forces;*** *I have called My mighty ones for Mine anger, My warriors to carry out My wrath; even those who rejoice in My highness, they are eager for My triumph;* ***they're bursting with pride to carry out My angry judgment.***
>
> *"There is a loud noise on the mountain—it sounds like a large army! There is great commotion among the kingdoms —nations are being assembled! The Lord Who commands armies is mustering the army, His forces for battle.*
>
> *"They come from a distant land, from the horizon. It is the Lord with the weapons of His wrath to destroy evil and wickedness from off the whole land"* (Isa. 13:3-5 KJV/JB/MSG/NEB; emphasis mine).

In the natural, these verses are primarily referring to the army of the Medes and Persians who invaded and attacked Babylon, but upon close examination, there is more referenced here than a natural army. God is telling us about His army, those who will one day come forth and take on spiritual Babylon. Notice the soldiers are called God's sanctified ones, His sacred warriors. They rejoice to see God's purposes accomplished on the earth. They rejoice when His will is done and His kingdom triumphs.

> *"I have commanded My (blessed) saints, and called on the giants of My wrath and* ***those most loyal to Me****. The Lord*

has called out ***His proud and confident soldiers to fight a holy war*** *and to punish those He is angry with"* (Isa. 13:3 AB/GNT; emphasis mine).

There is no army in the natural realm like this. This is a spiritual army, an army the Lord is calling forth to fight His holy spiritual war by singing His war songs.

God's Horizon People

These blessed saints, these giants of God's wrath, these proud and confident soldiers come from the horizon, from the "end of heaven" (Isa. 13:5 NKJV). They are horizon people. The Hebrew word for horizon is *qatesh* and literally means the "end," the "edges," or the "lips (mouth) of heaven."[3]

The horizon is where heaven ends and the earth begins; where heaven and earth touch; where heaven and earth are one, are in unity and harmony. Horizon people are one with God and with each other. God's holy army is made up of men and women who live at the horizon. These people live at the "mouth of heaven" where they hear the word of the Lord and do it. They walk in the will of the Father.

These are the people who are in sync with the Kingdom of God. They are the fulfillment of Jesus' prayer, "[Father, let] *Your kingdom come, Your will be done on earth as it is in heaven"* (Matt. 6:10 NIV). The horizon is heaven on earth. *"That your days may be multiplied and the days of your children...as the days of heaven upon the earth"* (Deut. 11:21 KJV). The horizon is where the Kingdom of God is manifested upon the land.

Battle Ready

There is a war and we are the warriors, but God has given us the victory through His Son. Jesus *"stripped all the spiritual tyrants in the universe of their sham authority at the Cross, He shames them publicly by His victory over them on the cross"* (Col.2:15 MSG/NLT). Jesus has taken away the keys of death and Hades and given us authority over all the power of the enemy. We go into the fight already victors in Jesus. It is a fight, but God has not left us unprotected nor unprepared. He has given us His spiritual armor and his spiritual arsenal. We will need both to overcome.

In Ephesians 6, the apostle Paul puts forth the analogy of putting on the whole armor of God. It includes the helmet of salvation, the breastplate of righteousness, the belt of truth, the shoes of the gospel, the shield of faith, and the sword of the spirit (Eph. 6:10-18).

God is strong and He wants you strong.

"God is strong and He wants you strong. So ***take everything the Master has set out for you, well-made weapons of the best materials.*** *And put them to use so you will be able to stand up to everything the devil throws your way"* (Eph. 6:10-11 MSG; emphasis mine).

When we receive the full revelation of our salvation in Jesus, the helmet of salvation covers our minds, protecting us from the mental assault of the wicked one. This helmet deflects the doubts, the false accusations, and the depression of the enemy. In much the same way, the revelation that *"we are the righteousness of God in Christ"* (2 Cor. 5:21 KJV) becomes a breastplate around our heart. That revelation guards our hearts from fear, anger, jealousy, and other emotions the enemy has in his munitions store.

God's armor protects us as we send out God's judgment on His enemies. His armor allows us to intercede and then to stand against the assault of the enemy as he tries to come in like a flood. To battle successfully against the camp of our enemies in darkness, God's warriors must be clothed in His armor. It's not an optional accessory. Without it, you walk into the battle uncovered, naked, and exposed. Clothed in God's armor, we then take up the weapons He has fashioned and forged for our spiritual battle. Paul wrote to the church in Corinth:

> *"Because the weapons we use are not worldly, not of this world. On the contrary they have God's power for demolishing strongholds;* ***my weapons have the power of God to destroy the camp of the enemy, to knock down the devil's stronghold.*** *With these weapons we break down every proud argument that keeps people from knowing God, every barrier of pride which sets itself up against the true knowledge of God; with these weapons we conquer their rebellious ideas, and we teach them to obey the Messiah. We use our powerful God-tools for smashing warped philosophies,* ***tearing down barriers erected against the truth of God,*** *fitting every loose thought and emotion and impulse into the structure of the life shaped by the Messiah"* (2 Cor. 10:4-5, CJB/NIRV/NLT/NET/MSG/Knox emphasis mine).

Our safety and victory depend not on what we have but on Who has us. The battle is the Lord's. If He instructs us to *"stand still and see the salvation of the Lord"* (Exodus 14:13), then, bless God, we'll be wise to stand perfectly still. Don't move a muscle. Keep our eyes wide open.

Lord, show us Your weapons of Your divine wrath. Show us how to use them to tear down the devil's stronghold. Teach us to match our weapons to our warfare and set Your children free.

When we use God's weapons, we release God's power.

ENDNOTES

1. There are seven foundational spiritual weapons of God. Don't leave home without them:
   1. **The word of God:** There are three Greek words that refer to the concept of the word. The logos word is the title given to Jesus. He is the interior reality of the Father revealed. *Graphe* is the written word, and *rhema* is the act of speaking; both of these are powerful under the anointing of the Spirit, but logos is that expression that reveals the interior of the speaker. Logos is the substantial reality of the speaker that is actually IN THE WORDS EXPRESSED. This concept is a major principle in Greek philosophy and some of them felt that logos represented 'substance.' When we preach the Gospel as a logos word by the Spirit, then the substantial reality of His words is expressed IN THE WORDS themselves. The logos, the written Word of God is the Sword of the Spirit, and part of the Armor of God that we just talked about earlier. It cuts away the bonds of sin and of the enemy, washing and renewing our spirit, soul and body (Heb. 4:12).
   2. **The blood of Jesus:** The blood of Jesus: paid the price for our sins, and we are forgiven (Rom. 3:22-25); delivers us from the power of darkness and translates us into Kingdom of Light (Col. 1:12-14); allows us boldly come into the Father's presence (Heb. 10:19-22); thwarts every spirit of rejection and makes us accepted into the household of God (Eph. 1:3-7). "For you did not receive the spirit of bondage again to fear, but you received the Spirit of adoption by

Whom we cry out, 'Abba, Father.' The Spirit Himself bears witness to our spirit that we are children of God" (Rom. 8:15-16 NKJ).

3. **The name of Jesus:** The name that is above every name gives us His authority over all the power of the enemy (Luke 10:19). In His name we cast out demons and heal the sick (Mark 16:19, Acts 3:16; 4:10-12). *"That at the name of Jesus every knee will bow, of things in heaven, and things in earth, and things under the earth; and every tongue confess that Jesus Christ is Lord, to the glory of God the Father"* (Phil. 2:10-11).
4. **The baptism in water:** This is God's Holy Ghost "circumcision made without hands" and we exercise our faith in this "operation of God" (Col. 2:11-15 KJV) to cut off and separate us from our old sinful nature and bury it forever in the sea of forgetfulness (Mic. 7:19).
5. **The baptism in the Holy Spirit:** The Holy Ghost baptism releases God's power from on high among us. One of the last instructions Jesus gave His disciples was to *"tarry in the city of Jerusalem, until the Holy Spirit comes and fills you with power from heaven"* (Luke 24: 49b KJV/NLT).
6. **The nine gifts of the Holy Spirit:** The nine gifts from God's Spirit manifest His power on the earth (1 Cor. 12-14). Through the gifts of the Spirit, the church is given *"strength, encouragement, and comfort"* (1 Cor. 14:3 NCV).
7. **The Nine Fruits of the Holy Spirit:** The nine fruits of God's Spirit release God's character of love and mercy on the earth (Gal. 5:22-23) through His people. Without the character of God we are never worthy to carry His power. We are changed from glory to glory unto His likeness. If we are not changed by His grace and if we don't take on His love and mercy, we are like James and John the two 'Sons of Thunder' (Mark 3:17) going around wanting to call the fire of God's judgment on everything and everyone (Luke 9:51-56).

2. Strong's #7023 and #2789/2791 retreived at: http://www.blueletterbible.org/lang/lexicon/Lexicon.cfm?Strongs=H2791&t=KJV.
3. Retrieved at http://classic.net.bible.org/strong.php?id=07097

CHAPTER TWO

The Power of a Song

The Nine Songs of the World

Without doubt, music is powerful. We have examined already how the power of a song and a shout can not only crumble the walls of a stronghold, but also transform a gasping asthmatic into a fit United States Marine. In a recent book by Elena Mannes,[1] she puts forth the hypothesis that music, which she says existed before agriculture and possibly language, stimulates more parts of the brain than any other human function and may possess the power to change the brain and the way it operates. Ms. Mannes goes on to postulate that music may have the potential to help those who suffer from neurological problems, such as victims of stroke or Parkinson's disease. It is no wonder then, that the Lord would use something so powerful in His spiritual arsenal.

There are many kinds of songs in the world and these songs can be grouped by different methods. For example, they can be grouped by style, i.e., classical, jazz, rock n' roll, country, rap, or they can be grouped according to the era they were written, i.e., music of the '60s, '70s, '80s, and so on. Another way of cataloging the songs in the world is by separating them into the categories of who is singing the song and to whom it is being sung. Using this method for the purposes of understanding God's use of His war songs, we can divide the songs in the world into nine categories.

Music is powerful and God's music contains God's power!

CATEGORY 1: MANKIND SINGING TO MANKIND

The first category is the songs that men and women sing to other men and women. There are at least five subgroups in this category:

1. **Songs that men sing to men:** Like fight songs or chants—"We will, we will rock you!"[2] or for those from my generation, "Nah, nah, nah, nah, ... hey, hey, hey, good-bye!"[3]
2. **Songs that men sing to women:** "Baby, I need your lovin', got to have all your lovin."[4]
3. **Songs that women sing to men:** "Stop! In the name of love, before you break my heart!"[5]
4. **Songs parents sing to their children:** "Rock-a-bye baby, in the tree tops, when the wind blows, the cradle will rock."[6,7]

5. **Songs that children sing to their parents:** "I'm bringing home a baby bumble-bee, won't my mommy be so proud of me."[8]

Category 2: Mankind Singing to the Devil

The second category is songs that men and women sing to the devil and his demons. All over the world, men and women are singing and chanting songs to demons posing as the false gods of their false religions. Some people sing or chant five times a day. While for the sake of this list being comprehensive, these songs must be acknowledged, a brief acknowledgment of these elegies here (and in categories three and four which follow) is all the mention they will receive and more than they deserve. The enemy and his dirges are not worthy of more of your time. Instead, the focus in this section will be on God's life-giving songs.

Category 3: The Devil Singing to Mankind

The third class is the songs the devil sings (through men and women) to men and women. Here, the source of the singer's inspiration is uniquely demonic. Songs from the devil to mankind can occur in a remote desolate part of the earth or at a concert in a large modern city—wherever a suitable vessel of demonic influence can be found. The enemy uses these songs to glorify man over God, to exalt the creature over the Creator. These songs that flagrantly declare mankind's self-exaltation can result in actual demonic activity occurring. Isaiah 13:21b (AB) tells us "and there the demons shall dance," speaking of Babylon, a city whose name in Old Testament studies is synonymous with carnality, idolatry, self-worship, and blasphemy.[9]

CATEGORY 4: THE DEVIL SINGING AGAINST GOD

The fourth kind of song is the songs that the devil sings (through men and women) blatantly against God. One example that comes quickly to mind is the 1979 heavy metal "Highway to Hell."[10] Sadly, the words are true. We are all on a road to hell unless, through God's grace and mercy, we repent and turn to Jesus. The enemy uses this type of song through men and women against God to mock God's holiness and judgment. It's like they are bragging and are happy they are going to hell. They don't seem to care that they're on a highway to hell. But God cares! In Jesus, He places them on the King's highway of holiness where *"no predator will go up on it; only the redeemed will walk on it … with singing … joy will overwhelm them"* (Isaiah 35:8-10 CEB).

> *We are all on the highway to hell until Jesus rescues us and places us on the highway to the King.*

CATEGORY 5: THE ANGELS SINGING TO GOD

Since the creation of the universe the Lord has been praised and worshipped in song by His angels. This is the fifth category of song. It continues today and will continue through eternity.

God asked Job: *"Where were you when I created the earth? Tell Me, since you know so much! Who decided on its size? Certainly you know that! Who came up with its measurements? What supports its pillars at their bases? Who laid its cornerstone as all the morning stars were signing for joy, and* ***all the angels in chorus were chanting praise?"*** (Job 38:4-7 MSG/JB/TLB; emphasis mine).

At the birth of Jesus, mankind got a glimpse of what this worship of the angels was like. Unable to squelch their rejoicing, the angels, for a brief moment, let mankind witness their joy and excitement as they proclaimed to the shepherds near Bethlehem the birth of their Messiah, the King.

> *"Suddenly, the angel was joined by a vast host of others–the armies of heaven–praising God: 'Glory to God in the highest heaven, and peace to all men and women on earth who please Him'"* (Luke 2:13-14 NLT/MSG).

Notice it's the *armies* of heaven that proclaim this glorious event. Their Commander-in-Chief has come to earth, and He is going to win back God's children to their Father God.

CATEGORY 6: ALL CREATION (ANGELS AND MANKIND) SINGING TO THE LORD GOD

The sixth type of songs are the songs we will learn to sing in heaven, when all of creation, all of heaven and earth, and even "under the earth," will sing these songs of worship to God the Father and to His Son Jesus, the Lamb. The apostle John tells us:

"Then I heard ***every creature in heaven and on earth*** *and under the earth and on the sea, and all that is in them, saying, 'To Him Who sits upon the throne and to the Lamb be praise and honor and glory and power, for ever and ever!'"* (Rev. 5:13 TNIV; emphasis mine).

There will come a day when men and angels together will sing songs of praise and worship in chorus: Mankind will sing a verse and then the angels will sing the next one. There will come a day when all of creation will join in praise and worship to God the Father and to His Son Jesus, the Lamb.

"After these things I looked, and behold ***a great multitude which no one could number of all nations, tribes, peoples, and tongues,*** *standing before the throne and before the Lamb, clothed with white robes, and with palm branches in their hands, and heartily singing: 'Our God, Who sits upon the throne, has the power to save His people, and so does the Lamb.'*

"And ***all the angels*** *were standing around the throne and around the elders and the four living creatures; and they fell on their faces before the throne and worshipped God, singing:*

'Oh, yes! Amen! Blessing and glory and wisdom and thanksgiving and honor and power and strength belong to our God forever and forever. Amen!'" (Rev. 7:9-12 NKJV/MSG/NASB/NLT; emphasis mine).

CATEGORY 7: MANKIND SINGING TO GOD

The seventh class of song is the beautiful songs of praise and worship men and women sing to our Lord Jesus and our Father God—the songs we can sing today while we are still living upon this world. We may have to wait awhile until we get to sing with the angels, but praise God that doesn't stop us from worshipping Him with all our heart now. These are the life-giving songs that uplift our hearts and fill us with peace and joy.

Songs sung from a sincere, worshipful spirit can reach such a depth that they touch the very heart of Jesus. At this point, our Savior joins us in our praise and worship of our Father: *"I will declare Your name to my brothers; in the midst of the assembly I will praise You,"* or *"Where Thy people gather, I will join in singing Thy praise"* (Ps. 22:22 Knox). Beautiful words, in any translation, written by David the psalmist, but they take on an even more profound meaning when quoted by the writer of Hebrews.

Let our praise and worship be so glorious that Jesus joins us in our song to the Father!

> *"But we see Jesus Who … experienced death on behalf of everyone … bringing many sons to glory and He is not ashamed to call them brothers and sisters saying 'I will proclaim Your name to My brothers, in the midst of the church I will praise You! **With the Church around Me I will praise Thee'"*** (Hebrews 2:9-12 KJV/Knox; emphasis mine).

Here we see that it is not David who joins in the praise with the throngs, but Jesus Himself who desires to sing praises with us in the assembly to the Father.

CATEGORY 8: GOD SINGING TO MANKIND

The eighth category of song is the songs that God the Father sings to His children. One of the most encouraging words in the Bible comes in Zephaniah 3:17. Here are a few translations:

> *"The Lord your God is in your midst.* ***He is a Warrior Who can deliver;*** *His power gives you the victory. He will rejoice over you with joy, He will renew you in His love, He will calm all your fears."*
>
> *"**He will exult over you by singing a happy song,** He will delight you with His songs, He will exult over thee with shouts of triumph."*
>
> *"**He will dance with shouts of joy** for you as on a day of festival."*
>
> *"Cheer up, don't be afraid. For the Lord your God has arrived to live among you. He is a mighty Savior. He will give you the victory. He will rejoice over you in great gladness; He will love you and not accuse you."*
>
> *"Is that a joyous choir I hear? No, it is the Lord Himself exulting over you in happy song"* (MSG/RHM/JB/TLB; emphasis mine).

To catch hold of just how powerful this passage is, take a look at the phrase *"He will rejoice over you with joy."* The Hebrew word for rejoice is *suws* and literally means "to go in a circle," "to leap," or "to spring."[11] The word for joy is *giyl* and it means "to dance" or "to leap with joy."[12] The picture this paints for us is of Father God so overcome with delight in us that He is unable to suppress the impulse to run and leap and dance and jump in circles.

This should be the goal of our worship, both corporately and personally: that our Father is so overjoyed with us that He is moved off of His throne and onto the dance floor of heaven where He runs in circles, jumping and leaping and dancing for joy! As He does so, He is shouting and singing songs of joy over His children. The results of His songs are peace and serenity on His family. Yes, everything is right in the world. Papa is dancing tonight. Dance, Papa, dance!

Papa is dancing tonight. Dance, Papa, dance!

CATEGORY 9: GOD SINGING TO THE DEVIL

There is one type of song left that answers the question: What songs does God want to sing to the devil and his demons? This last category is the songs God wants to sing through His children to declare the doom and destruction of the devil and demons. They are the war songs of God and their time has come.

The Bible is full of songs God has given us to defeat evil forces on this earth. God desires for us to sing and rejoice in His victory of light over darkness, of blessings over curses, of healing over sickness, deliverance over demonic possession, delight over depression, freedom over bondage, and life over death.

There is a roar going forth from the throne room of heaven for those who will open their mouths and sing the war songs God has prepared for just this time. God is roaring out of Zion (Joel 3:16-26). He is calling for His children to sing the powerful word of the Lord against the hordes of hell, declaring their doom and destruction by the blood of Jesus, by the name of Jesus and by His resurrection power.

This one sentence defines the war songs of God: The war songs are the songs the Lord wants us to sing against the devil and his demons proclaiming their doom and defeat by the power of God's grace and word.

Singing War Songs is One of God's Weapons

Although science is now documenting the influence of music and song on the human condition, no one needs a doctor to tell them that powerful things happen when we sing. One of the Hebrew words for singing is *za-mar* and it literally means "the weapon that cuts off bitterness, rebellion and chaos."[13] All nine songs of the world produce some sort of effect. Whether it's men and women singing to each other, mankind singing to satan, mankind singing to God, or any of the other categories, songs produce intense emotional reactions and even physical responses. God's powerful war songs are His spiritual weapons to cut off bitterness, rebellion, and chaos.

God's powerful war songs are His spiritual weapons to cut off bitterness, rebellion, and chaos.

The Importance of Singing the War Songs

When a preacher preaches, or a teacher teaches, or a prophet prophesies, the anointing on that individual's faith is mixed with the word of God to set the people free. Consider that when a hundred or a thousand or tens of thousands of believers sing the same word of God at the same time, the combined anointing upon all of those individuals is mixed with the word of God—the power is magnified a thousand-fold!

God commands us to sing a taunt-song against the kingdom of darkness.

When you walk into a dark room, you don't have to rebuke the darkness and you don't pray for God to push the darkness back. You simply turn on the light. At the presence of light, darkness has no choice but to flee. It's not up for debate and there's not even a split second of decision-making. Light overcomes the darkness every time. Music is a powerful weapon of light. Too long it has been used by the evil one to create darkness, to influence mankind and lead them astray. God says it's time to stop these songs of death. When we sing the war songs of God, we silence the songs of the devil.

> *"And it shall come to pass in that wonderful day when the Lord gives His people rest from sorrow and fear, from slavery and chains, you shall raise this taunt-song against the king of Babylon, crying, 'How the tyrant is hushed, his mad rage is hushed! For the Lord has crushed your wicked power, and broken your evil rule'"* (Isa. 14:3-5 KJV/NLT/Mof/TLB; emphasis mine).

There's an old adage that says "You can't take it with you." God made an exception when He cast lucifer "down to hell, to the sides of the pit" (Isaiah 14:15 KJV). God sent satan packing with two things—his pride and his music.

> *"Your magnificence has been flung down to Sheol* ***with the music of your harps,"*** *or "Brought down to Hades thy pride,* ***you and your peals of music"*** (Isa. 14:11a JB/Rhm/Mof; emphasis mine).

God detests unholy pride and unholy, demonic music so much so that He casts them to the depths of hell, to be forever separated from His holiness. As God's people sing the "taunt-songs," referred to in Isaiah 14:4-5 earlier; God breaks the power of the enemy and casts him down.

Loud Songs of Triumph

Music is like a knife: The effect it has depends upon who's using it and to what end. A scalpel in the hands of a skillful surgeon, cutting out a cancerous tumor, is a good thing, a life-saving thing. But that exact same scalpel in the hands of a rapist is evil, and a tool of death. It's time to stop the death chant of the enemy, to silence the dark songs of the cruel, the unmerciful, and the unjust with God's songs of light.

The Lord wants to shut, once and for all eternity, the mouths of violent and evil men and women, those who are under the control of the devil and his hordes of demons, who sing their songs of chaos, tyranny, and cruelty. He wants to silence the cacophony of the devil and replace it with His harmony of peace, joy, and life. The Lord, singing His war songs through us, is the only One to do it.

It's time to release the songs of God's light and life; to sing God's war songs and bring disaster and devastation upon the demonic spirits who shout their death chants over His children and over His creation. Death is silenced by life as it flows out of God's divine songs. Just as the light always conquers the darkness, so the divine always overcomes the demonic. God's songs of life and glory silence the songs of death and wickedness every time.

Death is swallowed up by life as we release the war songs of God.

God is pouring out His life-giving songs in an unprecedented way. We are blessed in this age to sing songs of unparalleled praise and worship to Jesus and our Father. The Lord is pouring out His songs, singing over us of His love and mercy. But now He is also pouring out His songs of victory over the evil one on a grand scale that has never been seen or heard. He is opening up His arsenal and bringing forth the weapons of His glorious wrath, His war songs of doom upon the demonic enemies that are set against Him, His Anointed One, and His children. His war songs muzzle the death songs of darkness while they proclaim life over death, healing over disease, wholeness over despair, and adoption over rejection.

Now is the time for us to let Him sing through us, to the hordes of hell, their defeat, doom, and destruction by the blood of Jesus, through which we have gained the victory.

> *"Thus saith the Lord, thy Redeemer, the Holy One of Israel: I am the Lord thy God, training you for your good, leading you by the right way...Come out of Babylon, hasten away from the Chaldeans,* ***with a voice of singing declare it, proclaim it***

with loud songs of triumph, *crying the news to the ends of the earth; tell them, 'The Lord has ransomed His servant Jacob'"* (Isa. 48:17, 20 KJV/NEB; emphasis mine).

Lord, teach us Your "loud songs of triumph," the war songs proclaiming Your victory! Sing Your war songs through us and cut off bitterness, rebellion, and chaos in our land. Replace them with Your joy and peace that are released as we sing Your songs of life.

Sing God's songs of war, use His weapon to cut off bitterness, rebellion and chaos.

ENDNOTES

1. Mannes, Elena, *The Power of Music: Pioneering Discoveries in the New Science of Song,* Walker & Company, 175 Fifth Avenue, New York, NY, 2011.
2. *We Will Rock You,* Queen, 1977, EMI, author Brian May.
3. *Na, Na, Hey, Hey, Kiss Him Goodbye,* Steam, 1969, Mercury Records, author Paul Leka.
4. *Baby, I Need Your Lovin',* The Four Tops, 1964, Motown Records, author Holland-Dozier-Holland.
5. *Stop! In the Name of Love,* The Supremes, 1965, Motown Records, author Holland-Dozier-Holland.
6. *Rock a bye Baby, Mother Goose's Melody,* London, UK, 1765.
7. My wife changed the words to this lullaby, "Rock a bye Baby, in mommy's arms, Jesus will keep you safe from all harm. And when your sleep comes, it will be sweet, and Jesus will give you all the rest that you need."
8. No copyright.
9. Retrieved at http://www.enduringword.com/commentaries/2313.htm
10. *AC/DC Highway to Hell,* 1979, EMI and Albert Productions; authors Bon Scott, Angus Young, Malcolm Young.
11. Retrieved at http://www.blueletterbible.org/lang/lexicon/lexicon.cfm?Strongs=H7797&t=KJV.
12. Retrieved at http://www.blueletterbible.org/lang/lexicon/lexicon.cfm?Strongs=H1523&t=KJV.
13. Seekins, p. 217.

CHAPTER THREE

WAR SONGS ARE THE NEW SONGS OF GOD

THE NEW SONGS OF GOD

Priests, prophets, and the King Himself decree to God's people throughout Scripture that we must "sing a new song to the Lord." The Hebrew word for new sometimes means "brand-new and fresh," but it comes from a root word that can also mean "to renew, repair, and restore."[1] Think of it in the same way that we use the phrase "new moon." It doesn't mean that the moon is brand-new each month, but that it comes out refreshed or renewed for that month. The Lord is bringing forth fresh new songs to renew and repair us. Nine times throughout the Old and New Testaments we are told to sing these new songs, and in each instance the instruction to sing is in the context of warfare, of battle, or of God defeating the enemy. There can be no doubt that these new songs that the Holy Spirit is encouraging us to sing are the war songs of God.

Close examination of these nine instructions from the Holy Spirit is crucial to our understanding the power and the importance of singing these new war songs.

1. *"Sing to Him a **new song**! Play skillfully as you shout out your praises to Him! ... Because no king is delivered by his vast army: **a warrior is not saved by his great might, we wait for the Lord; He is our Deliverer and Shield"*** (Ps. 33:3, 16-20 NET; emphasis mine).

   We sing a new song because, quite plainly, no king is saved by his army nor any warrior by his might. It could not be clearer that it is the Lord who gives the victory, and He does so when we sing a new song and shout out our praises to Him. As the prophet Zechariah puts it, *"Not by might, nor by power, but by my Spirit, saith the Lord of hosts"* (Zech. 4:6 KJV).

2. *"He gave me a reason to sing a **new song**, praising our God … **Your loyal love and faithfulness continually protects me.** Please be willing, oh, Lord, to **rescue me... 'Save me, Lord! Help me now!'** May those who are trying to snatch away my life be totally embarrassed and ashamed! But those who come to You be glad and joyful. You are My Helper and My Deliverer! Oh, my God, do not delay"* (Ps. 4:3, 11-17 MSG/GNT; emphasis mine)!

   The Holy Spirit teaches us the latest "God-songs," and we sing them to our Protector the Father, our Helper the Holy Spirit, and our Deliverer Jesus. We sing a new song so that God will rescue us from those who would snatch away our life, physical or spiritual.

3. *"Sing to the Lord a **new song**, Sing to the Lord all the earth … **He is to be feared above all gods, He is terrible to all the gods, because all the gods of the nations are demons,** but the Lord made the heavens. The Lord reigns,*

shout with joy ... for He comes to judge the earth" (Ps. 96:1 and 4-13 NET/NASB/NETS; emphasis mine).

Sing new songs proclaiming that all false gods are demons and they fear our God, for He is the Creator, He reigns, and He is coming to judge them.

Sing a new song, for all the false gods are demons, and they fear the Lord our God!

4. *"Oh, to sing to the Lord a **new song**! For He has done marvelous things. **His right hand and His mighty arm have gained Him the victory. The Lord demonstrates His power to deliver; He has saved us from our enemies in the sight of the nations**"* (Ps. 98:1-2 KJV/NET/CW; emphasis mine).

   Sing new songs praising God's right hand of might, demonstrating His power to deliver over all the earth.

5. *"The Lord, my Protector deserves praise, **the One who trains my hands for battle and my fingers for war.** Who loves me and is my Stronghold...**Who subdues nations under me** ... After our victory oh, God, I will sing a **new song** to You! ... **Save me from my cruel enemies**"* (Ps. 144:1-2, 9, 11 GNT/CW; emphasis mine).

   As God trains our fingers for war through playing our music, new songs of victory will emerge. Today's pianists and guitarists are the harpists of Old Testament times. The Hebrew word for harp is *kinnowr* and literally means "to open or allow the life of the man who was nailed to come forth."[2] When musicians strike the strings of their instruments in new songs to God, they are striking a blow to the hordes of hell. They are releasing the life, the power of "the Man who was nailed" into that place. They are doing battle with their hands and war with their fingers, sending a musical message to the enemy that his demise is on the horizon.

6. *"Praise the Lord! Sing to the Lord a* ***new song!*** *... Let the high praises of God be in their mouth and a two-edged sword be in their hand ...* ***to bind their kings with chains and their nobles with fetters of iron. This honor is given to all His saints"*** (Ps. 149:1, 6-9 NET/KJV/BBE; emphasis mine).

   With God's new song of high praise in our mouths we are equipped to do battle against the principalities and powers of darkness. We are not binding up the human leaders, we are binding up those spiritual forces behind the scenes attempting to manipulate and control them. Just as David played before King Saul, we sing to drive away the demonic oppression of the evil one. The very words that come from our mouths in the form of these new songs, the war songs of God, actually bind our enemies, making them powerless, ineffective, and immobilized in the battle. Once your enemy is rendered helpless, the final victory follows. That is the honor for all of God's saints.

7. *"Sing to the Lord a* ***new song****. Praise Him from the ends of the earth ...* ***The Lord emerges like a Hero, like a Warrior****, He inspires Himself for battle,* ***He shouts His war cry****, He yells, He shows His enemies His power ... To open the blind eyes, to bring out prisoners from the dungeon and those who dwell in darkness from the prison"* (Isa. 42:10, 13, 7 (NASB; emphasis mine).

   The Lord Himself advances as a mighty warrior, emerging amidst the echoes of His people praising Him with a new song. He joins passionately into the battle where He demonstrates His power to open the eyes of all who have been blinded to the truth, to set free all who have been bound by the enemy, releasing them from the darkness into His glorious light.

8. *"And they sang a* ***new song****, saying, 'You are worthy to take the scroll and to open its seals because You were killed, and* ***to the cost of your own Blood You have purchased for God people from all nations ...*** *and appointed them as a priestly kingdom to serve our God and* ***they are reigning on the earth'"*** (Rev. 5: 9-10 BBE; emphasis mine).

Even in heaven new songs are sung. New songs of praise to the One by whose power we are reigning now on the earth, as God's kingdom of priests, victorious over the enemy. When we sing new songs to the Lord, we reign.

As we sing the new war songs of God we release God's rule on the earth.

9. *"And they sung, as it were, a* ***new song*** *before the throne, and before the four beasts, and the elders: and no man could learn that song but the hundred and forty and four thousand, which were redeemed from the earth"* (Rev. 14:3 KJV).

As a result of the 144,000 singing a new song, three angels are released, each one with a different message to proclaim over the earth. Those three angelic messages are that the eternal gospel is declared (Rev. 14:6) that Babylon (the antichrist system) collapses (Rev. 14:8), and that judgment is meted out on the beast and those with his mark (Rev. 14:9).

This last new song in Revelation 14 sums it up nicely. The new songs, the war songs of God, declare the deliverance of

God's people through the gospel, the doom of the demonic strongholds in the land, and the destruction of the devil and all who still cling to him. It is not new preaching or new teaching that releases these three Revelation 14 angels. It is the new songs that are sung. We must step out in faith and sing the new songs of God and believe God to release His angels as we sing to Him, releasing the word of God in song, to accomplish His victory on the earth.

Nothing New Under the Sun?

Before we go on, we need to study what the "Preacher" of Ecclesiastes says. He says, *"There is nothing new under the sun"* (Eccl. 1:9 JB). Does this mean that nothing new can come upon the earth? No, his statement must be taken in its context. If there is nothing new, then how did God give us a New Covenant to replace the Old Covenant, how did we get born again and become a new creature in Christ, and how will we have a new heaven and a new earth? The Preacher uses the phrase "under the sun" 28 times in Ecclesiastes. He's referring to the work of man on the earth. He never uses the phrase "above the sun," that is to say, what comes from the throne room of God. Man cannot produce anything new under the sun, but as we can see in our New Covenant and new birth, new things can come from the heart of God (Isa. 48:6-7).

The Songs of God Change Things

When we sing the war songs of God something happens in the spiritual realm. God's word does not return to Him void. His word is like the rain that falls on the earth; it changes that parched land into a fertile garden and the desert can now blossom like the rose.

> *"That's how it is with My Words. They don't* ***return to Me without doing everything I send them to do****"* (Isa. 55:11 CEV; emphasis mine).

Whether it's preached, prayed, prophesied, or praised in song, the word of God changes things. These changes occur in the external, physical, seen world as well as in the internal, spiritual, unseen realm. God's new songs produce His new things. When we sing the new songs of God they release the power of God to make all things new. *"Then the One on the throne said, 'And now I make all things new!'"* (Rev. 21:5a GNT). When we continue to say and sing the same words, we continue to see the same results, but when we open our mouths to sing God's new songs, we will finally see God's new results, namely, the total defeat of the devil.

When we begin to sing the war songs of God, proclaiming the victory we have in the name and blood of Jesus Christ against all the demonic powers of hell, then we'll begin to see in the Spirit God's victory over all the earth—not just on an individual level but on a national level. We'll see whole nations delivered from the kingdom of lies and darkness where the evil one rules. We'll see people around the world freed to join us in the kingdom of truth and glorious light where Jesus reigns as King of Kings.

NEW SONGS CALL FOR JESUS THE WARRIOR KING TO APPEAR

God tells us in Isaiah, *"Behold, the former things are come to pass, and* ***new things*** *do I declare: before they spring forth I tell you of them"* (Isaiah 42:9 KJV; emphasis mine). In the very next verse God tells us how these new things will come about: We release God's new things, by singing His new songs. *"Sing unto the Lord a new song and His praise from the end of the earth!"* (Isaiah 42:10a KJV). As we sing His new songs the Warrior King comes forth to triumph over evil. *"The Lord will go forth as a warrior; He will rouse the frenzy of battle like a man of war.* ***He will raise a war-cry and triumph over His enemies!"*** (Isaiah 42:13 NEB/Rhm; emphasis mine).

Until we start singing God's new songs, we will never see God's new things. We'll never see the Lord Jesus come forth as the victorious Warrior King. The Lord is fed up with the devil having his way, harassing God's children, spreading wickedness and perversion. God desires to make all things new on the earth. This starts when we sing the new songs of God, when we cry out for the Lord to appear in our midst with His power and glory, confirming the word of God with signs following.

NEW HEAVENS AND NEW EARTH

Not only do God's new songs create and produce His new things in the earthly and spiritual realm, they also create His new heaven and His new earth. As we sing the new songs of God, we release God's power to produce these around us. *"Then I (John) saw a new heaven and a new earth. The first heaven and the first earth had passed away"* (Rev. 21:1 NLV; parenthetical mine).

When a man is born again through faith in Christ, he becomes a new creature. As a result he becomes a new husband, a new father, and a new family is created around him. But the powerful word of the Good News in Jesus must not stop there. There will be a new church transformed more and more into the glory of the Lamb, full of believers spreading the word and glory of God, creating new neighborhoods, new towns, new states, a new nation—a new earth.

God's new songs release God's new heaven and new earth!

As we sing the war songs of God, the demonic strongholds that besiege our families, our friends, our churches, our towns, our nations will fall like the walls of Jericho. There is no stopping the power of God released through His people.

> *"I, the Lord, will speak. What I say will be done, and It will not be delayed"* (Ezek. 12:25 NCV).

God promises *"I am watching to make sure My words come true"* (Jer. 1:12b NCV). Of course God watches over all of His word and does hasten to perform it, but read in context, that promise becomes even more powerful. Just two verses before this powerful promise God has revealed His call upon Jeremiah: He is to be a prophet to the nations—a very particular prophet.

> *"Look! Today I have appointed you as the overseer of the nations and over the kingdoms, in accord with My words spoken through your mouth, I will tear down some and destroy them, and plant others and nurture them and make them strong and great,* ***with a word you shall build them up and plant them anew"*** (Jer. 1:10 MLB/Amp/Knox; emphasis mine).

Jeremiah was an overseer, a prophet with a God-ordained anointing that gave him oversight authority for the nations. By the word of God Jeremiah was to tear down or build up entire nations. These words of judgment or mercy are the words God is watching over to hasten their fulfillment.

God watches over His word sent out to tear down strongholds and over His word to plant and build His kingdom.

"Then the Lord said to me, 'Look Jeremiah! What do you see?' And I replied, 'I see a whip made from the branch of an almond tree.' And the Lord replied, 'You are a close observer! And I too have My eyes open, watching for the opportunity to carry out the threats I utter.'" Another translation says: "That's right, and it means that I will surely carry out My threats of punishment'" (Jer. 1:11-12 TLB/ Knox).

These are the prophetic words over which God was keeping watch, to hasten their fulfillment. The prophetic spoken word has the power to tear down or build up whole countries. God is yet watching over His declared word to fulfill it.

The Five Megillot

Jesus and the Jews knew the power of singing songs. The Jews had a tradition of reading one of the Five Megillot (scrolls) before their five major Jewish festivals. One Megillot scroll was read during each feast.[3] Ruth was read at Pentecost, Lamentations was read at the Ninth of Av, Ecclesiastes was read at the Feast of Tabernacles, and Esther was read at the Feast of Purim (or Lights). The most beautiful song of all songs was reserved for the Feast of the Passover.

The Song of Songs was read on the Sabbath during Passover. Since it is a song, it is logical to conclude that it was not actually read but sung. One can only imagine what must have been in Jesus' heart and mind as He led His disciples in that song, at that time, as He prepared for His sacrifice. Jesus, His disciples, and no doubt the hosts of heaven, sang the love song of the Bridegroom going to fetch His bride. "I'm going to prepare a place for you, My bride, My love! I love you so much that I will die the death of all deaths to win your heart, win your love for Me!" As beautiful a picture as that paints for us as the bride, it is even more beautiful as a reminder to Jesus of the purpose of the suffering, sacrifice, rejection, death, and burial He would soon endure.

Jesus knew there is power in singing the word of God. The Song of Songs reminded Him of the joy to come, ***"Who, for the joy set before Him, endured the cross"*** (Heb. 12:2 KJV; emphasis mine). The joy that was set before Jesus, that drove Him willingly to the cross, was the joy of seeing multitudes of children that would come to the Father through the ages because of His sacrifice. Jesus sang God's word in the Song of Songs just before embarking on the road to Calvary, where He would engage in the battle of eternity for the lives of all mankind. And He was victorious! Church, now is the time—it's way past the time—to take up the war songs of God and be victorious too!

Now is the time to take up the war songs of God and be victorious!

Lord teach us Your New Songs and release Your new things upon the earth. As we sing Your new songs: the gospel is preached, the antichrist system falls and the beast is judged. As we sing Your new songs You bring forth Your New Heaven and New Earth.

Sing God's new songs over the nations,
build them up and plant them anew.

ENDNOTES

1. Retrieved at http://www.blueletterbible.org/lang/lexicon/Lexion,cfm?Strongs=H2318&t=KJV.
2. Seekins, pp. 10-11.
3. http://www.jewishvirtuallibrary.org/jsource/judaica/ejud_0002_0018_0_17898.html.

CHAPTER FOUR

A Prophetic Burden from the Lord

The Burden of the Lord

Throughout the Old Testament, God, through the Holy Spirit, would instruct His prophets to declare a message from the Lord. All of the books we call the minor and major prophets are such messages delivered at the direction of the Lord to address specific people in regard to specific circumstances or situations. Most often the Hebrew word *dabar* was used to designate this type of "word"[1] from God. A few times in the Old Testament an entirely different Hebrew word was used to designate a special message from God. That Hebrew word is translated "burden" in the King James Bible. This word for burden comes from the Hebrew root word *nasa,* which means "to lift up, to carry and to forgive;"[2] hence, it was translated "burden," as something that was to be "lifted up." In this case it is the word of God, heavy with His glory, that was to be lifted up and placed upon to whomever it was addressed.

The word for burden was used because what was being spoken was a unique word from God. It was unique because it was heavy. It was heavy because it carried the weight of God's glory. The Hebrew word for glory is *kabowd* and comes from the Hebrew root word *kabad,* which means "to be heavy, to be weighty."[3] These prophecies from God were laden with the wrath of God, and it was the obligation of the prophet to lift up this weighty word filled with God's glory and place it upon the demonic stronghold the Lord directed. The Hebrew word for burden transliterated into English is *massa.* Since this is my last name, you can bet that nugget of truth grabbed my attention.

God's burden is His heavy word of glory that we are to lift up and drop upon His adversaries.

The Massa Prophecies

The Hebrew word *massa* means a "burden, a load, to lift up, to carry, a prophetic word, a song."[4] It is applicable to three distinct situations in the Old Testament:

1. First, it could be a load or burden to be lifted up or carried. There are four subcategories for this meaning.
   A. It could be a physical burden or load carried on the backs of donkeys (Ex. 23:5), mules (2 Kings 5:17), or camels (2 Kings 8:9). It could apply to carrying a physical burden, such as the furnishings of the Tabernacle of Moses that the sons of Kohath were charged to carry (Num. 4:15-49).
   B. It could be an emotional burden of carrying (i.e. caring for) people (2 Sam. 15:33 & 19:35). Moses

complained to God that there were too many people for him to carry (lift up), so the Lord took some of His Spirit from Moses and placed it on 70 of the leaders to help Moses share the "load" of caring for the people (Num. 11:11-17).

C. It could be a <u>spiritual burden</u>, as in the case of King David's guilt that weighed him down and was conveying God's anger upon him. *"For my inequities are gone over my head; as a weighty massa (burden) they are too heavy for me"* (Ps. 38:4 NASB/OJB).

D. It could be a <u>financial burden</u> such as taxes or tribute. *"Some of the Philistines brought Jehoshaphat presents and silver massa (tribute)"* (2 Chron. 17:11 NRSV/OJB).

2. Second, it could be a prophecy or an oracle from God. The prophet would "lift up" his voice and declare the word of God's wrath as a burden to be lifted up and dropped on His enemies. Nearly every *massa* prophecy is negative, at least from the receiver's point of view, but very positive for the one imparting it because the "burden" releases God's vindication for the righteous. A burden from the Lord is like the gospel. Paul said it like this:

   "I am grateful that God always makes it possible for Christ to lead us in one perpetual victory parade. God also helps us spread the knowledge about Christ everywhere, and this knowledge is like the smell of perfume. ***But this fragrance is perceived differently by those being saved and by those perishing.*** *To those who are perishing, we are a fearful smell of death and doom. But to those who are being saved, we are a life-giving perfume"* (2 Cor. 2:14-16 CEV/MSG/NLT; emphasis mine).

The Gospel carries the aroma of "life-giving perfume" to those who accept its message, but to those who reject it, it bears the stench of "death and doom." The same is true of the *massa* prophecies. They spawn fear and rebellion in the demons, on which they are pronounced, but hope and rejoicing in the hearts of God's people who will reap righteous vindication by the prophet's pronouncement.

3. Third, it could be a song accompanied with music. The prophet would lift up his voice and sing God's word to the people. One such person who used these songs was Chenaniah. He was the chief musician and the one who led God's people in praise as they brought the Ark of the Covenant into Jerusalem to be placed in the Tent of David.

   "Chenaniah, chief of the Levites, was in charge of the ***singing*** *(Hebrew word massa): he gave instruction in the* ***singing*** *(massa) because he was skillful"*, or he was *"in charge of the* ***music*** *(massa), because he was skillful. Chenaniah was the* ***music master*** *(massa) with the singers"* (1 Chron. 15:22 NASB/NKJV & 1 Chron. 15:27 NJKV; emphasis mine)

In Ezekiel, God describes the heart's desire of His people, that on which their eyes and hearts are set—their sons and daughters (Ezek. 24:25). It was their children who "lifted up" (i.e. *massa)* their soul. In Young's Literal Translation it is translated, their children were "**the song (i.e. *massa*) of their soul.**" What parent's heart does not sing and is not uplifted at the mere sight of their child.

In summary, a *massa* could be a burden that could be a physical, emotional, spiritual, or financial load to bear, a word to proclaim, or a song to sing. For the purposes of understanding God's war songs, the definition of *"massa"* is a combination of the second and third applications. More precisely:

"A *massa* is a prophecy that is sung, a war song (usually with musical instruments), declaring the doom and destruction of God's demonic enemies."

A *massa* is a prophetic word of the Lord that is sung, a war song to declare the doom of our demonic oppressors.

The three Hebrew letters for *massa* literally mean "the power or authority to destroy chaos."[5] It is God's prophetic war song proclaiming His obliteration of the evil one and all the demonic forces. It is a song that destroys the chaos of evil from our land.

The Burden-Master

In 1 Chronicles 15 we are introduced to the "head Levite" Chenaniah. As the head Levite, Chenaniah had a very important responsibility. He was the *"burden-master chosen for his excellent skill"* (1 Chron. 15:22 Knox). The Knox translation contains a footnote that explains that the word "burden-master" is "possibly in connection with the singing, but it may be the 'burden' was the carrying of the Ark. The Latin has 'was in charge of the prophecy, as a precentor.'" A precentor is a person who helps facilitate worship. Literally, a precentor or cantor is "the one who sings before, or the first singer."[6]

The Amplified Version translates this verse:

> *"Chenaniah, leader of the Levites in singing,* ***was put in charge of carrying the Ark and lifting up song.*** *He instructed about these matters, because he was skilled and able"* (1 Chron. 15:22 Amp; emphasis mine).

This rendition in the Amplified Bible is inclusive of both the meanings put forth by Knox and the most accurate translation: Chenaniah was in charge of both carrying (lifting up the Ark), and singing (lifting up the song).

The time during which Chenaniah served as head Levite was a major transitional period for the Levites. It was a huge paradigm shift in the spiritual world. The ark no longer was to reside in Moses' Tabernacle, but rather it was to rest in the Tent of David. The Levites would no longer need to carry the Ark in the natural; instead, going forward, they would carry the Ark in song (1 Chron. 23:26 & 25:1 ERV). They would now "carry" the Ark, the very presence of the mercy of God, by their praise and worship. Chenaniah was responsible for the Levites in "carrying the Ark," but also he was the one in charge of singing the prophecies. He was a prophet and a priest, who "was charged with the striking up of the song—he carried on the instruction in singing because of his skill" (1 Chron. 15:22 MLB).

As another translation reads, *"Chenaniah was the chief of the Levites in the chanting. He directed the chanting, for he was skillful"* (NAB). Or *"Like the Levites who carried the Ark, the singers, and Chonenias that went as burden-master among the singers, as the* ***leader of the chant****"* (1 Chron. 15:27a Knox/NAB; emphasis mine).

God's Prophetic Songs

Chenaniah was the ruler of the prophecy. He took the lead in the prophetic songs. We see him here portrayed as the chanter, as the one in charge of leading the singers in singing the prophecy (the burden, the *massa,* the word) of the Lord.

> *"And Chonenias, chief of the Levites,* ***presided over the prophecy, to give out the tunes (massa),*** *for he was very skillful" (1 Chron. 15:22 CV emphasis mine). "And David was clothed with a robe of fine linen, and all the Levites that carried the Ark, and the singing men, and Chonenias,* ***the ruler of the prophecy*** *among the singers"* (1 Chron. 15:27 CV emphasis mine).

Another translation of these two verses reads

> *"Chenaniah, a Levite leader,* ***instructed others how to sing prophetic songs (massa)*** *because he was skillful at it." (1 Chron. 15:22 GOD'S WORD emphasis mine). "David was dressed in a fine linen robe, as were all the Levites who carried the Ark, the Levites who were singers, and Chenaniah,* ***the leader of the musicians' prophetic songs (massa)"*** (1 Chron. 15:27 GOD'S WORD emphasis mine).

Both times the Hebrew word *massa* is translated not just as prophecy but as "prophetic songs." So we see that this weighty, prophetic word of God comes and the Lord instructs them not to speak it but to sing it. God's burden is a prophetic war song, accompanied with musical instruments. These burdens are His spiritual weapons that will wipe out all the demonic hordes that oppose Him and oppress His people.

The burden of the Lord is a prophetic word to be sung.

We have the privilege of singing these prophecies, declaring the defeat of the evil one and all those aligned with him.

> *"Let the godly ones exult in glory: Let them sing for joy on their beds. Let the high praises of God be in their mouth, and a two-edged sword in their hand, to execute vengeance on*

> *the nations and punishment upon the peoples,* ***to bind (the demons oppressing) their kings with chains and (the ungodly forces manipulating) their nobles with fetters of iron,*** *to execute on them the judgment written; 'This is an honor for all His holy ones'. Praise the Lord"* (Ps. 149:5-9 NASB; parentheticals and emphasis mine)!

We are called to sing against the principalities and powers working behind the scenes not against people, just as David played his harp against the evil spirits oppressing King Saul, not against Saul the man.

The Rhapsodies of Isaiah

There is another reason these *massa* prophecies are songs. Dr. Richard Moulton, professor, prolific author, and lawyer, called such prophecies in Isaiah the "Isaiahan Rhapsody." Dr. Moulton goes on to say we "find in his (Isaiah's) writings a fusion of all other literary forms in that new form which is here called a rhapsody."[7] Dr. Moulton calls the conclusion of Isaiah's prophecies the "Dooms of the Nations" (i.e. the *massa* prophecies), the "Rhapsody of Judgment."[8]

Dr. Moulton was cognizant that his new term, "Isaiahan Rhapsody," would need clarification. In defense of this new terminology he wrote, "I am sensible of the awkwardness of attempting to introduce a new technical term in connection with literature so sacred and so familiar. But the new term (i.e. rhapsody) is needed *because the matter to be described is not paralleled in other literatures.*"[9] To Dr. Moulton, an utterly new form of prophecy was being introduced in Isaiah and the closest definition, in his opinion, was to call it a rhapsody.

The definition of rhapsody is an "enthusiastic or extravagant song, speech or composition; instrumental music of irregular form that suggests improvising." To be "enthusiastic" literally means to be "in theos" or to be "in God." Webster's definition of enthusiastic is to be filled with enthusiasm, or the belief of a special relationship with God or revelations from Him.[10] If you are "in God," meaning you are in fellowship with Him, and you're receiving revelations from Him, you can't help but be enthusiastic. Rhapsodies also convey the idea of improvising, much like singing in the Spirit. The Lord has some spontaneous rhapsodies to release to His children as we praise and worship Him. Ask God, trust Him to release these war songs by revelation.

The Old Testament Massa Prophecies

There are nearly 30 *massa* prophecies in the Old Testament, with one of them given by Isaiah (Isa. 21:9) quoted twice in the New Testament (Rev. 14:8 and 18:2). More than half of these prophecies are in the book of Isaiah. To get a better understanding of these songs, we'll start by looking at the first *massa* prophecy given in Isaiah. The first burden in Isaiah is 13:1 through 14:23. It is sung by God, through Isaiah, against Babylon. Babylon here represents the antichrist system, the one-world government—satan's attempt to establish another tower of Babel. And God doesn't waste any time. He starts at the top. He goes for the killing blow, crushing the heads of His enemies.

> *"The massa (or burden, oracle, prophecy, vision, divine revelation, message) of Babylon,* ***concerning Babylon's doom****, which Isaiah, the son of Amos, saw"* (Isa.13:1 OJB/KJV/RSV/TNIV/TLB/GOD'S WORD /NET/AAT; emphasis mine).

From this point in Chapter 13:1 all the way to Chapter 30, Isaiah blasts away with a series of burdens against the spiritual forces working behind the scenes in the nations around Israel and against those spirits operating in Israel herself. The Lord desires to expose and destroy these spiritual forces operating hidden in the background. As He told Ezekiel, *"Son of man, sing this funeral song, this mournful prophecy against the Evil One who works behind the scenes to work through men like the prince of Tyre"* (Ezek. 28:12 NLT/CW). The war songs are against these unseen forces.

But before we delve into the bad news for God's enemies in the *massa* prophecies, we need to put things in perspective. To do so, we need only take a look at chapter 12 preceding.

Chapter 12, which leads into the burdens of the Lord, is sometimes titled "Thanksgiving for God's Salvation" (RSV) or "Songs of Praise for Salvation" (NLT). In this brief yet beautiful chapter, Isaiah begins to thank and praise God for His salvation, protection, and deliverance. Repeatedly the prophet tells us to sing, rejoice, and shout.

> *"**A day is coming when people will sing**. I **praise** You, Lord! The Lord is my strength and **song**. He is my Savior! With joy you will draw water from the wells of salvation. God's people **rejoice** when He saves them.*
>
> *"**A day is coming when people will sing. Give thanks** to the Lord! Call for Him to help you! **Sing** to the Lord because of the great things He has done. Let the whole world hear the news. Let everyone who lives in Zion **shout and sing**! Israel's Holy God is great, and He lives among His people! **Shout and sing aloud**, oh, inhabitant of Zion, for Great is He among you, the Holy One of Israel"* (Isa. 12:1-6 GNT/KJV/AB/TNIV; emphasis mine).

Twice we are told in Isaiah 12 "a day is coming when people will sing." Then in the next eighteen chapters of Isaiah (13-30), the Lord introduces us to the songs of deliverance we can sing against the demonic forces oppressing us. The Lord is telling us "Here are the songs that I want you to sing against the powers working through those nations!" It is not the physical nation God is calling us to sing against. It is the demonic power operating behind that nation. Remember, our battle is not against an enemy of flesh and blood *"here on earth that we can see or get our hands on, but with the darkness of spiritual beings who were once in heaven and are now using their authority and power to try to rule the world. Therefore ... stand your ground,* ***making use of all your weapons****"* (Eph. 6:12-13 CW/CCB; emphasis mine). That day to sing as prophesied in Isaiah 12 is today. Today is the time for the children of God to sing His war songs of deliverance.

> *"Behold, God is my salvation. I will trust and not be afraid, for the Lord Jehovah is my strength and my song"* (Isa. 12:2 KJV).

It's no accident that Isaiah quotes from Exodus Chapter 15 here: *"My song is of the Eternal, He is my strength, of Him I sing"* (Exod. 15:2 Mof). This verse is quoted one other time in the Bible, in Psalm 118.

> *"****The Lord gives me strength and a song****. He has saved me. Shouts of joy and victory come from the tents of those who do right: 'The Lord has done powerful things.' The power of the Lord has won the victory"* (Ps. 118:14-16 NCV emphasis mine).

Moses and the children of Israel sang this song of deliverance to the Lord after Pharaoh and his army were destroyed in the Red Sea. God gives us strength *and* a song—they go together.

In Chapters 13-14, Isaiah proceeds to deliver the words of God's wrath and doom upon the spiritual force affecting the Babylonian kingdom, telling how the Lord will punish him for what he had done to God's people. ***"I'll put a full stop to the evil on the earth,"*** *and "terminate the dark acts of the wicked"* (Isa. 13:11 MSG; emphasis mine). God then pulls back the curtain in the spirit realm so we can clearly see the real power operating behind the scenes through Babylon in Isaiah's day. It is lucifer who boasts against the Lord.

A day is coming when God's people will sing, walking in Jesus' steps, destroying the works of the devil. That day is today!

The five "I wills" of lucifer:

> *"You have said in your heart, '<u>I will</u> ascend to heaven; <u>I will</u> raise my throne above the stars of God: <u>I will</u> sit enthroned on the mount of the assembly, on the utmost height of Mount Zaphon; <u>I will</u> ascend above the tops of the clouds; <u>I will</u> make myself like the Most High"* (Isa.14:13-14 TNIV).

And God's most apt commentary:

> *"How you have fallen from heaven, Morning Star; son of the dawn! You have been cast down to the earth, you who once laid low the nations"* (Isa. 14:12 TNIV).

GOD'S TAUNT-SONGS, HIS WAR SONGS OF DOOM

In Isaiah 14 God extends His grace to His people. With compassion He will bring them back to their land and they will *"rule over those who had ruled them, they will oppress those who had oppressed them"* (Isa. 14:2 NASB/MSG). Then God gives some interesting instructions to His People. He tells them, *"To take up this parable,* ***this taunt-song, this bitter song of doom*** *against Babylon.* ***You will make fun of the king of Babylon by singing this song"*** (Isa. 14:3 CEV/Mof; emphasis mine).

Moulton tells us that this "doom-prophecy" against Babylon is written on the basis of the "taunt rhythm," and the last part is a "fully developed ode on fallen Babylon."[11] God is telling the Jews to openly taunt Babylon. The word taunt comes from a Persian root word that simply means "to pierce with words."[12] When we are called upon by the Lord to taunt the enemy, we are simply called to pierce him with the Word of God. We declare the truth to the enemy:

- "You are insane and crazy, Jesus is the Invincible Conqueror."
- "You are a loser, Jesus is the Lord."
- "You are doomed, Jesus is Divine."

These truths pierce the enemy to his core of his empty life.

Taunts and taunt songs are not new in the Bible. The Lord Himself laughs from His throne and mocks the plans of the rebellious:

> *"The kings of the earth form a united front; the rulers collaborate against the Lord and against His Anointed King. They say, 'Let's tear off Their shackles They have put on us! Let's free ourselves from Their ropes.'* ***The One enthroned in heaven laughs in disgust; The Lord taunts them"*** (Ps. 2:2-4 NET; emphasis mine).

GOD'S WAR SONGS ACTIVATE GOD'S POWER

This taunt-song from the Lord is called "one of the boldest prosopopoeias (i.e. proclamations) that was ever attempted in poetry."[13] We see a beautiful progression here in Isaiah 14. First, in obedience to the Lord, God's people begin to sing against the evil one (vs. 4-6). Second, the whole world begins to sing and break out with cries of joy (vs. 7). Third, creation (the trees) joins in the celebration as the evil one falls (vs. 8). Fourth, the world of the dead rise up and mock the evil one's demise (vs. 9-10). Last, the Lord God Himself joins in mocking the downfall of the evil one (vs. 12-23).[14]

Our praise and worship sets off a chain reaction ... even God Himself will join in rejoicing of the defeat of the devil.

The key revelation given here is that as we praise and worship the Lord, we set off a chain-reaction in the Spirit. Everyone and everything, including God the Father, joins in on the celebration of the doom, defeat, and destruction of the evil one.

BEWARE RAILING ACCUSATIONS

When Michael the archangel came against the devil concerning the body of Moses, Michael did not give a "railing accusation" against satan. He simply said, "The Lord rebuke you" (Jude 1:9 NJKV). Here Michael was taunting satan, piercing him with the word, by quoting the prophetic word of God that Zechariah spoke against satan:

> *"And He showed me Joshua the high priest standing before the Lord, and satan standing at his right hand to oppose him. And the Lord said to satan, '**The Lord rebuke you, satan!** The Lord Who has chosen Jerusalem **rebuke you!**"* (Zech. 3:1-2a NJKV; emphasis mine).

When Jesus was tempted by the devil in the wilderness, He responded in much the same way. Each time the devil came at Him with a temptation, Jesus' response was the word of God. Jesus would counter-attack satan's assault with "It is written," "It is written," "It is written" (Matt. 4:4, 7, 10; Luke 4:4, 8, 12). This is how we overcome the evil one, by the word of our testimony, by the blood of Jesus, and by being willing to die for Christ (Rev. 12:11 KJV/MSG).

GOD'S WORD—VERBATIM

God warns against adding to or taking away from His word. He tells Israel that if they are to *"live and go in and take possession of the land which the Lord, the God of your fathers is giving you,"* then they must follow His decrees. He immediately gives them this decree: ***"You shall not add to the word** which I am commanding you, **nor take away from it,** that you may keep the commandments of the Lord your God which I command you"* (Deut. 4:1-2 NASB emphasis mine). Again in Proverbs 30:6 we are cautioned, *"Don't add to His words, lest He rebuke you and you be found a liar"* (NKJV). And finally, the last words of Jesus in the Bible warn us:

> *"I testify to everyone who hears the words of this prophecy of this book: **If anyone adds to them,** God will add to him the plagues which are written in this book; and **if anyone takes away** from the words of this book of this prophecy, God will take away his part from the tree of life and from the holy*

> *city, which are written in this book"* (Rev. 22:18-19 NASB; emphasis mine).

God doesn't want us twisting, taking away from, or changing the meaning of His word. We would be "taking away" or watering down the word of God if we didn't completely follow God's instruction. If God is saying taunt, we are to taunt. Like Jesus, we are simply saying, "It is written." Like the angel Michael, we are quoting the word of God and nothing but the word. When we sing the war songs, we are singing the words of the Lord, exactly as God tells us to sing them.

We would be "adding to" the word of God if we included railing accusations against satan. To do so would be singing out of offense and pain, resulting in rage and unholy vengeance. God's children don't speak, act, or sing out of self-indulgence. We speak, act, and sing out of obedience. Jesus, our firstborn brother, spoke the words the Father told Him, both the "what" and the "how" (John 12:49 NIV/MSG/BBE). We'll do well to do the same. If God says to sing these "taunt songs," we better sing these songs exactly as He tells us.

The words of God against His enemies are to be sung, not just read, not just preached. God has chosen singing as part of His spiritual arsenal, and He shows us this throughout His word.

A WORD OF CAUTION

Before we begin to sing these war songs we must pay close attention to the Lord's instructions. He says we need to be at a certain place in Him before we can sing these war songs.

> *"**When** the Lord gives you rest from your pain and turmoil and harsh service to which you have been enslaved, **then** you will sing this song and taunt the King of Babylon"* (Isa. 14:3-4 NASB/NCV/GOD's WORD; emphasis mine).

Take note of the "when" and the "then" in God's word. The Lord is cautioning not to step out and sing these war songs until we receive rest and healing in and through Him. We must be whole in the Lord. Whole is not perfect; whole is healed. We must have rest in our spirit; no turmoil, no bondage to any demonic slavery. Singing from a heart that is still wounded can lead to the trap of railing accusations against the enemy, of which we have been warned. Such singing can be a snare to our soul and will not invoke the power necessary to defeat the evil against which we battle.

The war songs of God are to be sung out of faith. They are songs sung from a heart that is free from anger, free from bitterness, free from the desire for vengeance. They are songs that when born from the lips of those redeemed and restored by the Almighty God can and will demolish devilish dominions. God is the avenger (Rom. 12:19). He will repay. We sing in faith and our singing releases His vengeance. We sing; God gives payback. Nowadays there are warning labels on CDs (and for good reason). The war songs of God need warning labels on them: "Warning! These songs are not for the faint of heart or wounded."

The war songs of God are to be sung out of faith.

I know what it's like to be wounded, to be "hit by friendly fire." After graduating from college and Bible school, I went into the ministry as a pastor for a campus ministry. Sadly, circumstances with the leadership of that ministry made it necessary for me to step down as pastor after serving for five years. It took another five years before I went back to any service for the Lord. I know what it is like to be wounded by your own family in the Lord. But praise God, He is the restorer of our souls. He restores what the enemy tries to destroy. He is the God of the resurrection. He brings back to life things in our heart we thought had died.

If you are wounded and hurting, go and receive the rest and healing found in the Lord's presence. Get your healing from the Lord before you step into the fray. This is a principle of the natural world that applies to the spiritual as well. In the natural, we never send wounded warriors into the heat of the battle. They must be well and strong if they are going to be effective. If just thinking about going into spiritual warfare stirs up a "twinge" in your spirit, it's not time for you to fight … yet. When your spirit is healed, healthy and ready for the fight, that "twinge" will be replaced by a sense of excitement and anticipation. A war cry will rise up within you as you learn more about God's war songs, and when it's time and you are ready, you will take that war cry to the front lines.

When it is time and you are ready, you will take that war cry to the front lines.

Lord, reveal the power of Your word to destroy demonic strongholds. Heal us, equip us and train us with the weapons of Your Divine wrath. Jesus, sing with us as we declare the war songs of God in our praise and worship and see those demonic walls fall!

The weight of God's glory is unloaded on the demons' head as we sing.

ENDNOTES:

1. Retrieved at http://www.blueletterbible.org/lang/lexicon/lexicon.cfm?Strongs=H1697&t=KJV.
2. Retrieved at http://classic.net.bible/org/strong.php?id=05375.
3. Retrieved at http://classic.net.bible/org/strong.php?id=03513.
4. Retrieved at http://www.blueletterbible.org/lang/lexicon/lexicon.cfm?Strongs=H4853&t=KJV.
5. Seekins, pp. 10-11
6. Retrieved at: http://en.wikipedia.org/wiki/Precentor.
7. Moulton, Richard G., The *Modern Readers Bible,* (MacMillan & Company, 1940), 1,392.
8. Moulton, p. 1,393.
9. Moulton, p. 1,392.
10. http://www.webster1828.com/websters1828/definition.aspx?word=Enthusiasm.
11. Moulton, p. 1,570.
12. Webster (Hardcover Edition) 1828.
13. Smith, Jerome H., ed., *The New Treasury of Scriptural Knowledge,* (Nashville: Thomas Nelson Publishers, 1992), 760.
14. Smith, 760-762.

CHAPTER FIVE

The Purpose of the War Songs

The Essence of a War Song

After Isaiah proclaims God's word of wrath against Babylon and lucifer, he goes on to deliver a series of more than twelve more burdens (i.e. war songs) against the principalities and powers operating behind the scenes to manipulate the unhappy inhabitants of these countries. In the last few verses of Isaiah 30 we find a prophecy that explains the essence and mission of the war songs of God. It reveals the purpose of why we sing and what happens in the Spirit when we sing. A thorough understanding of this particular burden of the Lord will be valuable ammunition when you find yourself in a firefight with the adversary.

> *"Behold, the name of the Lord comes from afar, burning with His anger, and* ***the burden (massa) thereof is heavy:*** *His lips are full of indignation, and His tongue as a devouring fire: And His battle cry overwhelms, like a flooding river"* (Isa. 30:27-28 KJV/NET; emphasis mine).

Other versions translate the Hebrew word *massa* in verse 27 as the Lord comes and *"His doom is heavy"* (NEB/REB), or *"His wrath burns and is heavy to bear"* (DRB). Most translations have some reference to smoke *"rising up"* (as *massa* refers to "lifting up") from the Lord's fire or a *"heavy smoke is rising"* from the Lord, or as *"the lifting up of smoke"* (see NIV/TLB/RSV). Read in context (found on preceding page) we see that these words are about the Lord's lips, His tongue, and His breath or voice. It's clear that this "heavy burden" is not about smoke but about a word out of the heart of God.

God is coming with the burden of His Word, and it is heavy with the weight of His glory.

Other translations read:

> *"See, the name of Yahweh comes from afar, blazing in His anger, heavy His exaction" or "heavy His threat"* (JB/NJB).

Exaction means "the act of demanding with authority, and compelling to pay or yield; an authoritative demand."[1]

Yet another translation reads:

> *"Look, from afar the name of Yahweh is coming, burning in anger,* ***with a heavy hand****. Filled with fury are His lips, like a consuming fire is His tongue" (CCB emphasis mine). Still another translation says, "Behold the name of the Lord comes after a long time, burning wrath;* ***the word of His lips is with glory, a word full of anger,*** *and the anger of His wrath shall devour like fire"* (CAB/Sept; emphasis mine).

In summary, God is angry and He's about to pay a visit, bringing with Him something weighty and ominous. That "something" is the word from His lips, and that word is heavy with His glory to set things straight in the world.

The most accurate translation of this all-important verse would be *"The Lord comes ... and His massa, His prophetic war song of doom is heavy."* We know it's a song He brings with Him by looking to the next verses:

> *"His wrath pours out like the floods upon them all, to sweep them all away. He will sift out the proud nations and bridle them and lead them off to their doom.* ***But the people of God will sing a song of joy****. They will celebrate and be happy when the Lord takes action.* ***You will sing happy songs*** *as in a night set apart for a festival, and gladness of heart as he who is going with a flute, to come into the mountain of the Lord, to the Rock of Israel"* (Isa. 30:28-29 TLB/NLT/ERV/ISR/CW; emphasis mine).

God is coming down from His throne in anger and wrath, but His children don't tremble in fear. Instead, they sing. They sing because their Lord is singing. God is coming, singing one of His war songs of wrath upon the enemies of His children. When we hear our Lord sing, we can't help but join in the song. We can't help but rejoice because the Lord is coming to set things right that were wrong, make paths straight that were crooked, and shine light into the darkness.

God's people are singing because God is singing!

The entire context of Verses 27 and 28 is God speaking forth or singing His word. Just look at the terminology used: His *massa* (prophetic word), His lips, His tongue, and His breath or battle cry. God is declaring an important word here, and we need to hear it.

The Majestic Voice and Rod of God

Reading on it becomes crystal clear that there is singing, music, and dancing in this battle against God's enemies:

> *"And the Lord will cause His **majestic voice** to be heard and shall crush down His mighty arm in anger upon His enemies, with angry indignation and with devouring flames, and tornados and terrible storms and huge hailstones" and "the voice of the Lord will shatter Assyria, as He strikes them with the rod. And it shall come to pass, that every stroke of the staff of doom which Yahweh shall lay upon him, shall be to the **music of tambourines and harps: and in battles of shaking will He attack them with His weapons"*** (Isa. 30:30-32 Rhm/CEV/KJV/NET; emphasis mine).

Here God calls our tambourines and harps His *weapons* of doom. Worship leaders, choir and orchestra members, whether you like it or not, you're in God's Army now. That instrument you hold in your hand is your M-16 rifle, your RPG launcher, your LAW. Remember that on Sunday morning as you take it in your hand. You're not just leading the congregation in some lovely, feel-good melodies. You are engaging the forces of darkness in hand-to-hand mortal combat.

The Hebrew word for shaking is *tenupah* and means "to swing or wave."[2] One version reads "a warfare of waving." *Tenupah* is used primarily in reference to presenting the wave offering to the Lord (Ex. 29:24; Lev. 8:27). So in the midst of this warfare we have a sacrifice, a wave offering of worship to the Lord. Some Bible versions translate this word for shaking as "with **dancing**!" (JB/NET, emphasis mine), and another *"So it is decreed that the Rod should pass over him, brought down on him by the Lord's hand to the music of your tambourines and harps. A 'strange warfare' this is that* ***shall quell them****."* (Knox; emphasis mine). The word "quell" isn't used much in our modern day language. It's an old-fashioned term that means "to kill, stifle, stop, vex, suffocate, and to reduce to peace."[3] The mental picture here is of God coming down, beating the tar out of the enemy, then leaving peace where chaos once reigned. Indeed, the music of tambourines and harps and dancing make for "strange warfare," but they are the exact weapons God has designed for this battle.

Other translations put it like this:

> *"And as the Lord beats Assyria,* ***His people will keep the rhythm with their drums and harps****"* (ERV; emphasis mine).
>
> *"Every blow God lands on them with His club is in time with the music of drums and pipes!"* (MSG)
>
> *"And every blow of the rod of His punishment, which the Lord will send on him,* ***will be to the sound of music****"* (BBE; emphasis mine).

That's what it means for the hills to be "alive with the sound of music." The mountains of the Lord are alive with the glorious sound of battle music, a/k/a our praise and worship. *"He will beat them to the music of tambourines and harps; He will fight against them with His mighty weapons"* (NCV). Our worship and our music are an attack on the strongholds of the evil one. Our praise and worship sound like a

God strikes the adversary to the beat of our praise and worship.

funeral dirge to the devil—*his* funeral. Each time we strike the guitar or beat the drum, the Lord strikes the adversary in the spiritual realm.

Give God All You've Got

In 2 Kings we read of Joash, the king of Israel, coming to the prophet Elisha for guidance. During Joash's day, Israel was being oppressed by the nation of Aram also called Syria, and the king needed God to deliver them. Elisha instructed King Joash to take some arrows and strike the arrows on the ground (2 Kings 13:18). King Joash took the arrows and struck them three times on the ground and stopped. Elisha was fuming!

> *"And the man of God was furious with him and said, 'You should have struck five or six times; then you would have defeated Aram (I.e. Syria) utterly; as it is, you will strike Aram three times and no more'"* (2 Kings 13:19 KJV/NEB).

Here's the point: We're in a battle. We *can't* hold back. We *must* go all out, give it all we've got. As we praise and worship the Father with *all* of our heart, soul, mind, and strength, He strikes a blow to each beat of our music. Remember, the violent take the kingdom by storm:

- We Cry—God Crushes
- We Praise—God Pounds
- We Worship—God Wallops
- We Sing—God Smashes
- We Rejoice—God Ruins
- We Declare—God Dooms, Defeats, and Destroys

The Mission of the War Songs

There is one more very important point in the last verse of this war song that is vital for us to understand. It begins with these few simple words: *"Long ago was Topheth made ready"* (Isaiah 30:33 NEB). Topheth was the place where the Jewish people burned their rubbish, but it was also the place where they, at one horrible time in their history, sacrificed their children to the demonic god Molech (Lev. 18:21, 2 Kings 23:10, and Jer. 7:31). We see in this final verse of Isaiah 30 that God is preparing this shameful place for something else.

> *"Yes, it has been made ready for the king (the Hebrew word here for king is Molech). The funeral pyre has long been ready,* ***prepared for Molech the Assyrian god;*** *it is piled high with wood"* (Isa. 30:33 NLV/TLB; emphasis and note in parentheses mine).

For years this demon had deceived the Jewish people and driven them to sacrifice their very sons and daughters to Molech. *Molech* in Hebrew means "king," but it is very similar to the Hebrew word for "shame."[4] Both meanings are applicable, as Molech could be called the demon king of shame, in stark and undeniable contrast to our true and living God, the Lord of glory and honor. Now God says He is preparing Topheth for Molech. God is causing this demon to reap what he has sown. God Himself will prepare the funeral pyre, and by His own breath *"like fire from a volcano, will set it all on fire"* (Isa. 30:33 TLB).

This is one of the characteristics of our God we see throughout scripture: He turns the tables on His enemies. The very place of their assumed victory—in this case Topheth—becomes the place of their definitive defeat. Just as the cross

God turns the tables on the evil one. The place of satan's so-called victory will become the very place of his defeat.

was supposedly satan's ultimate defeat over Jesus, in reality, it is the everlasting place of the devil's absolute, unmitigated defeat, doom, and destruction (1 Cor. 2:6-8). God does this not just on the corporate level, but also on the individual level, for all of His children. Those areas of weakness and sin in our life become our greatest areas of strength and victory when Jesus takes control.

The Pleasant Warfare of Worship

Each time we come before the Lord in praise and worship we must be sensitive to the Holy Spirit, just as an orchestra member carefully watches each wave and subtle gesture of the hand of the conductor. As our Great Music Director, the Lord may direct us to move into spiritual warfare through our praise and worship. He may lead us into this pleasant warfare of praise to sing His war songs of wrath against a specific enemy. He will join us in our faith as we sing these taunt songs and strike the enemy to the beat of our praise.

David knew the power of our praise and worship. The Lord wants even our children to join in His victory. David proclaims, *"You have taught children and nursing infants to give You praise, toddlers shout the songs that drown out enemy talk. They silence Your enemies who were seeking revenge"* (Psa. 8:2 NLT/MSG). Even the songs of our children drown out and silence the evil one.

The prophecy in Isaiah 30 is not just about God delivering Israel from the physical bondage of the Assyrians. It's much better than that. He was delivering them from that demonic stronghold of Molech as well. Through their praise and worship in faith, God was able to pay Molech back for the death and destruction he had wrought upon God's people. This same deliverance is available for us today, as we open our mouths in faith and let loose the weapons of our warfare of worship on our adversary.

The war songs of God create a spiritual retaliation from God upon the hordes of hell. They must be put to music because we are not only preaching, praying, and prophesying God's word against the enemy, we are also praising God for the victory. We don't do this with railing accusations, from a hurt and wounded spirit, but from a heart filled with love, passion, praise, and worship to our Father God. We do it in faith, standing on and obeying His word. And something happens in the Spirit when we step out and believe God: we are changed. The word of God not only changes the world around us but it changes us as well. There's a release of God's power when we sing His war songs of wrath, when we put on God's armor of light, when we are clothed with Jesus Himself. We become the weapons of God's hands against the forces of darkness.

The war songs of God create a spiritual retaliation from God upon the hordes of hell.

Lord, lead us as our Conquering Conductor in our praise and worship. Release Your war songs, Your weapons to destroy the chaos of sin and rebellion. Open our eyes to see Your mighty arm smashing down the fortresses of

wickedness to the beat of our music. Turn the tables on the evil one, and make the areas of our weaknesses become the places of our strength in You.

During our warfare/worship, God beats the devil to the beat of our music!

ENDNOTES:

1. Webster 1828.
2. Retrieved at: http://classic.net.bible.org/strong.php?id=08573#.
3. Webster 1828.
4. Retrieved at: http://www.newadvent.org/cathen/10443b.htm.

CHAPTER SIX

The War Songs Applied

If any person in all of history has known the power of praise and worship, it was King David. David was a singing warrior. He is the one we must look to if we are to learn how to apply these war songs of God.

King David knew God. He recognized his Father God, and in his beautiful songs (psalms) we hear David's heart of worship. The Psalms are full of praise and worship expressing David's love to the Lord, but they're also full of rejoicing and exaltation because of the defeat of his enemies and the victory he had in God. David was a lover and a fighter, and best of all he knew when it was time to love and when it was time to fight (Eccl. 3:8). He also knew how to subdue and overcome not only his fleshly enemies, but those forces of evil in the spiritual realm as well.

The Little Picture

David knew how to fight off a demonic attack. We see this in the example of him playing on the harp to refresh the tortured soul of King Saul. Saul was tortured because of his own failure and his disobedience to God. You see, Saul had blatantly disobeyed the Lord (in a battle, no less). As a result of his disobedience, God rebuked him, through the prophet Samuel. *"For rebellion is as the sin of witchcraft and stubbornness as the evil of idolatry. So because you have rejected the word of the Lord, He has rejected you as king"* (1 Sam. 15:23 NIV/NASB/NLT).

Samuel is then directed by God to go and anoint David as the next king. As soon as Samuel anointed David, *"the Spirit of the Lord rushed upon David from that day onward"* (1 Sam. 16:13 NET). At the same time, just the opposite was happening to Saul: *"Now the Spirit of the Lord had turned away from Saul, and an evil spirit from the Lord tormented him"* (1 Sam. 16:14 NET).

There is no vacuum in the natural realm of the earth, and there is no vacuum in the spiritual world. When Saul rejected the Lord, he lost God's kingly anointing which now was given to David. When Saul lost the Spirit of God's anointing, something had to take its place.

Jesus warns us:

> *"When the unclean spirit goes out of a man, it passes through waterless places seeking rest. Not finding any, it says 'I will return to my house from which I came.'... It goes and takes along seven other spirits more evil than itself, and they go in and live there; and* ***the last state*** *of that man becomes worse than the first"* (Luke 11:24-26 NASB; emphasis mine).

Saul's "last state" definitely became "worse than the first." He became overtly "anti-God's anointing." He had become infected, as it were, with the spirit of "antichrist," which literally means anti-Messiah or anti-anointing.[1] What started out as stubbornness, which God likens to the evil spirit of idolatry, transmutes into the evil spirit of envy, which then gives place to the even more destructive demonic spirit of murder. Talk about going from bad to worse.

Find a Man Who Can Play Skillfully

Saul's servants recognized that their king was being tormented by an evil spirit and advised him to let them find a man who could play skillfully and refresh the King, *"Why don't you let us find someone who can play a lyre and sing to you? When the evil spirits come, he can sing songs about the Lord, and the evil spirits will stop bothering you"* (1 Sam. 16:16 CW). Apparently, the power of music to thwart evil spirits was acknowledged in Israel in those days. Saul's servants found David and employed him to come and play for the king.

> *"David would take the harp and play songs of praise to the Lord with his hand; Saul would be refreshed and be well and the evil spirit would depart from him"* (1 Sam. 16:23 NASB/CW).

The Hebrew word for "evil" conveys the ideas of bad, afflicted, displeasure, grief, distress, misery, sorrow, wicked, and wretched.[2] The Hebrew word for "evil" comes from a root word meaning to spoil, break down, hurt, and vex.[3] Saul was definitely vexed and breaking down. The word "torment" means to be terrified or troubled. When David's anointed music was released, Saul was refreshed and made well. "Refresh" means to breathe, enjoy, and accept. The word "well" conveys the idea of being better, cheerful, gracious, joyful, kind, merry, pleasant, prosperous, favor, and sweet. One translation of this scripture reads *"new life came to Saul"* (BBE).

David's worship drove off the demonic spirits and brought rest and peace to King Saul.

Scripture says David played for King Saul on a daily basis to bring relief to his tormented (i.e., terrified and troubled) soul and spirit. Most often, David's music would soothe Saul, but there are two times in scripture where Saul's hatred for David was so overwhelming it couldn't be placated, even by the anointing on David's best harp playing. The evil spirits of envy and murder were at work in Saul's life.

The first time David's music failed to overcome Saul's evil spirit occurred shortly after David returned to Jerusalem with Saul after defeating Goliath. Word of David's amazing victory over Goliath and the ensuing defeat of the Philistines at the hands of Israelites had already reached the city. Scripture tells us that the women of Jerusalem greeted the returning army with dancing and tambourine playing and singing, *"Saul has slain his thousands and David his tens of thousands"* (1 Sam. 18:7 NIV). But the song they sang enraged the spirit of envy within King Saul. From that moment on, the Bible says Saul *"kept a close eye on David with suspicion and envy from that day on"* to kill him (1 Sam. 18:8-9 TNIV/NASB/BBE).

The "jealous spirit of murder" that permeates Saul's being hated the attention given to David. It rose up in Saul so much so that when David came in to play for him as before, instead of being soothed, the spirit erupted.

> *"The next day an evil spirit from God came forcefully on Saul. And he raved in his house like a madman, while David was playing the lyre, as he usually did. Saul had a spear in his hand and he hurled it, saying to himself, 'I'll pin David to the wall.' But David eluded him twice"* (1 Sam. 18:10-12 NIV/GNT).

David's Three Options

Because God's Spirit was with David, he again went victoriously into battle against the Philistines and returned, unharmed. Once again he entered Saul's court to play the lyre for the king and found Saul again being tormented by an evil spirit and "with his spear in his hand" (1 Sam. 19:9). The scene was all too familiar to David. No doubt, he started weighing his options.

1. **Take a rain check.** David could leave and come back later, preferably when Saul was unarmed. A king needn't hold a spear while sitting in his throne room. Saul's sole purpose for arming himself was to kill David.
2. **Proceed with the plan to play.** David could believe that God would deliver him, just as He had in the past. He could go in to Saul with his lyre and play—being ready to duck and run as before. This is the option David chose. As before, Saul tried to kill David, so David ducked the spear again and ran out (1 Sam. 19:10).

There is a third option that merits examination.

3. **<u>Go and get backup.</u>** David could have brought in some backup singers: Heman, Asaph, and Ethan, singers in the Tent of David (1 Chron. 15:16-17), and Chenaniah, the chief musician (1 Chron.15:22). With David out front, playing on the harp, the backup singers' song for Saul could have gone something like this:

"Do-Do-Do-Do-Do, De-Do-De-Do-De-Do
Oh, my lord Saul, yes, you are the king,
But there's One above, He's Master of everything.
"He's called you forth, to do your part. But above all
else, give Him your heart. Oh, king Saul!
Do-Do-De-Do-Wa."

Application of Option 3

For a while David was able to appease the demonic spirit in Saul, but over time, Saul became worse. He continually rejected the rest and refreshing of the Lord through David's anointed playing. David was growing and advancing in life. He became more and more successful, because he was walking in loving obedience and worship to the Lord. At the same time, Saul was getting worse, holding onto his jealousy and hate. Our walk in the Lord is not stagnant. Jesus said that we are either "with Him or against Him" (Matt. 12:30; Luke 11:23). There is no neutral ground. There is no coasting in the Kingdom. We go forward or we slide backward. In his book James W. Moore said it well, *"You can get bitter or better."*[4]

When ministering to God's children, if there is no success, go get backup.

Saul was definitely getting bitter. No matter how often or

how well David played, Saul chose to continually reject God's anointing. The lesson here as it relates to our warfare is that when ministering to God's children, if there is no success, go get backup. Go find other "heavy-hitters" in the spirit to assist you in ministering to someone. Jesus tells us if someone will not listen to you, go and get another brother or sister, have them join you in talking with him (Matt. 18:15-17). This is wisdom. The same is true in the natural. A solitary soldier is not sent to try to overpower an enemy battalion. We match the weapon to the warfare and have other warriors join us in the battle.

The Big Picture

These stories from King David's life show us how we can use the word of God in song as a weapon for deliverance from the oppression of evil spirits; however, there is a bigger picture as it relates to the war songs of God, and it is revealed to us, again, through a story about King David.

King David desired to bring the Ark of the Covenant from the house of Obed-Edom to Jerusalem (1 Chron. 15; 2 Sam. 6). David choreographs the glorious procession that will lead the Ark to its newly appointed dwelling place. He is very specific about who will do what and where in this praise parade. Because David is a military leader, it is a military procession. The procession consists of King David, the priests, the Levites, the military leaders, the singers, musicians and dancers, all of them making a joyful sound of praise to the Lord as they usher the Ark to its new resting place.

One man stands out in this group: Chenaniah, whom we have met in an earlier chapter. Chenaniah's name means "he whom God defends"[5] (1Chron. 15:22; 27).

As the leader of the Levites, the chief musician, he is:

- "in charge of the singing" (NASB);
- "in charge of music" (MSG);
- "master of the song" (OJB).

The Hebrew word translated song, music, or singing is *massa*. As we saw in chapter four, *massa* also means "to lift up." Because of this meaning, some translators have proposed that it had something to do with the physical act of lifting up the Ark, while other translators suggest it had to do with lifting up the voice in song.

Another excellent translation, and possibly the closest to the true meaning, is the God's Word Translation. It reads, *"Chenaniah, a Levite leader, instructed others how to sing prophetic songs because he was skilled at it"* (1 Chron. 15:22), and *"Chenaniah, the leader of the musicians' prophetic songs"* (v. 27).

The Chenaniah Anointing

Everything we know about Chenaniah is given to us here in 1 Chronicles 15. He is called the leader or chief of the Levites. He was in charge of the singing and music because he was "skillful" in it, or as one translation defines it, he was skillful because "he understood it" (1 Chron. 15:22 RSV). Chenaniah understood the song and the music. He understood the burden of the Lord, these prophetic war songs.

Chenaniah alone is listed by name as being present with David in verse 27. You see, David had learned a valuable lesson when he played for King Saul years ago. David learned that sometimes you need backup. And here, facing the city of Jerusalem with the Ark of God in tow, David realized he needed backup—and plenty of it. So David brings along a "heavy hitter" in the spirit, a man whose only mention in scripture is as one who understands and is skillful in singing and leading the singing of these prophetic war songs. As a commander so well acquainted with battle, David could have called up his army to lead the way for the Ark's voyage into Jerusalem. Instead, David brought the priests, the choir and musicians, and leading them all, Chenaniah, he whom God protects.

David called for backup singers, not soldiers, to accompany the Ark's entrance into Jerusalem.

These war songs release the power of God against His enemies. They are songs of God's wrath. David and his backup are not singing wrath songs against Jerusalem. They are singing the war songs against the demonic stronghold over Jerusalem. For years Saul had reigned as king over Israel, and the demonic spirit of jealousy and murder that consumed King Saul had flooded the city of Jerusalem, from the top to the bottom. Jerusalem was no longer a city of peace, but had become a city of murderous envy. That demonic jealousy flowed down from the commander to the cook, from the leader to the lowest in that place. Anointing always flows from the head to the feet. Just as the oil with which Aaron, the first priest, was anointed flowed down from his beard to the edge of his priestly garments

Chenaniah was leading the army of David in war songs against that religious stronghold over Jerusalem.

(Ps. 133:2), so, too, the anointing of Saul had soaked through the entire city of Jerusalem.

The whole time Saul was King, he never once made an effort to retrieve the Ark of the Covenant and return it to God's people. His ignoring of the Ark was not by accident. Saul was not right with God. He was not near to the Lord, nor near to the things of God. He was perfectly content to have God's Ark as far away as possible (1 Chron. 13:3). But a new sheriff was coming to town. King David was correcting that long-standing wrong. David's praising army was driving the demonic force out of the city of God and back into the waterless places where it belonged.

The picture here is of David and his backup courageously, joyfully singing and dancing their way into Jerusalem, escorting the Ark of the Covenant to a tent where it will be once again in close proximity to God's chosen people. In the midst of this celebration, something tragic happened. David's wife, Michal, the daughter of Saul, was watching this praise parade through a window. When she saw her husband, the king, jumping and leaping and worshiping God, instead of rejoicing with him we are told she "despised him in her heart" (1 Chron. 15:29 NASB); she was "filled with contempt" (MSG) for her own husband.

Why would a wife not laugh and smile and rejoice along with her husband at such a time of great success and elation? The answer is in her lineage. The spirit of Michal's father, Saul, maintained a stronghold in his daughter. In this moment, Michal had a choice to make. She could either let go of her father's familiar spirit or cling to it. Sadly, she made the wrong choice.

In the parallel story recorded in 2 Samuel, scripture tells us that David was going home to "bless his family" (2 Sam. 6:20 AAT). As David entered his home, ready to spread the joy of the day to his wife and household, he was not greeted by the loving, joyful arms of his spouse. Instead of rejoicing and receiving her husband's blessing, she cursed him. Her evil attitude caused her to miss out on the blessing, not only of that day, but of all her days thereafter. She began to mock and sarcastically criticize David. She accused him of exposing himself before his slave girls like "one of the vulgar fellows" (2 Sam. 6:20 RSV). David responded, I "will act even more foolish before the Lord" (2 Sam. 6:22 NLT).

If Michal had repented, there is no telling how many children she and David might have had.

For her harsh words and unwillingness to let go of the evil spirit of jealousy, Michal was cursed with barrenness. *"And Michal the daughter of Saul, had no child to the day of her death"* (2 Sam. 6:23 NRSV). God made her barren because she was still holding on to that family spirit, that familiar spirit which had ruled her father. It's as though God was saying, "I will not allow that demon to reproduce in My city. Michal, I'll let you live, but I will not allow that demon of jealousy and murder to be fruitful and grow in My town. That demon stops with you." Her child would have been the next king, but because she did not repent, no child from Saul's family line would ever again sit on the throne of Israel. Had Michal repented, that curse of barrenness would have lifted and she would have been fruitful and increased to the end of her days. Sorry to say, she did not repent.

A Paradigm Shift in the Spirit

When the Ark was brought into Jerusalem, it was a monumental time in the history of God working with His people. It was a time of transition for His spiritual leaders. For years, the sons of Kohath, (Kohath was one of the three sons of Levi) had carried the furnishings of the Tabernacle of Moses (Num. 4:1-49). We read about their responsibilities in Numbers 4, and in this one chapter the Hebrew word *massa* is used nine times. Each time it's used, it is referring to carrying the furniture of the Tabernacle. Beginning here in 1 Chronicles 15 and 2 Samuel 6, a significant transition takes place. No longer will the Levites "carry" the Ark and its furnishings. From now on their service will be in bearing the burden of the presence of the Lord by "lifting up" His prophetic word in song. A shift in the Spirit takes place and the Ark is no longer carried from one camp to another as it was in the past. No longer were the priests required to lift up the Ark, God's mercy seat in the natural (1 Chronicles 23:26), but now they lifted the mercy seat up in the Spirit with praise and worship 24/7/365 (1 Chron. 25:1-31).[6] The Ark now resided in the Tent of David, waiting the day it would be permanently placed in the Temple of Solomon.

From the Tabernacle to the Tent to the Temple

Probably 99 out of 100 of believers are awaiting the Lord Jesus' return to His temple in Jerusalem. However, examining scripture, we find that the priority of God during this age of grace and the gospel of the new covenant is not the temple, but rather, the tent. God's word tells us that He must restore the tent before we'll ever get to the temple.

The Lord proclaimed through His prophet Amos.

> "***On that day I will set up David's fallen tent***. *I will repair the holes in it. I will restore its ruined places. I*

> *will rebuild them as they were a long time ago, that they can conquer the remnant of Edom and all the nations that belonged to Me. This is the very word of the Lord, who will do this"* (Amos 9:11-12 GOD'S WORD/NEB/JB; emphasis mine).

"That day" is today. Amos is prophesying about the day of God's grace and His new covenant in the blood of Jesus. James, an elder in the church, confirms this during the believers' meeting in Jerusalem when conflict arose concerning the Gentiles and the requirement of circumcision for them to become a member of the church. Peter, Barnabas, and Paul have all spoken, and when they are finished, James stands up and begins to speak.

> *"Brothers, listen to me. Simon (i.e. Peter) has described to us how God first showed His concern by taking from the Gentiles a people for Himself. The words of the prophets are in agreement with this, as it is written: '***After this I will return and rebuild David's fallen tent.*** Its ruins I will rebuild, and I will restore it, that the remnant of men may seek the Lord, and all the Gentiles who bear My name, says the Lord, who does these things'"* (Acts 15:13b-17 NIV/NKJV; emphasis mine).

This age, when the gospel of the Kingdom of God is preached, is the time when God is restoring the Tent of David that has fallen. Now is the time for the Tent of David to be rebuilt, a time full of praise and worship, a time of rejoicing and dancing, a time full of music and the joy of the Lord. The prophetic war songs of the Lord must be included in that praise and worship. They are a vital part to bringing in the very presence of Jesus to a home, a town, or a nation. Jesus is the Ark of the New Covenant. He is the

Tent that contains the very presence and mercy seat of God. He is the Word made flesh among us.

> *"And the Word, entering a new mode of existence, became flesh, and lived in a tent [His physical body] among us," or "And the Word became flesh and did* **tabernacle** *among us"* (John 1:14a Wuest/YLT emphasis mine).

Just as the first Ark was ushered into God's city following the echoes of praise, worship, and war songs, so must Jesus, the new Ark, be ushered into our midst.

The Big Picture for the World

The prophetic war songs contain the very ammunition of God to attack and defeat our demonic oppressors. These war songs must be put to music and must be sung by God's children over the demonic hosts of hell set against us. From the small scale to the large, in both situations, they are equally powerful. We are to take the word of God and sing the Lord's release over individuals and families (the little picture) and over churches, cities, states, and our country (the big picture).

Today the Lord is restoring the fallen tent of David and our praise and worship ascends 24/7 before the throne.

When Jesus sent out the 12 disciples (Matt. 10:1-15) and the 72 disciples (Luke 10:1-12), they were instructed that as they came into a city, they were to stay in a home there. Jesus tells them to pronounce their blessing, their peace on that home.

This is what we are doing when we sing the war songs of God over a home, church, or town. The war songs release God's blessing and peace over that person or people, just as King Saul experienced God's peace when David played for him. The force of the power of the Spirit of God in specific, focused, Holy Ghost-directed and concentrated praise and worship drives the darkness back. Then, because that veil in the spirit is torn away, the people in that area are able to truly "hear" God's good news.

Like David, let's sing over our cities and nation.

This is the same principle as intercessory prayer for a place to receive God's anointing. The war songs just add more ammunition to the fight. We are releasing the specific weapon for that adversary. When the enemy comes at you or your family as a roaring lion seeking to devour you, you don't pull out a shotgun. It will only irritate him and make him madder. You pull out your most high-powered rifle and take him down. When faced with a fight, it's better to have all the "whomp" you can get your hands on.

There will be homes and cities that will reject the gospel, just as the region of the Gadarenes, where Jesus cast out demons and made a man well, only to have the entire town come out to Him and beg him to leave (Matt. 8:34).[7] We are not to be discouraged. Remember, we are simply singing to clear a path for the Ark of the New Covenant to enter. No matter what, we must be faithful and do our part. We must stand in the gap and believe for the release of God's power over the land. We must sing God's blessings over the nations and sing God's judgment of doom over His demonic enemies. We must not stop until we see the glory of the Lord cover the earth as the waters cover the sea.

A Prayer for Modern Day Chenaniahs

God bring forth Your army of modern day Chenaniahs: Those who will understand and be skillful at lifting Your burden against our enemies; those who will be able to lead others in the prophetic war songs of the doom and destruction of spiritual darkness. Those who will go forth with the anointing of Chenaniah to understand and skillfully use the war songs, realizing that God has His hand of protection on you as you sing and fight.

Rise up warriors of God!

It's time to go to war!

Endnotes:

1. Retrieved at http://classic.net.bible.org/strong.php?id=473.
2. Retrieved at: http://classic.net.bible.org/strong.php?id=07451.
3. Retrieved at: http://classic.net.bible.org/strong.php?id=07489.
4. Moore, James W., *You can get Bitter or Better,* (1989) Abington Press.
5. Retrieved at http://www.blueletterbible.org/lang/lexicon/lexicon.cfm?Strongs=H3663&t=KJV.
6. In 1 Chronicles 25 we are given a list of 24 praise leaders and musicians who would play and sing before the Lord in the Tent of David. The number 24 is not an accident. It implies they were to praise and worship the Lord all day long. Each group would worship the Lord for an hour and then the next group would come in. It was to be a constant flow of worship 24/7.

   The meanings of the names of these 24 praise leaders are also not an accident. They tell us what each group was to focus on during their hour of worship. Notice that their responsibility was "to prophecy God's message" (1 Chronicles 25:1-3 ERV; emphasis mine). These were not just worship songs but prophetic "inspired songs" (NAB) going forth. Here are the names and meanings of the 24 leaders who conducted praise, worship, and prophesying in the Tent of David 24 hours a day:

1. **Joseph** means "Jehovah has added, He is adding" (Focus on the blessings that God is adding to us).
2. **Gedaliah** means "Jehovah is great, the greatness of Jehovah, whom Jehovah has made great, magnified of Jehovah" (Focus on how God's greatness magnifies and makes us great).
3. **Zaccur** means "remembered, mindful" (God remembers us).
4. **Izri (or Zeri)** means "created, my imagination, my thought, my formation, my fashioner (or distillation, balm, formation), a man or woman of a firm mind" God's thoughts form our thoughts; they are a balm to our soul.
5. **Nethaniah** means "the gift of Jehovah, given of the Lord" (We are the gifts that God gives to the world).
6. **Bukkiah** means "Jehovah has emptied, emptied out by Jehovah, emptying of the Lord" (God empties us so He can fill us with His good things).
7. **Jesharelah (or Asarelah)** means "these are upright, upright toward God, right towards God (or upright towards God, an upright or straight oak, guided towards God)" God makes us righteous and we are guided towards Him.
8. **Jeshaiah** means "Jehovah has saved, the salvation of Jehovah, the safety of Jehovah" (God's salvation and safety).
9. **Mattaniah** means "the gift of Jehovah" Focus on the gifts that God gives to us.
10. **Shemei** means "hearing, renowned, famous" (God hears us and we hear Him).
11. **Azarel (or Uzziel)** means "God has helped, the help of God (or the strength of God)." God helps us and makes us strong.
12. **Hasbahiah** means "the reckoning of Jehovah, whom God has considered or esteems." God is focused on His people.
13. **Shubael** means "the return of God, the captive of God" (God returns and we are free to be His servants).
14. **Mattihiah** means "the gift or reward of Jehovah" (God gives to us, and we give the gifts of God to the world).
15. **Jeremoth** means "He is Most High, high places" (The Most High places us on His high places).
16. **Hananiah** means "whom Jehovah gave, the grace of Jehovah, graciously given of the Lord, whom God has favored" (Rejoice in God' mercy, grace and favor that He has given to us).
17. **Joshbekashah** means "a hard or sharp seat, seated in a hard place, dwelling or seated in hardness" (Even in hard times, we dwell safely).
18. **Hanani** means "My grace, gracious" (God's mercy, grace and favor).

19. **Mallothi** means "I have uttered, I have spoken, I speak, My fullness. (We speak about the fullness of God, and we speak out by the fullness of God).
20. **Eliathah** means "to whom God comes, God of the coming one, my God has come" (The beauty of God's presence).
21. **Hothir** means "abundance," from the word "has made abundant, a surplus, who remains, or who abounds, to excel, to gain the victory or one who is undaunted" (God's abundance makes us undaunted, courageous, fearless, and brave).
22. **Giddalti** means "whom I have made great, whom I have magnified, whom I have trained up" (God magnifies and makes us great by His training).
23. **Mahazioth** means "visions, seeing a sign" (God gives us signs, visions and prophecies).
24. **Romamti-ezer** means "I have exalted help, exultation of help, I have heightened help, or I have exalted the Helper." We exalt the Helper, the Holy Spirit, Who walks with us.

Imagine the joy if we would again take up this practice of praise and worship to our Lord 24/7/365 in the Tent of David that the Lord is repairing in our day.

7. According to history, a strong church was later founded in this area. It was believed to be the result of this one man who was so demonized but then so gloriously delivered by Jesus. This one man brought God's grace to the area that in the past had demanded Jesus to leave.

PART 2
THE WAR SONGS OF GOD

" ... that I may conquer by His song ..."

—Habakkuk 3:19 CAB

Habakkuk

God's War Song to Defeat Violence

CHAPTER SEVEN

WE NEED ANOTHER FLOOD!

"It is the Lord's glory men must learn to know,
that shall cover the earth, flooding over
it like the waters of the sea"
—Hab. 2:14 Knox

A DEMONIC ATTACK OF VIOLENCE COVERS THE LAND

You drive to the mall, get out, look over your shoulder, lock your car and walk hastily to the nearest entrance, avoiding eye contact with the group of young people huddled around the back of an SUV. Back home and ready to call it a day, you turn out the lights, take a peek out the back window as you pull the curtains tight, lock, double lock, and chain your doors before you can rest. The next morning, the lead news story reports another shooting at a school and the little children who were ruthlessly murdered. The next tells a story of a young man who commits suicide after being the victim of bullying and emotional abuse. That piece is followed by new statistics that show the murder rate is up in your town, as is the incidence of rape and robbery. The final story of the morning tells of a child pornography ring being busted one town over and the rescue of several children who had been held captive by the perpetrators.

There is a demonic attack of violence running rampant over our land. We see it all around us. We see it on our televisions every morning and every evening—wars and conflicts raging among the nations. We see the fear, the loss, the sorrow and heartbreak it produces. Its death and destruction are everywhere. This demon of violence is operating unbridled not just in other countries; it is loose in our nation, in our cities and towns. It has slithered its way into every area of our lives, where even our schools, movie theaters, and places of worship are not safe.

This is not the will of our Father God. God with His "furious love"[1] desires to destroy that oppressive violence and set His children free. The Lord is calling for men and women to join Him in this war. It is not a battle involving hate and violence, but one of love and forgiveness. He is looking for warriors to bring His love and liberation to our nation.

A CALL TO BATTLE

The Lord is declaring "Who will stand in the trenches and fight? Who will stand in the gap to stop this onslaught of violence?" This problem of violence we face today is not a new problem. The prophet Habakkuk cried out to the Lord concerning this same demonic spirit of violence that we face today. This was the cry of Habakkuk's heart: *"Oh, Lord, how long must I call for help before You listen, before You save us from violence? Why do You make me see such trouble? How can You stand to look on such wrongdoing? Destruction and violence are all around me, and there is fighting and quarreling everywhere"* (Hab.1:2-3 GNB).

The entire book of Habakkuk is a burden from the Lord against this spirit of violence. In reading Habakkuk's words, we discover the same spirit is trying to destroy our nation today, and in this discovery we also find our hope. Through the words of this prophet thousands of years ago, God clearly and beautifully instructs us how to defeat this demonic oppression.

The name Habakkuk means "to embrace."[2] We are called to be like Habakkuk and embrace those devastated by violence. Embrace them and bring them to the Father, where He will heal and restore their hearts and lives. But that is only part of the victory in this battle. The complete victory is won when we embrace those prisoners of war who have been entrapped and used by this vile demon. We are called not only to embrace and reach out to the wounded, but also to the wrongdoer. We do that by singing God's songs of deliverance over them, by singing God's word, by singing His "It is written." As we sing, the word of God shatters that demonic stronghold over their lives, and they are set free. It's time to fight with God's heart of war and release the love of our Father God.

The Lord's Solution to the Violence Problem

Like us, Habakkuk saw violence all around him. He cried out to the Lord for His deliverance: *"How many times do I have to yell, 'Help! Murder! Police!' before You come to the rescue?"* (Hab.1:2 MSG). Because the problem of violence is a spiritual problem, it will never be resolved by our police force, our government, and our court systems. These manmade institutions can only attempt to curb the spread of this plague on our land, but they will never cure it. They may help in specific situations as they arise, but they will never heal it. Spiritual problems demand spiritual answers.

We have prayed for the families devastated by violence, but who is praying for that demon of violence to be devastated?

God has a way to resolve this problem of violence, and He demonstrates it in His word. The Hebrew word for violence is *chamac* and pronounced *hamas.*[3] The first time we encounter this term is in Genesis, during the days of Noah. Here we have the first example of God's total resolution to the problem of violence run amok.

> *"The earth also was corrupt, ruined before God, and* ***the earth was filled with violence****"* (Gen. 6:11 NKJV/NET; emphasis mine).

> *"Man's wickedness is out of control and needs to be stopped"* (Gen. 6:7 CW).

> *"And God looked upon the earth, and behold it was corrupt; for every mortal on earth had corrupted his life. And God said unto Noah, 'The end of all flesh is come before Me, for the earth is* ***filled with violence*** *because of them, the time has come for Me to take action'"* (Gen. 6:12-13 KJV/CW; emphasis mine).

The earth was "filled with violence." Violence had infected and ruined all of creation and God's only solution was to send a flood to wash the world clean with His baptism of water. A flood is God's spiritual cure for this spiritual attack. This is the same answer He gives to Habakkuk. The only way to stop this attack of violence during Habakkuk's day was for God to send another flood. This is also God's response to us today. The only way to stop the demonic attack of violence we see all around us is for God to send a flood. Our only hope is another flood from God.

God answers Habakkuk's cry, and everything He tells Habakkuk is the same answer He has for us today. He tells Habakkuk: *"Write the vision, and make it plain upon tablets that he may run that reads it"* (Hab. 2:2 NKJV). One translation says *"so those who read* ***may be able to soar!"*** (AEB; emphasis mine). The vision the Lord showed Habakkuk is the same vision He shows us today: **The Lord is going to send another flood, a flood to wash this demonic violence from our land.** But this flood will be very different from the flood of Noah's day, because the Lord has promised in His covenant with Noah that *"all flesh shall never again be cut off by water of the flood, neither shall there again be a flood to destroy the earth"* (Gen. 9:11 NASB). The next flood God sends will not be a flood of natural waters. It will be a flood of the glory of the Lord.

God's answer to demonic violence is to send another flood—a flood of His glory!

The Lord is sending a spiritual flood and as a result, *"It is the Lord's glory men must learn to know, that shall cover the earth,* ***flooding over it*** *like the waters of the sea"* (Hab. 2:14 Knox; emphasis mine). This impending flood of God's glory is our only hope of deliverance. Let's pray, preach, prophesy, and praise our Lord to release this flood of His glory over our country and our world. Let's persist in praising until God opens up the windows of heaven and pours out a flood of the *"knowledge of the glory of the Lord"* that will power-wash the unclean spirit of violence from the face of the earth, once and for all.

The Glory of God is His Heart of Compassion

To understand exactly what Habakkuk is telling us in this phrase "the *knowledge* of the glory of the Lord," we look to Moses. In Exodus 33, Moses cried out to the Lord, "Please, show me Your glory" (Ex. 33:18 WEB), and the Lord answered and revealed to Moses His glory. The Lord told Moses He would pass by and Moses would behold the glory of the Lord (Ex. 33:19-22). When the Lord passed in front of Moses, He proclaimed His name, His glory to Moses.

> *"And He passed in front of Moses, proclaiming, 'I am the Lord. The Lord is a God Who is* ***a compassionate, merciful, and gracious God****. I am slow to anger and abounding in unfailing love and faithfulness, maintaining covenant, faithful love to a thousand generations, forgiving wrongdoing, rebellion, and sin'"* (Ex. 34:6-7a NLT/NIV/WYC/HCSB; emphasis mine). [4]

Moses asked to see God's glory and that is exactly what God revealed to him. God showed Moses—and us—oh, so clearly what is His glory. The Lord proclaimed that He is a merciful God. He is a God full of love and forgiveness. He is a compassionate God, rich and abounding with covenant love. This is the knowledge that will flood the earth. This is the revelation the Lord will release upon our land. And it is this knowledge of God's glory, the power of the revelation of His nature, His character of love and grace that will drive back violence. The enemy has no defense against the love of God.

We "must learn to know" the glory of God's character as He revealed it to Moses. We must learn to truly know Him in all of His love, mercy, grace, faithfulness, and forgiveness. It is a flood of His character that must overflow from His children to show an imprisoned world His divine, victorious compassion to drive out demonic, violent condemnation. When we truly know Him and are filled with His mercy we will drive out malice. When we truly know Him and are filled with His grace and faithfulness we will drive out greed and fear. It is this revelation of God's character displayed through His children that will flood the earth and wash away the noxious demon of violence forever.

Sing for God's glory—His grace and compassion—to cover the earth!

The Attack is Everywhere

Just as it was in the days of Noah when violence was everywhere, so it was in the days of Habakkuk, and so it is today. As Habakkuk, we cry out to the Lord about the violence we see everywhere:

- **In our marketplaces (Hab. 2:5-8)**: We see that spirit causing men to get "rich by stealing and extortion" (2:6b MSG). This violent greed results in their "murders" and "*violence* against the people" (2:8b GNB).

- **<u>In our homes (Hab. 2:9-11):</u>** We see greed and violence operating. We see those who "obtain wicked gain for his house" (2:9a Amp), who make their "family rich with what you took by *violence*" (2:9a GNB). This violence released outside the home soon turns inward against the family members themselves.
- **<u>In our civil government (Hab. 2:12-14):</u>** We see, "him who builds a city with bloodshed and founds a town with *violence*" (2:12 NASB).
- **<u>In our country (Hab. 2:15-17):</u>** We see the "*violent* acts" (2:17 NET) that are manifested by those who make people drunk. In their rage, they force people to drink from the bowl of their "furious anger" to see their nakedness (2:15 NET).
- **<u>In our church (Hab. 2:18-19):</u>** We see makers of idols, who trust in a "teacher of lies" (2:18 NKJV). Those who worship false gods fill the land with "*violence* and deceit" (Zephaniah 1:9b CEB).

Take heart. For every demonic attack, God has His divine acclamation. In Habakkuk 1:8-11, we read God's response to Habakkuk's complaint. God tells the prophet that even though the enemy comes in with his demonic army, and his intention is *"to do violence and everyone is terrified as they approach"* (1:9 NET/GNB), though *"they mock kings and rulers are a joke to them, and laugh at every stronghold"* (1:10 NET/HCSB/HNV). God encourages Habakkuk

For every demonic attack, God has His divine acclamation.

(insert your name there) to taunt the enemy with His songs of victory because the Lord will cause the enemy to be swept *"on like the wind and they shall fall down and are gone, for their own strength was their god"* (1:11 GNB/WYC).

Then the Lord declares that the *"conquered people will take* ***up a taunt-song*** *against him. Won't they laugh, even mock and insult their oppressors?"* (Hab. 2:6 GNB/NASB/NET; emphasis mine). When kings and rulers of the world rise up against Him and His Anointed One, we are told, *"The One enthroned in heaven laughs in disgust; the Lord taunts them"* (Ps. 2:4 NET).

The Hebrew word used in Habakkuk 2 for taunt-song is *mashal* and means a parable or proverb. It can also mean a derisive poem or song.[5] It is the same word used by the Lord in His burden to Isaiah when He told that prophet, *"Then* ***you will mock*** *the king of Babylon with* ***this taunt-song.*** *You will sing this song [of contempt] about the king of Babylon"* (Isaiah 14:4 GW/CJB/HCSB; emphasis mine). The devil and his demons may laugh, but they will laugh for just a little while. The Lord has His own laughter against His adversaries, and He will release this laughter through His people: *"From His throne in heaven* ***the Lord laughs and mocks*** *their feeble plans"* (Ps. 2:4 GNT; emphasis mine). The word for mocks used here is *la'ag* and literally means "the benefit of knowing (Who is in) control."[6] We can laugh because we know Jesus is in control and has already won the war. We can laugh because our Lord is laughing.

GOD'S WORD ARROWS

God's war songs are victorious because they contain the word arrows of His glory and power. The shepherd king

David tells us, *"If evil people don't change their ways, God will sharpen His sword; He will string His bow and take aim. He takes up His deadly weapons; He makes His arrows flames of fire"* (Ps. 7:12-13 NIRV/NCV/GNB/BBE). Let the word of God come out of our mouth as His arrows of fire to defeat the enemy.

Most believers are familiar with the "fiery darts of the wicked one" (Eph. 6:16 KJV), but remember, the devil cannot create, he can only counterfeit. His fiery darts are just a perversion of the Lord's burning arrows of fire. God sends His word like flaming arrows to pierce our hearts. God's word arrows convict the world of sin and convict believers of righteousness. The arrows of truth from God are full of love, hope, and mercy; they cause us to repent and return to the arms of our Father. The enemy's fiery darts are full of his lies, false accusations, slander, and condemnation. They cause those wounded by them to despair. God has given His people a shield of faith to quench these poison arrows.

The devil does not have a shield of faith to stop God's word arrows of fire.

Not only do we quench the devil's fiery darts, we turn around and shoot God's word arrows of fire right back at him. With God's word flying with lethal accuracy from our mouths, we not only counter the adversary's attack, we also drive him back into his own territory—back to the pit, back to hell. God revealed this beautiful revelation about the enemy's pathetic, weak condition to my wife who shared it with me. The Lord showed her "The evil one does not have a shield of faith; therefore, the devil cannot stop My arrows of fire." When we shoot, shout, and sing the word of God against the devil, he is defenseless. He has no choice but to turn tail and make a run for it. So fire away, army of God! Fire away!

Send another flood, oh Lord! Release the flood of Your glory, wash away the filth of violence on our land and fill the earth with the knowledge of Your compassion and grace.

Send another flood, Oh Lord!
Release the flood of Your glory!

ENDNOTES:

1. *Furious Love* is the name of a powerful documentary by Darren Wilson. To learn more about the film, visit www.furiouslovefilm.com or www.wanderlustproductions.net.
2. Retrieved at http://www.zianet.com/maxey/Proph7.htm.
3. Retrieved at http://www.blueletterbible.org/lang/lexicon/lexicon.cfm?strons=H2555&t=KJV.
4. The last part of Exodus 34:7 is left out intentionally. This latter part of the verse concerns God punishing the guilty for their sins, and the children being punished for their parent's sins to the third and the fourth generation. It is left out because later in scripture (Ezekiel and Jeremiah) the Lord declares that He has removed this proverb. To wit: *"The life of the parent and the life of the child belong to Me. Only the one who sins will die"* (Ezek. 18:1-4 CEB). He explains in Jeremiah that He will do this because of the new covenant He will establish with Israel (Jer. 31:29-34). Even the part about the guilty being punished and dying for their sins will be removed. It will be removed if they repent and return to the Lord in this New Covenant. In the New Covenant of the blood of Jesus, God *"will forgive their wrongdoing and never again remember their sins"* (Jer. 31:34b CEB). This revelation of God's love is the knowledge of the glory of God that will cover the earth. The Lord declares: *"They will no longer need to teach each other to say, 'Know the Lord!' because **they will all know Me**, from the least of them to the greatest"* (Jer. 31:34a CEB emphasis mine).

5. Retrieved at http://classic.net.bible.org/strong.php?id=04912
6. Seekins, pp.10-11

CHAPTER EIGHT

VICTORY ON EVERY BATTLEGROUND

"How long, Lord, will You be deaf to my plea? 'Violence!' I cry out to You ... The Lord gives me this answer: 'Write down the vision, inscribe it clearly on tablets, so he that reads it may soar.'"
—Hab. 1:2a and 2:2, REB/AEB

WAR SONGS FOR VICTORY EVERYWHERE

For instruction in defeating violence on every battleground, we simply look to the burden the Lord gave Habakkuk. The Lord told the prophet "Write down this message and make it plain!" The message is for us to send the fiery word arrows of God into the enemy's camp, piercing him with our words (a/k/a to taunt him, *Webster's 1828, Hardcover Edition*). We are called upon, to shoot, shout, and sing into the strongholds of violence coming against our land. The Lord instructs His people to *"take up a taunt-song against them, mocking riddles, in scoffing derision show your scorn for them and say"* (Hab. 2:6 NASB/NRSV/RSV/GNT). The Lord proceeds to give five woes of doom for us to proclaim in song over these spirits of violence:

1. **Victory Over Violence in the Marketplace**
2. **Victory Over Violence in our Homes**
3. **Victory Over Violence in Civil Government**
4. **Victory Over Violent Drunkenness**
5. **Victory Over Violence in the Spiritual Arena**

We will discuss each of these in depth in this chapter.

1. Victory Over Violence in the Marketplace

(Hab. 2:5-8)

Sing God's word against the spiritual attack of hamas, greedy violence, in the marketplace. Rise up and take back what the enemy has stolen from us, from our families, and from our friends. Declare God's words to the wicked one, *"Let those who have been plundered and robbed, rise up and plunder you!"*

> *"Doom to the one who piles up stolen goods and makes himself wealthy by extortion"* (Hab. 2:6, CEB/NKJV).

> ***"Suddenly, your debtors will rise up in anger. They will turn on you and take all you have, while you stand***

trembling and helpless" (Hab. 2:7 NLT; emphasis mine).

"You have plundered the people of many nations, ***but now those who have survived will plunder you*** *because of the murders you have committed and* ***because you have filled the countryside with violence*** *against the people of the world and its cities"* (Hab. 2:8 GNB/NLT; emphasis mine).

Where is the War Song?

God is very economic, He doesn't waste words. His truth is like hidden treasure. Let's study this woe of doom and find His treasure. As we look at this first doom, we find three things to put to music in our war song:

1. We're called to proclaim God's doom and destruction over this demonic spirit of violence. We don't just pray for the families subjected to violence but also proclaim the doom and defeat of that demon.
2. We entreat the Lord to wake up His people, cause them to rise up and say that is enough! No more violence in the name of Jesus.
3. We not only stop this reign of violence, we release the terror of the Lord upon them and plunder the "strong man" who stands trembling and helpless.

When Jesus was casting out demons and revealing the kingdom of God had come, He explains that the devil is a strong man. But now, Jesus the Stronger One, is here! He said, *"So long as a strong man like satan is fully armed and guards his own palace, his goods are safe; but when someone stronger attacks and overpowers him, the stronger man takes away all the weapons he relied on and carries off his belongings"* (Luke. 11:20-22 JB/NLT). In the power of Jesus, the Stronger One, we can plunder the strong man's goods. We take back what he has stolen. The devil is a thief, and when you catch a thief, he has to pay back seven times what he has stolen (Prov. 6:30-31).

Release the Whip of Jesus

The marketplace can be infected with greed and violence. The people of God are called to invade the marketplace and cause God's rules of love to prevail. The Lord says, *"Enough, you princes of Israel!* ***Stop all your violence*** *and oppression and do what is just and right...****You must only use honest weights and scales"*** (Ezek. 45:9-10 NLT; emphasis mine). It is never the other way around. The marketplace should never invade God's temple. Whenever it does, we ask Jesus to show up with His whip and clean out His temple (John 2:14-17). As we sing God's war songs, see Jesus moving in our midst driving out ungodly spirits of greed and violence with His Holy Ghost whip!

In all of this, we look with New Covenant eyes. We do not sing against the person who has robbed, plundered, and extorted. We sing against the demonic spirit of greed-fueled hamas. In the words of Jesus, *"If someone takes your coat, let him have your shirt as well"* (Luke 6:29b GNB). *"And when someone takes what is yours, do not ask for it back"* (Luke 6:30b GNB). This is the heart of our Father. This is the way God's children do warfare. We don't react with revenge and violence and try to take back what is ours.[1] Instead, we sing the Lord's deliverance for those who have been oppressed. We go forth rejoicing in the power of our God as we sing against the darkness of violence and greed and break its demonic hold over people. We rise up against our oppressors and actually terrify them, not by our muscle or our might, but by the revelation of God's glory in us. We stop the violence and bloodshed by singing against that spirit. That demonic power will be broken and flee from the terror of the Lord and individuals will be set free.

Another Hebrew word for violence that relates to this is *gazal* and it means "to rob or plunder with force or violence."[2] It specifically refers to robbing by violence in the marketplace which the Lord hates (Isa. 61:8). This particular act of violence—that is, violent robbery—is one of the sins that cause a "gap" in the wall of a nation's spiritual defenses. When people are thieves, the Lord looks for a person to stand in the gap for the land (Ezek. 22:23-31). The Lord is calling for men and women to "stand in the gap" and "rebuild the wall of righteousness that guards the land," to shore up the spiritual defenses of our country, that have been destroyed by greedy violence.

Stand in the gap and rebuild the wall of righteousness.

2. Victory over Violence in Our Homes

(Hab. 2:9-11)

In Habakkuk 2:9, the Lord declares His judgment against the man *"who builds his house by unjust gains and made your family rich with what you took by violence"* (Hab. 2:9a NET/GNB). Violence that begins in the market place can quickly and easily spill over into violence in the home. A man who has fallen prey to the spirit of violence in the marketplace (i.e., his job) has opened the door for the spirit of violence to enter the sacred fortress of his home. Once it's entered in, it will undermine the very foundation of the home and rot out the roof. It's the sad story of the man who is frustrated at work that comes home and kicks the dog or hits the wall with his fist. He will soon be taking out his anger and frustrations on more than the family pet and the plaster.

Every nine seconds a woman in America is battered by her partner.[3] Research on what causes domestic violence asserts there are "trigger factors," that is, situations that may produce a violent reaction. There are six trigger factors that can cause a man to act violently at home. The top two on the list are stressful situations. These are usually defined as financial problems or problems at work, and frustrations, usually stemming from underachieving in work or other problems encountered at the place of employment.[4] Another trigger factor is if there are abusive-prone attitudes and beliefs such as "I'll show her who's boss."[5] This abusive-prone attitude combined with frustrations creates an "If I can't be the boss at work, I'll at least be the boss at home" volatile environment. Wives and children often find themselves in the wrong place at the wrong time when this explosive combination detonates.

God commands us to sing against this demonic spirit of violence bent on destroying families. As we sing God's word arrows excerpted from Habakkuk, we release the soul-convicting power of God's Spirit upon the person acting in violence in their home:

> ***"You are doomed!"*** (Hab. 2:9a GNB, emphasis mine).
>
> *"Trouble is coming to you who bring confusion to your house and are sinning against your own soul.* ***You will self-destruct!****"* (Hab. 2:10 DRB/BBE/NET/JB, emphasis mine).

> ***"The bricks of your house will cry out against you and accuse you,*** *and the boards that support the roof* ***will agree that you are wrong"*** (Hab. 2:11 NCV/MSG; emphasis mine).

God's word tells us that the house of the violent will rise up against them. As we sing, we unleash the power of the Holy Spirit to inhabit the very homes and convict the hearts of those who have become ensnared by this demonic spirit. The house becomes a "haunted house"—haunted by the Holy Ghost.

Sing for that home to be "haunted" by the Holy Ghost!

The word "ghost" was an old English term meaning guest.[6] When the Holy Ghost enters and becomes a holy guest in the homes of the violent, He fills them with conviction that they are destroying themselves and their families. Once this Holy Guest takes up residence in a place, there is no place to run, no place to hide. What a powerful picture the prophet paints for us! The violent man's very house—the walls, the foundation, the roof—cry out, warning him of the impending doom he faces. The goal of this convicting "haunting" is, as always, salvation and deliverance for the violent, as well as God's healing for the victims.

The Lord says that those who have been abused, like Abel, that He can hear the voice of their blood crying out to Him from the ground (Gen. 4:10). Others who have been oppressed, their ***"voice will whisper like a ghost out of the ground ... but suddenly your ruthless enemies will be driven away like chaff before the wind.*** *In an instant, I, the Lord of Hosts will come upon them... and all the nations fighting Jerusalem will vanish like a dream"* (Isa. 29:4-7 AAT/TLB; emphasis mine). Let our voice release the voice of the

Holy Ghost and convict anyone moving in violence. Their violence will come back upon them, *"The trouble they plan will return to punish them, and **their violent acts will come back to haunt them**"* (Psa. 7:16; Voice emphasis mine). Those are powerful word weapons to put in our war songs and sing against the spirit of violence.

MASS MURDERER OR MIGHTY MISSIONARY

In Mark 5:1-20 God shows us exactly how we are to deal with this demon. This is the story of a man completely consumed by a violent demon that called itself "Legion." The man was so violent and so shameful he had been exiled to the tombs outside the city to live among the dead bodies. Seeing with our natural eyes, we would take great pains to avoid this man. Jesus saw a man not to avoid but to go after. Where we see perversion, Jesus sees potential. Where we see the next mass murderer, Jesus sees His next mighty missionary. Pray for the heart of God to abide abundantly within His children so that we will see with His eyes of love. There is no limit to the love of our God.

> *Where we see perversion, Jesus sees potential.*

3. VICTORY OVER VIOLENCE IN CIVIL GOVERNMENT

(Hab. 2:12-14)

Adolf Hitler. Just the mention of his name evokes emotions of fear, disgust, disbelief, grief—the list goes on. This horrific leader of the Nazi party of Germany, without a doubt, operated under the influence of the demon of hamas. Under his leadership, an entire race of people were systematically hunted and exterminated. His bloodlust was matched, regrettably, by his influence. His influence flowed not only to his fellow Germans, who betrayed and turned over their fellow citizens to the Nazis and Gestapo in droves, but to other countries as well. Even the French, when their country fell into Hitler's power, gave up their own Jewish citizens for extermination.

The reign of Hitler is a perfect example of the horrors that ensue when the spirit of violence overwhelms government leadership. When leaders establish their regimes by bloodshed, even their own people are not safe. The government of a nation represents the head of that country. If demonic violence can attack and overwhelm the head, the anointing of violence flows down upon the nation and it becomes covered in darkness.

Tyrannical leaders who exert corrupt control over the law enforcement and military under their rule place the entire citizenry of a country in peril. One need only turn on the evening news to see this spirit of hamas still dominates the leadership of many nations. When violence holds sway over the leadership of a country, the death of its citizens and the destruction of its land always follow. This is why the beautiful promise of God's glory is given to us here in this war song in the context of violence trying to overtake a government. We must sing against the spirit of violence in the leadership of countries. Countless lives are at stake. Sing for their sakes:

> *"You are doomed! They kill people to build their city and do wicked things to make their walled city strong.* ***The Lord All-Powerful will send fire to destroy what***

> ***those people have built, all the nations' work will be for nothing****, for they shall all fail. The* ***peoples weary themselves only for emptiness, falseness and futility.*** *The Lord Almighty has done this. For the earth shall be filled, that men may know the glory of the Lord, as the sea is covered by the waters"* (Hab. 2:12-14 DRB/BBE/ ERV/ NCV/WYC/GNB/Amp; emphasis mine).

As we sing God's war song, see what is happening in the Spirit. Our songs, full of the word of God, go flying through the air. Those word arrows, full of God's fire, are salting the heavenlies. As the heavens become full of God's splendor, they release an outpouring of His glory upon the earth, especially upon the leaders. The Lord repeats His promise to Habakkuk, *"God comes from Teman, the Sovereign One from Mount Paran. Selah. His splendor covers the heavens,* ***His glory fills the earth****"* (Hab. 3:3 NET/NIV; emphasis mine). The work of evil, violent men will come to an end, because the glory of God will pour out from His throne in heaven and wash the violence away.

The War Song

Some verses for this war song would proclaim:

- That spirit of violence operating in our government is doomed by God.
- The Lord has determined to destroy all their ungodly work by His fire.
- They weary themselves on their futile efforts, all of it will fail. Sing for them to come to their senses, return to the Lord and work for His kingdom.
- The glory of the Lord to flood the world and wash away all violence!

"DON'T TOUCH A HAIR ON THEIR HEADS"

We charge into battle without fear because we have the assurance of God's word that His divine protection goes with us. We are sheltered from oppression even from our governmental leaders:

> *"God did not let anyone mistreat, hurt, or oppress our people. Instead* ***He protected us by punishing rulers.*** *To keep them safe, He gave a warning and a command to kings,* ***He told kings to keep their hands off****: 'Don't you dare lay a hand on My anointed, and don't hurt a hair on the heads of My prophets. Do not ye touch My anointed servants, My christs; and do not ye harm My prophets'"* (Ps. 105:14-15 CEV/EXB/MSG/WYC; emphasis mine).

You and I are His anointed servants. We are Jesus made manifest to the world and we have God's protection. ***"He will defend the oppressed*** *among the people, He will deliver the children of the poor;* ***He will crush the oppressor****"* (Ps. 72:4 NET/NIV; emphasis mine). The Hebrew word for oppressor is *ashaq* and means "to oppress or treat anyone unjustly or violently."[7] Call upon God's promises to crush our demonic oppressors and bless our land with peace: *"The Lord does what is fair and executes justice for all the oppressed"* (Ps. 103:6 NET). *"You will live under a government that is just and fair. Your enemies will stay far away; you will live in peace. Terror will not come near. You shall be far from even the thought of oppression (or) destruction"* (Isa. 54:14 NLT/AMP). If you take this word from God and believe it, you will live in peace.

Godly Government Reflects King Jesus

The responsibility of our civil government in God's plan is to reflect King Jesus to the people of their nation. Solomon tells us the job of the king is to, *"liberate them from the fierce sting of persecution* ***and violence****, for their lives are precious to him"* (Psa. 72:14 TLB/Voice). Jeremiah tells us that godly civil government is to, *"Administer justice each morning; save the victim from the hand of the thief"* and *"**Stop the violence** and the shedding of blood in this place"* (Jer. 21:12 & 22:3 Voice; emphasis mine). Against ungodly government we cry out to the Lord, *"Throw them off, O Lord, Confuse their speech, and frustrate their plans,* ***for violence and contention are building within the city;*** *make these enemies begin to quarrel among themselves –* ***destroy them with their own violence and strife****"* (Psa. 55:9 Voice/TLB; emphasis mine). Sing for the Lord to send confusion and their own violence back on the heads of these violent spirits. More beautiful word weapons to add to our war song.

> Sing for God to destroy this demon with its own violence.

We must sing for the release of this revelation over our government leaders. The revelation that work for the glory of man will always fail, only the work for the glory of God will endure. We sing that the knowledge of God's love and mercy will fill our land like a flood washing and driving away every trace of violence.

4. Victory over Violent Drunkenness

(Hab. 2:15-17)

Every day we hear of people falling victim to sexual violence. Everywhere we see the problem of drunkenness and the use of "date rape" drugs to sexually abuse others.

> *"You are doomed! In your fury you humiliated and disgraced your neighbors. Giving them too much to drink of the wine of your wrath, who keeps filling their cup with* ***your anger and malice, pouring out your anger*** *and* ***[by] rage making drunk; like an angry drunk,*** *you knock others to the ground and strip them naked, roping them into your sexual orgies" (Hab. 2:15 BBE/MSG/NET/ERV/Voice; emphasis mine).*

What a nightmarish image! These words tell of a man full of rage (a/k/a violence) enticing and entrapping others through drunkenness to participate in unthinkable sexual exploits. Sadly, it sounds like it comes right off the front page of one of today's newspapers. God tells us to sing a taunt song against that spirit of violence that motivates men and women to lure others into their trap of drunkenness and sexual assault. Rape is not an expression of sexual passion. Quite the contrary, it is an act of violence, designed to debase, demean, and degrade the victim. The pain and suffering caused by this debauchery is impossible to measure. No wonder our Father judges this violence so harshly:

> *"You will be filled with disgrace rather than honor. Now it's your turn to drink and* ***expose your own nakedness,*** *you lack God's mark and fall to the ground*

> *like a drunk person. The cup of anger from the Lord's right hand is coming around to you, and* ***shameful vomiting will cover your glory****"* (Hab. 2:16 NASB/NCV/Voice/TNIV; emphasis mine).

The writer of Proverbs warns us that, *"violent people try to recruit their neighbors, wanting to lead them down the vile path of evil they have chosen"* (Prov. 16:29 Voice). But the Lord says to them, you will "d*rink until you are drunk enough to vomit; stagger and fall to the ground, never to rise again; so well shall My sword do its work among you"* (Jer. 25:27b Voice/Knox). Even in this judgment we see the grace and mercy of our God because He can use this fallen state as a "wake-up call" to draw such a one away from violent actions and back to their Father. We sing for the power and glory of God to assault those demons enslaving these people. We pray for God's furious love to beat back those spirits and for the Lord to pour out His Spirit upon that individual to lead them to repentance. Through this vile vomit, the veil is ripped off, exposing their miserable state for everyone to see. Like the prodigal son in the pigpen, they "come to their senses" and return to their Father, who runs to welcome them with open arms and a kiss and throws a glorious party for His lost child who has come home (Luke 15:11-24).

Of course, there may be some who still don't return. For those, we sing the rest of God's judgment, praying for God to reveal to them the death and destruction they cause to the hearts and souls of those they have violently violated.

> *"****For the violence done against*** *Lebanon*[8] *will now overtake you, you will be hurt. You terrified the wild animals you caught in your traps.* ***Now terror will strike you because of your murder and because of your violence against the people of the world and its cities!****"* (Hab. 2:17 NCV/NLT/Voice/GNB; emphasis mine).

The death grip of this spirit must be broken. As we sing, we believe the Lord to release His "terror" upon them so that they will see the true horror of what they have done. They have terrified many young girls and boys with their traps of alcohol and drugs. They have "murdered" the heart and soul of many through sexual abuse and molestation.[9] Now it's their turn. They will be the one terrified when they fully realize what they have done. There is nothing quite like the terror of God to slap a man back to his senses and to his knees.

The prophet Micah had this same problem during his day. He declares, God's *"Doom to those who plot evil, who go to bed dreaming up crimes … They bully the neighbor and his family, see people for what they can get out of them. God has had enough. He says, 'I have some plans of My own: Disaster because of this interbreeding evil! ... It's doomsday for you.* ***Mocking ballads will be sung of you'"*** (Mic. 2:1-4 MSG emphasis mine). God has called us to love our neighbor. He does not put up with evil and abuse.

The War Song

Some word weapons the Lord gives us to sing against angry drunks are:

- God's doom upon that violent spirit.
- God's exposure of the wickedness and vileness of this demon.
- God's violence to fall and overtake them. That demon reaps the violence it has sowed.
- God's terror will cause that unclean spirit to flee in terror.

The Lord is looking to us, His children, His advocates to be the ones to reach out and set the enslaved free. He is calling us to be His healing hands of love to those who have been abused. But we don't stop there. We must also reach out to the abuser. We must reach out to those who are imprisoned by this demon of violence and deliver them, as well. This is what the war songs of God are all about. We are at war to set both the captives and the captors free.

5. Victory over Violence in the Spiritual Arena

(Hab. 2:18-20)

One thing we can be sure of as children of the Most High is that we will be the relentless target of spiritual violence. Habakkuk warns us against the overt spiritual violence of idolatry, which is nothing short of the worship of demons. David tells us, *"great is the Lord and greatly to be praised; He is terrible to all the gods,* ***because all the gods of the nations are demons****"* (Psa. 96:4-5 KJV/NETS; emphasis mine). Let that sink in for a moment. The Lord says all the gods, all the idols of the world are demons. Then consider the Apostle John's familiar warning *"Little children, guard yourselves from idols"* (1 John 5:21 Wuest).

Putting the two together, John's warning becomes more ominous, "Little children, guard yourself against demons!" But that's just half of it. We don't just avoid demon worship; we are never to be afraid of demons. Another translation puts John's exhortation this way, "My children, ***keep your souls from fearing the idols***!" (ARTB). John says to guard our souls from the fear of demons. We don't fear the devil, but we have a big dose of healthy, holy fear of the Lord.

Looking now to the words of Habakkuk, we understand not only the severity of the problem, but also the gravity of God's word against it. God's word condemns those involved in actively seeking to arouse demonic spirits to rise up and lie to the world but especially to His people:

All the false gods of the nations are demons.

> *"Doom to the one saying to the wood, 'Wake up!' or to the silent stone, 'Be exalted!'"* (Hab. 2:19 NETS/CEB).

In this arena of spiritual violence, the responsibility and authority of the church is evident: We are to rise up and destroy. We are the only ones equipped to conquer the "teachers of lies" (Hab. 2:18 CEB) embodied in idols, to declare that the voices of these false priests and false prophets shut up and be still. The devil is the father of lies and the Lord *will* shut his mouth. This is the song we sing to hush the voice of the evil one: *"The Lord is in His holy temple; let all the earth hush and keep silence before Him"* (Hab. 2:20 AMP).

This is the same response the Lord gave Zephaniah to declare against those who were worshipping demons. There were people in Israel who were worshipping Baal, the host of heaven, and Molech (Zeph. 1:4-6). The Lord declares, *"On that day, I will punish those who jump temple thresholds fearing pagan demons, who fill their master's house with violence and fraud"* (Zeph. 1:9 Voice/NRSV).

By worshipping demons, idols and false gods, these *"priests make vile holy places and **do violence to God's teaching**"* (Zeph. 3:4 Voice; emphasis mine). False gods do violence to the Word of the Lord. God's answer is His divine "hush", His powerful "shut up" to those spirits: *"Hush, be silent at* *the presence of the Lord God, for the day of the Lord is at hand"* (Zeph. 1:7a YLT/HNV).

Again in the book of Zechariah, when Israel was oppressed by the demon worshippers of Babylon (Zech. 2:7), the Lord declares: *"Let all flesh be quiet and make no sound before the Lord: because the Lord is coming. He is getting ready to come from His holy temple in heaven"* (Zech. 2:13 BBE/NIRV).

The same Hebrew word is used by all three of these prophets. It is the word *hacah,* and it means "Be silent! Silence! To hush." It is a *command* to be silent before the Lord.[10]

God refuses to let the voices of these demons be heard. He simply tells them "Shut up!" We see Jesus do the same thing when He encountered an unclean spirit in the synagogue:

> *"In the synagogue there was a man possessed by a defiling spirit-wind of devils, and it shouted at the top of its voice, 'Ha! What do you want with us, Jesus of Nazareth? Have you come to destroy us?* ***Have You come to make us disappear?*** *I know who you are – the Holy One of God!' 'Be quiet!' Jesus said sharply, '****Your mouth be muzzled*** *and come out of him at once!' Then the demon threw the man down before them all and came out and did not injure him in any possible way"* (Luke 4:33-35 JB/Wuest/ARTB; emphasis mine).

There will be words spoken in our places of worship that confront the truth, just as the demon confronted Jesus in the synagogue. It is our assignment to silence the teachers of lies in the midst of God's people and end their violent assault against the church. We sing God's word to usher in His presence and silence the spirit of idolatry. When the lies of these spirits are silenced, when we only hear God's words of truth, we are changed. As we are changed, we can bring hope and redemption to a world led astray to worship false and futile gods.

What is our war song against that spirit of violence in the church? "In the Name of Jesus, shut up!"

The Lord tells us to *"Sing for joy and be happy, oh, daughter of Zion; for behold I am coming and I will dwell in your midst"* (Zech. 2:10 BBE/NIRV). God is coming down to dwell with and protects us. Like Jerusalem, we don't need any physical walls because *"the Lord has promised that He Himself will be a wall of fire around the city to protect it and that He will live there in all His glory"* (Zech. 2:5 GNT). The Lord is coming to protect us, our homes, and our cities. He will be that wall of fire around us and will fill our land with His glory. And when the glory of God inhabits a place, violence has to leave.

Later, we see that Habakkuk rejoices at the effects God's arrows of fire will have on the enemy:

> *"You rode upon the clouds; the storm cloud was Your chariot, as You brought victory to Your people. Your bow is ready for action; You commission your arrows (literally, "sworn in are the arrow shafts with a word")* ***Uttering curses for the arrows,*** *You cause* ***flash floods*** *on the earth's surface. When the mountains saw You, they trembled.* ***Flood*** *waters poured in, the deep roared and lifted up its hands on high. At the flash of Your speeding arrows and the gleam of Your shining spear, the sun and moon stood still. You furiously stomp on the earth; in fury You trampled the nations. You went out to save Your people, to save Your anointed one. You struck down the leader of the wicked and completely*

destroyed his followers. Your arrows pierced the commander of his army" (Hab. 3:9-14a CEB/GNB/MSG/WEB/NET with footnote; emphasis mine)

Forge a Chain!

In Israel's past, the wicked were punished by a rod (Psa. 89:30-34). Because of all the violence, the Lord told Ezekiel, ***"forge yourself a chain: for the land is filled with bloody murderers, and the city is full of violence"*** (Ezek. 7:23 KJV/JB; emphasis mine). Today, once again our land is filled with violence, and the Lord is commanding us to "forge a chain!" Now in the power of the name of Jesus, we bind up these demon spirits of violence with our praise and worship. The psalmist informs us that this is the honor for all of God's saints, *"Let the high praises of God be in their throats and two-edged swords in their hands...* ***to bind their kings with fetters and their nobles with chains of iron...****this is the glory for all His faithful ones"* (Psa. 149:6-9 NRSV; emphasis mine).

When we sing God's words they fly like arrows, bringing the glorious curses of God upon His demonic adversaries. As these word arrows of fire fly through the heavenlies, they "salt the clouds"[11] of heaven and release the flood of His glory upon the earth. The demonic high places tremble as they see the Lord approaching because "His splendor covers the heavens, and His glory fills the earth" (Hab. 3:3b GNB/NET).

Lord, as we sing Your war songs of praise and thanksgiving against these demonic spirits of violence, let Your arrows fly. Silence the voice and the power of these violent spirits. As we sing forge a chain of Your glory! Bind them by Your power, and we will take back what the thief has taken

from us and our nation. Let violence be replaced with Your peace. Let Your glory fill the earth.

There is nothing like the terror of God to slap a man back to his senses and bring peace to our homes.

ENDNOTES:

1. In the natural army, soldiers are taught not to let their anger control them as they fight. This is vital instruction. A skilled warrior channels his anger and contains it in a controlled counterattack against his enemy. The same is true in God's army. If someone close to us is the victim of violence, as God's warriors, we don't come against that abusive person in uncontrolled anger. Instead, we attack in the Spirit the demonic influence over the offender and fight against it in the peace of our God. That individual needs divine help and intervention, and we are the ones God is calling upon to bring it.
2. http://www.blueletterbible.org/lang/lexicon/Lexicon.cfm?Strongs=H1497&t=KJV
3. Domestic or family violence is ravaging our homes. In America alone, "approximately four million women are believed to be battered each year – one every nine seconds – by their partners. It is so common now that it is now the leading cause of injury to American women, accounting for more hospital emergency room visits than auto accidents, muggings, and rapes combined" http://www.nursece.com/courses/72, "Family Violence", p. 29.
4. Catalog 99 KAN, National Center of Continuing Education 2012; Hudson, Shelda L., RN, BSN, PHN, "Family Violence", p. 31, http://www.nursece.com/courses/72.
5. Ibid.
6. Webster's 1828 Ed., (hardcover), definitions for "ghost" and "ghastly".
7. http://www.blueletterbible.org/lang/lexicon/lexicon.cfm?Strongs=H6231&t=KJV
8. Of all the nations to which Habakkuk could have alluded, the Holy Spirit picks Lebanon as the country being oppressed. This is not an accident. Just as there are generational curses, there are national curses. National curses can be the result of an evil leader or unjust laws. The blood of Jesus

dissolves the law that says the children must pay for the sins of the father, yet there is still sickness and poverty in our country and corruption in our governments. Jesus has won the victory, but it is up to us, His disciples, to fight the fight against these raging demonic spirits whose sole ambition is the destruction of God's creation. Lebanon is still under a national curse. They are still being harassed by the spirit of hamas today. We need to sing not only over individuals and cities, but we must sing over whole nations to break any curse that is trying to operate in their land. The United States of America is under some national curses. The manner in which our forefathers treated the Native Americans and African Americans is still affecting our country. These curses must be broken as God's people humble themselves before the Lord and ask for His forgiveness. The Lord will reveal what we need to do for restitution and His healing in our land.

9. Unless this cycle of violence is broken, the end result will be some type of "death." When the psychologist Lenore Walker, Ed.D., ABPP researched more than a 1,000 battered women and a smaller group of abused men, she found a pattern. She labeled this pattern the "Three Phase Theory" of family violence. The three phases of this cycle of violence are the tension-building phase, resulting in the violent explosion phase, followed by the reconciliation phase. This cycle of violence is repeated again and again, but "each time the pattern is repeated, the level of lethality increases and leads to possible death of the victim, either a physical death or a kind of psychological death." (Catalog 99 KAN, National Center of Continuing Education 2012; Hudson, Shelda L., RN, BSN, PHN, "Family Violence", pp. 30-31, http://www.nursece.com/courses/72). While Walker's comments are specific to domestic violence, the same pattern and end result are observed in sexual abuse and violence. By the power of the Holy Spirit, we must break this cycle of violence, before it is too late.
10. Retrieved from: http://www.blueletterbible.org/lang/lexicon/lexicon.cfm?Strongs=H2013&t=KJV.
11. "Salting the clouds" is the manmade process of producing rain. The process involves releasing salt, dry ice, or other particles, usually via an airplane, over clouds to increase the possibility that the clouds will produce rain. This is what we do when we release God's word into the heavenlies. As we shoot, shout, and sing His words we are salting the clouds of heaven to release the "rain" of God's glory upon the earth.

CHAPTER NINE

GOD'S MIGHTY STAG

TREADING DOWN THE STRONGHOLDS OF VIOLENCE

"The Lord God is my strength. He makes me sure-footed as a deer; He mounts me upon high places that I may conquer by His song"
(Hab. 3:19 CAB/GNB)

REJOICE IN THE POWER OF OUR GOD

It's obvious that Habakkuk was a man who studied the word of God, especially the Psalms of David. We know this by examining the verses Habakkuk chooses to reference in his prophecy. God ends Habakkuk's prophecy in Chapter 3, as a prayer to be sung, *"This prayer was sung by the prophet Habakkuk"* (Hab. 3:1 NLT). Chapter 3 is a song according to *shigionoth*. This term is used only one other time in the Bible, in the title of Psalm 7 by King David.

The meaning of *shigionoth* is uncertain but one translator says it means a "wild passionate song, with rapid changes of rhythm" (NET). Another translation says the prayer of Habakkuk the prophet was to be "set to wild, enthusiastic, and triumphant music" (Hab. 3:1 Amp). What a beautiful definition of a war song. They are wild, enthusiastic songs of triumph. *Shigionoth* comes from the root word *shagah,* which means to "swerve or reel as drunk with wine or love."[1]

So we have two songs—or psalms—in the Bible called *shigionoth.* One is Psalm 7 by King David and the other is the song in Chapter 3 by Habakkuk. We know Habakkuk is all about defeating violence in the land. Psalm 7 is a song of David asking God to deliver him from men of violence. Coincidence? I don't think so.

In Psalm 7 David declares that unless the Lord comes to his rescue, violent men will *"come rushing on my soul like a lion, wounding it, while there is no one to be my savior"* (Ps. 7:2 BBE). David finds he does have a Savior, and He is our Savior too. The Lord prepares *"His deadly weapons; He makes ready His flaming arrows"* (Psa. 7:13 NIV) and comes to our rescue as our Savior. Again we have God's word telling us he will deliver us with His bow and arrows of fire.

The Lord our Savior thunders down on the evil one oppressing us. As a result, our enemy *"becomes the victim of his own destructive plans and* ***the violence he intended for others falls on his own head****"* (Psa. 7:16 NET; emphasis mine). Another translation declares:

> *"That's what happens:* ***mischief backfires; violence boomerangs****"* (Psa. 7:16 MSG; emphasis mine).

Habakkuk echoes this boomeranging of violence. He says, the enemy came in "like a ***violent storm*** to scatter me, ***but***

You smashed their heads with their own weapons" (Hab. 3:14 GOD'S WORD/CEV; emphasis mine). Knowing God is our Savior and having His word that the evil of the violent will boomerang, we can enthusiastically and triumphantly sing these war songs.

Become the Mighty Stag of God

What we see in the final verses of this prophetic, instructive book is that Habakkuk has been changed. No matter what violence Habakkuk sees around him, he is able to rejoice. Though the trees are not producing and the crops are withering and there are no cattle in the stalls, still Habakkuk declares beautifully and triumphantly: *"I will exult in the Lord; I will rejoice in God my Savior"* (Hab. 3:18 NETS). Habakkuk cries out *"The Lord my God gave me strength! The Lord God is my power, and He caused my feet to be secure like the deer"* (Hab. 3:19a NETS/CEB)! No wonder Habakkuk can rejoice. God has made him strong–Army of God strong.

God makes us strong: Army of God strong!

In the natural, the commander of an army doesn't send his warriors into battle until they are well trained and fully equipped. The Lord does the same with His army. Habakkuk is a perfect example of this preparation. The prophet is rejoicing in the power of God because the Lord has *made* him strong and *given* him the feet of a deer. This is not a picture of a fawn frolicking merrily on the mountaintops that we're talking about here. The Hebrew word for deer is *ayalah* and refers to a great stag. These great stags in the wild can weigh upward to 700 pounds. This is not Bambi! This is Stagzilla! These mighty stags are not lumbering clods. They are sure-footed, strong, and swift.

Stags can run—actually bound—40 miles an hour and leap up to nine feet high.

God transforms Habakkuk. He makes his feet strong and agile as the mighty stag and then causes him *"to walk upon mine **high places**"* (Hab. 3:19 KJV; emphasis mine). This last beautiful verse of Habakkuk is chock-full of revelation. The Hebrew word for walk is *darak* and it means to "tread upon, to tread down and to march."[2] God changes Habakkuk—and now us—into His Mighty Stag. He gives us the powerful spiritual feet of His stag to bound over and tread down the demonic high places of violence set against us. Remember our warfare is not against people but *"against spiritual wickedness **in high places**"* (Eph. 6:12 KJV; emphasis mine). God makes us His Mighty Stag so we can tread upon these high places of demonic strongholds and conquer them.

When God Repeats a Word, Pay Attention!

When Habakkuk ended his song with Verse 19, he was quoting King David. Of course, this is not by accident. Not only did Habakkuk pattern this last chapter as a psalm mirroring David's Psalm 7, according to *shigionoth,* but this last verse where he comprehends his transformation into God's Mighty Stag is a direct quote from David in 2 Samuel 22, and that is repeated in Psalm 18. (Note to self: When the Lord repeats a verse in His word it is very important, but when He repeats a whole chapter twice, it is very, very important. Pay attention!)

So we end our study of Habakkuk by examining this very important word of David found in 2 Samuel 22, repeated in

Psalm 18, and then quoted by Habakkuk in 3:19. It is a song rejoicing in God's protection from violence and violent men. No wonder Habakkuk was encouraged. He could rejoice for the same reasons King David rejoiced. David rejoiced that the Lord was his "Protector," "strong fortress," and "shield" (2 Sam. 22:2-3 GNB). David begins his song with singing that the Lord *"is my Savior;* ***He protects me from violence"*** (2 Sam. 22:3b GNB; emphasis mine), and he concludes the song with *"Oh, Lord, You give me victory over my enemies* ***and protect me from violent men"*** (2 Sam. 22:49 GNB; emphasis mine).

In God's strength and by God's power, David declares *"I can run through a troop* (at 40 miles an hour*); by my God I leap* (bound like a deer) *over a wall* (nine feet tall)" (2 Sam. 22:30 AMP; notes in parentheses mine). Habakkuk quotes from David about the Lord making his feet sure-footed as the deer (2 Sam. 22:34), but David goes on after this verse:

> *"He trains my hands for battle!* ***He shows me how to fight!"*** (2 Sam. 22:35a NET/MSG; emphasis mine).

Our General will never send His warriors into battle until we are trained to fight and equipped with the proper weapons. Just what weapons does David say God has trained him to use against the violence all around him? Does He give David a sword, a spear, or a slingshot? No, it's a bow. And not just any bow made of wood, but *"a bow of bronze"* (2 Sam. 22:35b NLT). God not only makes our feet firm and secure so we can stand on and tread down the high places, He also makes our arms strong to bend a bronze bow to shoot His arrows of fire. With a bronze bow His word arrows can fly farther and penetrate deeper. And remember, the devil has no shield of faith to stop them.

As David and Habakkuk, we can rejoice that the Lord is training and enabling us for the battle. We can proclaim that the Lord *"gives me strength for the battle and victory over my enemies"* (2 Sam. 22:40 GNB) and *"I crush them; they become like dust: I trample them like mud in the streets"* (2 Sam. 22:43 GNB). God makes us strong in Him and the enemy becomes dust under our feet as we engage in battle to free His children and His world from the dark forces of violence in high places.

The devil has no shield of faith to stop God's words of fire shot from our bow of bronze.

Two Thermonuclear Words

The last phrase in Habakkuk is easy to overlook. It appears to be just a footnote of musical instruction: *"To the chief singer on my stringed instruments"* (Hab. 3:19b KJV). But this is so much more than just a word of instruction on how to sing this war song. My prayer is that the revelation of this last verse in Habakkuk will change the fundamental nature of God's church forever; just as one other verse from Habakkuk has already changed the heart of the church.

The other verse in Habakkuk I reference is *"The just shall live by his faith"* (Hab. 2:4 KJV). When Paul grasped this word from Habakkuk, it became the foundation for his letters concerning his revelation about the grace of God. Grace comes by our faith not by our works. Paul tells us *"For in the gospel a righteousness from God is revealed, a righteousness that is by faith from first to last, just as it is written, 'The righteous will live by faith'"* (Rom. 1:17 NIV). In his letter to the believers in Galatia, Paul repeats this important cornerstone of our beliefs, *"Now it is clear no one is justified before God by the law, because the righteous one will live by faith"* (Gal. 3:11 NET).

Centuries later a German monk named Martin Luther would receive the Holy Spirit revelation of this verse from Habakkuk expounded by Paul concerning faith as the singular way of living a life in right-standing with our Lord. On October 31, 1517, as a result of this revelation, Martin Luther would nail his *Ninety-Five Theses* to the door of the Castle Church in Wittenberg, Germany, and the protestant reformation would be born. Protestants around the world have Martin Luther, Paul, and Habakkuk to thank for this word.

We conquer our demonic high places by singing God's songs.

Once again one verse from Habakkuk can change the face of the church forever. It is this last phrase in the last verse in Habakkuk. It is made up of two Hebrew words: *Natsach* for the chief singer, and *negiyah* for stringed instruments. Two little thermonuclear words! *Natsach* means "to shine, be bright, to oversee and to conquer, the song leader."[3] *Negiyah or Negiynah* refers to "music, a taunting or mocking song."[4] Most translations of this revelation-power-packed verse miss the mark. The best, most complete translation is found in the Septuagint (a/k/a LXX).[5] Examine how some of the LXX versions translate this last verse of Habakkuk:

"That I may triumph with His song" (Sept).

"That I may conquer by His song" (CAB).

"By His song I will conquer" (AEB).

"And He the Conqueror will lead me upon my high places singing Psalms." (DRB).

The New English Translation of the Septuagint (NETS —not to be confused with NET, New English Translation) provides two alternate translations of Chapter 3 of Habakkuk. Both are wonderful.

> *"The Lord God is my power, and He shall establish my feet unto the end.* He causes me to mount the heights, ***to be victorious in His song."***
>
> and
>
> *"The Lord God gave me strength, and He caused my feet to be secure.* ***And upon the necks of my enemies He causes me to mount****; having been swift, He rested."* (Hab. 3:19b NETS; emphasis mine)

Jesus, our Singing Overcomer, leads us in our war songs of triumph. As we sing God's war songs, God causes us to tread on the high places and necks of our demonic enemies.

God's word weapons are found throughout scripture. They are not limited to just these words from Habakkuk. Habakkuk showed us what to do by writing down the vision the Lord gave him, but he just got us started. There are many more words of promise of God's deliverance from violence.

Make it your mission to search His Word and discover the vast arsenal He's given us to vanquish the evil one. Fill your quiver with an abundance of "It is written" to shoot, shout, and sing against this demon of violence declaring their doom, defeat and destruction by the power of our God. And just as David sang over King Saul, and *"Saul was refreshed and became well, and the evil spirit left him"* (1 Sam. 16:23b Amp), so too will our singing drive this evil spirit of violence out of our nation. Our nation will become refreshed and well once more.[6]

Lord, let the revelation of Your love and mercy flood our land! Fill us with the glory of Your furious love! Fill us with Your beautiful heart of war. Make us Your Mighty Stag and cause us to tread down the principalities and powers in the high places. Your heart will not be content until all the strongholds of the evil one are destroyed, Your children are set free, and Eden is restored. We will experience heaven on earth, when Your glory covers the land. For when Your glory falls, Your will is done, as it is done in heaven.

Lord, train our hands for battle,
and show us how to fight.
Train our hearts for a holy war,
and show us how to love.

ENDNOTES:

1. Gesenius Lexicon retreived from: http://www.blueletterbible.org/lang/lexicon/Lexicon.cfm?Strongs=H7686&t=KJV.
2. Gesenius Lexicon retreived from: http://www.blueletterbible.org/lang/lexicon/Lexicon.cfm?Strongs=H1869&t=KJV.
3. Retrieved from: http://classic.net.bible.org/strong.php?id=05329
4. Retrieved from: http://classic.net.bible.org/strong.php?id=05058
5. The Septuagint is the Old Testament translated from the Hebrew language into the Greek language. It derived its name from the supposedly 70 to 72 Jewish scribes who translated it while they were exiled in Alexandria, Egypt. Septuagint is the Greek word for 70 and the manuscript for this translation is usually indicated by the Roman numeral for 70 which is LXX. The Jewish scribes translated the Old Testament into Greek around the third and second century, and the Greek speaking Jewish

people who were exiled there used it. The early Christian church also adopted it. Jesus and the Apostles, including Paul, would often quote from the Septuagint when they quoted from the Old Testament. Like many of the other English versions available, I do not agree with everything in their translation. It is just another wonderful source for us to utilize as we dig into God's word for wisdom and understanding.

6. Here are more words weapons from scripture to sing against the demon of violence (hamas):
    - *"He has compassion on the weak and the needy; He saves the lives of those who are in need. He redeems their lives from oppression and violence; He will value their lives"* (Psa. 72: 13-14 CEB/NET).
    - *"Oh Lord, rescue me from wicked men! Protect me from violent men, who plan ways to harm me. Protect me from violent men, who plan to knock me over. O Lord, do not let the wicked have their way! Do not allow their plan to succeed when they attack! As for the heads of those who surround me – may the harm done by their lips overwhelm them! Calamity will hunt down a violent man and strike him down"* (Psa.140:1-2, 4, 8-9, 11b NET).
    - All of Isaiah Chapters 59 to 64 resonate with echoes of the violent days of Habakkuk. The people were sinful and violent and as a result there was no justice. No one intervenes, so the Lord Himself puts on His armor and comes down to deliver them. He puts His Spirit upon them and places His words in their mouths. He declares to them:
        - *"Arise, shine, for your light has come and the glory of the Lord is risen upon you!"* (Isa. 60:1 NKJV).
        - God will *"honor His footstool and violence will no longer resound throughout your land, nor devastation or destruction within your borders. You will call your walls salvation, and your gates praise!"* (Isa. 60: 13b, 18 CEB).
        - *"You, Lord, are our Father! You have been called our Protector from ancient times"* (Isa. 63:17 NET).
        - *"If only You would tear apart the sky and come down! Let Your adversaries know who You are"* (Isa. 64:1-2 NET).
    - As we sing we release the confusion of God in the camp of the evil one:
        - *"Confuse them, oh, Lord! Frustrate their plans! For I see **violence** and conflict in the city"* (Psa. 55:9 NET).
    - Stand on the promises of God's covenant of peace and protection:
        - *"Do not hand the life of Your dove over to a wild animal! Do not forget forever the lives of Your oppressed people! Look to Your covenant, for the dark places of the earth are full of dwelling places of **violence**"* (Psa. 74:20 NET, with footnotes).

    - *"My hand will support him, and My arm will strengthen him. No enemy will be able to exact tribute from him, and a son of* ***violence*** *will not oppress him. I will crush his enemies before him; I will strike down those who hate him. He will experience My faithfulness and loyal love, and by My name he will win victories. He will call out to Me, 'You are my Father, my God, and the Protector Who delivers me.' I will always extend My loyal love to him, and My covenant with him is secure"* (Psa. 89:21-28 NET, with footnotes)
    - *"'Because of the* ***violence*** *done to the oppressed (the victims of* ***violence****), because of the painful cries of the needy, I will spring into action,' says the Lord. 'I will provide the safety they so desperately desire'"* (Psa. 12:5, 7 NET, with footnotes).
- When the fear of violence and violent men come against us, we can boast in the protection and deliverance of our God:
    - *"Have mercy on me, O God, for men are attacking me! All day long hostile enemies are tormenting me. When I am afraid I trust in You. In God–I boast in His promise–in God I trust, I am not afraid. What can mere men do to me? Because they are bent on* ***violence*** *do not let them escape! In Your anger bring down the nations, O God! My enemies turn back when I cry out to You for help; I know that God is on my side! In God–I boast in His promise–in the Lord I boast in His promise–in God I trust, I am not afraid. What can mere men do to me"* (Psa. 56:1, 3-4, 7, 9-10 NET)?
- Violent men will reap what they sow:
    - *"The* ***violence*** *done by the wicked will sweep and drag them away because they refuse to do what is right"* (Prov. 21:7 NET/Amp).
- Many abusers of young girls and boys come from a line of abuse in their own family and relatives. This will stop:
    - *"Because you* ***violently slaughtered*** *your relatives, the people of Jacob, shame will cover you and you will be cut off forever"* (Obad. 1:10 NET).
- We respond to God's call to battle against demonic violence:
    - *"Proclaim this among the nations: 'Prepare for a holy war! Call out all the warriors! Let all these fighting men approach and attack! Beat your plowshares into swords, and your pruning hooks into spears! Let the weak say, 'I too am a warrior!' Bring down, O Lord, Your warriors! The Lord roars from Zion! Egypt will be desolate and Edom will be a desolate wilderness, because of the* ***violence*** *they did to the sons of Judah (literally "sons of praise"), in whose land they shed innocent blood. But Judah will reside securely forever, and Jerusalem will be secure from one generation to the next"* (Joel 3:9-11, 16, 19-20 NET, with notes).

MICAH & NAHUM

GOD'S WAR SONGS TO DEFEAT SORCERY & SEDUCTION

CHAPTER TEN

Know Your Enemy

"And the Breaker [the Messiah] will lead you out of exile, and the people will break through the gate and leave the city where they were held captive and go free, back to your own land; Your King will go before you—the Lord Himself will guide you"
—Mic. 2:13 (Amp/TLB/NCV/NLT)

A Dual Assault for a Double Demon

We'll study the books of Micah and Nahum together, because both deal with God's response to the demonic attacks of sorcery and seduction against His people. Both of these prophets use taunt songs—war songs of God—against these vile spirits. The word given these two prophets applies to the church today because God's people presently are being assaulted by these same two demons. The Lord desires to break their attack and show us how He has given us the authority and power to overcome them. In Jesus, we always have the victory.

The prophecy of Nahum, as Habakkuk, is called a burden from the Lord (Nah. 1:1 KJV), another war song of God. The book of Nahum is very poetic and has been compared to the Song of Songs in the excellence of its literary style. This is in agreement with our thesis that a burden is a song. Some Biblical scholars see the whole book as composed of two songs. Nahum concludes his prophecy "with a taunt song and funeral dirge of the impending destruction of Nineveh."[1]

Here we have another example of a burden from the Lord referred to as a "taunt song," just as the one given to Isaiah to sing against Babylon (Isa. 13:1-14:4).

The book of Micah is not called a burden. Instead, it is referred to as a *dabar,* a word from the Lord. *Dabar* is the Hebrew word that is used most often in the Old Testament to indicate a prophetic word. Micah may not be a burden in the sense that Nahum is a burden, but the Lord does tell Micah to use a taunt song against those who are practicing evil among His people. This taunt song was to be sung against *"those who plot evil, who lie in bed planning mischief and wickedness"* (Mic. 2:1 JB/NCV). We sing against that spirit at work in those who *"covet fields and take them by force; find homes and take them away; they are cruel to a man and his family, even to come between a man and his inheritance"* (Mic. 2:2b MSG/BBE/Knox). The Lord doesn't tolerate someone oppressing a man and his family, and He definitely doesn't tolerate someone harassing a man and his inheritance for his children. You just don't do it.

The Lord says, *"On that day they shall take up a* ***taunt song*** *against you; they will taunt you with this mournful song"*

(Mic. 2:4a NRSV/NIV; emphasis mine). As we have learned previously, the Hebrew word for taunt song is *mashal*. It is the same word used by Isaiah when the Lord instructs him to sing God's burden of doom against Babylon (Isa. 14:4), and the same word that is used by Habakkuk to sing God's burden of doom against the spirit of violence (Hab. 2:6). Remember, one definition of *mashal* is a *derisive* poem or song. Derisive means to show contempt by laughter, mocking, or ridicule. So even though Micah is not called a burden, God does tell him to incorporate a taunt song against those practicing evil and oppressing His children (Mic. 2:1-4).

God loves it when we put this all together and sing His taunt songs with joy against the enemy; when we pierce the evil one with God's word and with our laughter, as we enjoy and rejoice in Jesus. When we obediently sing His war songs, we place spiritual bonds and fetters on the principalities and powers of darkness (Ps. 2:3 with Ps. 149:5-9); therefore, let us sing joyfully the victory the Lord has given us over our demonic foes and bind the strongman (Matt. 12:29).

The Lord rejoices when we pierce the evil one with God's Word and our laughter.

The goal of God's heart of war and of our faith is the salvation of His children and to *"make disciples of all the nations"* (Matt. 28:18-20 NASB). By God's word, we are victorious in this battle and can rejoice with the Psalmist as in *"A Song of Ascents: When the Lord brought back the captive ones of Zion, we were like those who dream. Our mouths were full of laughter,* ***our tongues with songs of joy****. Then it was said among the nations, 'The Lord has done great things for them.' The Lord has done great things for us,* *and we are filled with joy"* (Ps. 126:1-3 NASB/NIV; emphasis mine). As we sing our war songs of deliverance, the nations will join us with their songs of joy and victory.

SORCERY AND SEDUCTION

Our nation is overrun by the influence of these dual forces of sorcery and seduction. These two spirits go hand in hand. Many times they are so intertwined that it's hard to distinguish where one ends and the other begins. A good definition for both of them is "manipulation or control." A person influenced by the spirit of seduction and/or sorcery is trying to control and manipulate others to do his or her will. The Lord never manipulates; He always motivates, and His motivation is always founded in His love for us. The revelation by the Holy Spirit of the Father's love for us causes us to surrender control of our lives over to Him. This surrender unravels the chains of darkness with which the evil one would shackle us. As we are free, we can now sing of His liberty to the world.

We see sorcery and seduction everywhere we look. We know *"the whole world lies in the power of the evil one"* (1 John 5:19b CEB), and it is the very nature of the evil one to control and manipulate people. This is not the will of the Father; He sent His Son Jesus to change all of this. Jesus came *"to destroy the work of the devil"* (1 John 3:8b CEB). Likewise, the Father has given us the victory in Jesus, so the evil one *"cannot touch"* us (1 John 5:18b CEB). This complete victory is what He wants us to share with the world.

Out of necessity, I will make a few statements explaining sorcery and seduction so that we may sing against them intelligently and effectively. Like Paul, who said, *"It is shameful even to talk about the things that ungodly people do in secret"* (Eph. 5:12 NLT), I would rather talk about the power, love, and mercy of our God. Talking about what the devil is up to saps your joy, gives an opening to doubt, and depression creeps in and tries to take up residence. However, since it's important in any warfare to know your enemy, we will briefly assess these two demonic spirits.

In reference to sorcery, we see people everywhere looking for power and influence. One definition of witchcraft is "intimidation by manipulation for domination."[2] The trouble is these folks are seeking the wrong thing in all the wrong places. In their frantic grasp at power, they turn to using lies, emotional exploitation, physical domination, and other forms of manipulation (i.e., sorcery) to attain their goals. There are those who delve even more deeply into the dark world of sorcery and turn to overtly seeking to satisfy their lust for power through the use of these spiritual channels.

We see sorcery functioning not only in the world, but shockingly we see it at work even within our churches. This spirit of sorcery is operating at both ends of the spectrum within the church. On one end, it comes under the guise of a legalistic, religious spirit; on the other end, this spirit operates under what some call "charismatic witchcraft." This must stop. The world must see the true, clean power of God working in love through His people. They must see a demonstration of His powerful love that encourages and motivates. Anything less only enslaves and manipulates.

Sadly, most people have no clue what depths of deception and ensnarement await those who dare dabble in all forms of sorcery. The evil one promises power, fame, and riches, but delivers deeper and deeper levels of enslavement to him. Nahum reveals this lie to the sorcerers in Nineveh, *"you tempted and lured the nations like a harlot, dangling the allure of immorality. You were a sorceress* ***promising control of the spirit world****, enslaving nations to lives of immorality and families to sorcery"* (Nah. 3:4 Voice; emphasis mine).

It is all a lie. The devil is a liar and the father of lies (John 8:44 NET). Lies are the only thing those bound by this demonic spirit will ever get from him. What they need is to see the truth of Jesus; see His merciful love and the victory of His blood. Once they have seen the genuine, they will never settle for the counterfeit. The more we get to know Jesus, the more we see how evil and corrupt the enemy really is.

The more we know Jesus, the more we see how evil and corrupt the enemy is.

In reference to seduction, all you have to do is turn on your television, open a magazine, or look at a billboard. It's a sad fact, but advertisers know that in America, sex sells, and it sells because of the power of the spirit of seduction.

Sexual allure is not the only form of seduction. Power is also very seductive. Many in our culture are seduced by greed and the desire for material gain. Again, you need only watch the news or read the day's headlines to see the destructive power this manifestation of seduction has on our society. Those in power who have become ensnared by this spirit abuse and take advantage of the poor and defenseless. This is in direct opposition to Christ's mandate to care for those in our society who are the weakest.

That's enough about the works of the devil. Let's look now to the Lord and to His word to learn how He desires to destroy the works of darkness by His light shining through us.

Lord, open our eyes with Your light that reveals the deception of darkness. Saturate us with the power of Your word to sing against the powers of evil. Show us how You desire to work through us by Your power, break the power of the wicked one off of Your children!

Sing the taunt-songs of God.
Pierce the father of lies with God's truth.

ENDNOTES:

1. Retrieved at: http://www.etsjets.org/files/JETS-PDFs/32/32-2/32-2-pp159-169_JETS.pdf and https://en.wikipedia.org/wiki/Book_of_Nahum.
2. Retrieved at: http://www.mcleanministries.com/custom.html.

CHAPTER ELEVEN

GOD'S BREAKER ANOINTING-I

GOD'S WILD OX SHATTERS SORCERY

"Arise and thresh, O daughter of Zion, people of Zion, get up and crush your enemies. I will make you like a threshing ox. I will give you iron horns and bronze hoofs. So you will crush many nations."
—Mic. 4:13a NIRV/KJV

GOD'S WORD-WEAPONS AGAINST SORCERY

During the days of Micah and Nahum, the leaders of the capital cities of Samaria, Jerusalem, and Nineveh had submitted to the spirit of sorcery. Because that spirit was controlling the leadership of the nations associated with the capitals, it was given free rein to flow down and control the citizenry as well. Micah gives the word of the Lord against Samaria, the capital of Israel, which composed the ten northern tribes (Mic. 1:5-7), and Jerusalem, the capital of the two southern tribes, Judah and Benjamin (Mic. 1:9). (The nations of Judah and Benjamin had turned from worshipping the Lord and had replaced Him with Nineveh's false gods of sorcery (Mic. 6:12-14). Nahum addresses his burden from the Lord against Nineveh, the capital of Assyria where the sorcery originated (Nah. 3:4-7). This malicious demon was wreaking havoc on the people of these nations.

The Hebrew word used here for sorcery is *kesheph*,[1] and it means to use "incantations, sorceries and witchcraft." It literally means "to speak a word that opens or allows destruction."[2] *Kesheph* is found only six times in the Old Testament. This word is first used by King Jehu to describe the witchcraft of Queen Jezebel as he rides out to destroy her (2 Kings 9:22-33). It is used twice by the prophet Isaiah concerning God's impending doom on the sorcery used by Babylon (Isa. 47:9, 12-15). It is used once by the prophet Micah describing the sorcery practiced in Israel (Mic. 5:12), and twice by the prophet Nahum describing the sorcery operating in Nineveh (Nah. 3:4).

It's interesting to note that Jezebel and Babylon, both associated with the word *kesheph* are still around today in the spiritual realm. Both are mentioned in the book of Revelation as still being major adversaries of our Lord. This is a very wicked demon. This spirit was manipulating and enslaving the people of Nineveh, Samaria, and Jerusalem, and the Lord came down to break its power and bondage over His children. He broke its power back then, during the days of Micah and Nahum, and He's doing it today.

To enchant means "to practice sorcery or witchcraft on anything; to give efficacy to anything by *songs of sorcery.*"[3]

An enchanter is "one who has demons at his command."[4] Sorcery refers to "enchantments, magic or witchcraft for the power of commanding evil spirits."[5] *Kesheph* comes from the Hebrew root word *kashaph*,[6] which means to use "enchantments or magical *songs*."

When we break them down and then put them all together, we come up with a comprehensive definition of sorcery. Sorcery is the practice of commanding demons by enchanting or singing "songs of sorcery" or "magical songs." Someone is using a spirit of sorcery by singing magical songs to command demons. Singing magical songs releases the power of the evil one, but glory to God, the Lord has an answer for this.

The Lord's plan is to silence these songs of sorcery with His songs of war! Hear the word of the Lord against Tyre as they rejoiced over the fall of Judah, ***"I will put an end to the noise of your songs****, and the sound of your instruments of music shall be heard no more, gone forever"* (Ezek. 26:13 BBE/Amp; emphasis mine). And to those who oppress with terror, Isaiah says the Lord will be, *"Like the heat of the desert, You stop their violent attack, You silence the roar of foreigners. As heat is reduced by the shadow of a cloud,* ***so the boastful, battle songs of the terrible, ruthless ones will be silenced****"* (Isa. 25:5 NIVUK/NKJV/NLT/OJB/CEB/EXB; emphasis mine). The cloud of God's glory will shelter us under His shade from the oppression of the terrible ones. As we sing His songs, God silences their terrible songs of sorcery.

Singing God's beautiful songs of war silences the terrible songs of sorcery.

WAR SONGS ACTIVATE GOD'S POWER

It is the will of the Father to silence these death songs forever. To that end, the Lord gives Nahum and Micah very specific instructions to confront the evil onslaught released by these magical songs. He gives His burden (war song) to Nahum to counter these songs of sorcery, and He tells Micah to sing a "taunt song" against this evil. We, too, are called to sing His war songs to shatter the enemy's songs of sorcery. The whole book of Nahum is God's burden "concerning the impending doom of Nineveh" (Nah. 1:1 TLB). We must sing these same songs against this spirit of sorcery operating in all the "Ninevehs" of our day. As we sing His war songs and proclaim the victory in Jesus in our corporate praise and worship, the Lord descends and treads upon the demonic high places (Mic. 1:3 KJV/Mof).

Nineveh was the capital of Assyria and had enslaved the two nations of Israel and Judah. But what was worse than their physical enslavement, both Israel and Judah had become spiritually imprisoned; both nations had submitted to Assyria's false gods of sorcery as well. Sorcery is like cancer: Left alone, it keeps on spreading, but by targeting the heart of the cancer cells, good medicine halts the disease and ends its ravaging effects. Our Great Physician has a cure not only for our physical diseases, but for the spiritual plague of sorcery as well.

The burden of God's word to Nahum is that God is coming down and that spirit of sorcery is doomed (Nah. 1:1-15). God addresses the city of Nineveh in this war song because it is the place of origin, the source of this attack of sorcery. In battle, a skilled warrior always goes for the kill shot. The

Lord always goes for the head because He wants to cut off our problems at their source; therefore, He takes aim at that principality and power of sorcery in Nineveh in order to silence these magical songs at their source.

In Chapter 1 of Nahum the Lord gives us a series of three beautiful promises. We can stand on these promises and sing them as we go into battle. Here are the three beautiful promises from the word of God that we can put to music and sing this war song against the spirit of sorcery.

PROMISE 1:

*"**With an overflowing flood, He will make an utter end of His adversaries**, and darkness shall pursue His enemies. What are you thinking of, Nineveh, to defy the Lord? Whatever you plot against the Lord, He will completely destroy! **He'll stop you with one blow**; He won't need to strike again."*
—Nah. 1:8-9 KJV/RSV/NET/TLB; emphasis mine

All demonic plots are useless against the Lord and His children. God will destroy all evil plans of sorcery with a flood of His glory, and He will cause all our adversaries to be pursued by the darkness. All it takes is one blow from the hand of God to stop them. As we sing, God strikes the enemy to the beat of our music and singing. When we mix our faith with this word, it becomes a hammer in our hand. Jesus said, *"If I cast out demons by the finger of God, then the kingdom of God has already overtaken you"* (Luke 11:20 NET). With just one blow from the hand of God this demon is shattered.

PROMISE 2:

"The Lord is not afraid of him, though he builds his army millions strong. Though they be strong and many, they will be cut off and pass away. They are going to be cut down, annihilated. ***Now I will break off your chains, and release you from the yoke of slavery.****"*
—Nah. 1:12-13 RSV/JB/TLB; emphasis mine

The Lord hates this chain of slavery to sorcery. His plan for the "whole earth" is to break this demonic Assyrian yoke (Isa. 14:24-27). The Lord is calling us to be His Holy Ghost empowered Chain-Breakers. As we sing our praise and worship to the Father, we release the power of God's light to cut through those chains of darkness like a laser.

PROMISE 3:

"The Lord has given a commandment concerning you [evil Assyrian counselor] that no more shall your name be perpetuated. Out of the house of your gods I will cut off the graven and molten images. ***For I'll destroy all your idols, then a time will be set for your funeral****... which will come very soon. I will make your grave; for you are vile,* ***I will make your grave a dunghill, and I will bury you!*** *For how you stink with sin!"*
—Nah. 1:14 Amp/KJV/Mof/AEB/TLB; emphasis mine

The Lord is saying to that wicked spirit who is leading the people astray, "You are as good as dead to Me. It's time for your funeral, and look who is coming to bury you!" God tells us in the next verse that someone is coming on the tops of the mountains, one who is treading upon the high places to bury our enemy. That someone is anyone who is preaching the gospel of Jesus.

> *"**Behold upon the mountains, the feet of him who brings good tidings; who publishes peace!** The invaders have been wiped out, and we are saved! Celebrate your feasts, oh, Judah, perform your vows! For never again will the wicked one **(Belial)**, pass through you. **He is cut off completely**"* (Nah. 1:15 Amp/TLB/TNIV/NET/NASB; emphasis mine).

The "wicked counselor" is the source of the sorcery operating in Nineveh. Here we are told the name of this wicked counselor of sorcery, "who plots evil against the Lord" (Nah. 1:11 NET). His name is *Belial,* which is another name for the devil. This name is most fitting because it means the *"good for nothing, the worthless one."*[7] Let's sing this chorus to remind the devil of just how loathsome he is in contrast to our Lord. "The Lord is altogether wonderful, and you, devil, are altogether worthless. The Lord is good for everything, and devil, you are good for nothing. Jesus and His heralds are proclaiming His good news, and they have come to bury you."[8]

Preaching the gospel buries demonic sorcery!

The War Song Against Sorcery

Here are a few word weapons from Micah and Nahum to sing against sorcery:

- God is sending another flood with darkness to drive you back.
- God is destroying all your demonic plans.

- God only has to strike you with one blow.
- God breaks your chains of sorcery off of His people.
- God tears down your strongholds and blots out your names forever.
- God annihilates Belial, the worthless one, the good for nothing wicked counselor. He will no longer invade God's children.
- God's burial crew, anyone preaching the good news, is coming to bury you under the weight of the glory and gospel of Jesus!

Now, that's a war song. Let's take these Divine truths and add more ammunition from God's word to sing the doom and destruction of sorcery.

Shout the Gospel of Jesus

We overcome this attack of sorcery by the precious promises of God. As we come preaching the Gospel of our Lord Jesus Christ, we are treading upon the mountains, the high places set against us. God dispatches these heralds of good news to the mountaintops to declare this message of the good news:

> *"Go up on a high mountain, oh, herald of Zion! Shout out loudly, oh, herald Jerusalem! Shout! Don't be afraid! Say to the towns of Judah, 'Here is your God! Look,* ***the sovereign Lord comes as a victorious Warrior; His military power establishes His rule'"*** (Isa. 40:9-10a NET; emphasis mine).

This is the good news: Jesus, the Messiah has come. As we proclaim the good news, Jesus as God's victorious Warrior will come down and establish His rule in the spiritual realm as well as in the natural world. As we preach the Gospel of the Kingdom we see "satan fall like lightning" from that high place (Luke 10:18 KJV). Sing and release the Warrior King and His Kingdom upon the earth. The Breaker is coming, and He comes to give us that same Breaker anointing.

GOD'S TWO-FOLD BREAKER ANOINTING

The Lord will shatter sorcery and seduction by pouring out His Breaker anointing upon His children. God's Breaker rises up and destroys the enemy's hold on us. *"He Who opens the breach will go up before them; the Messiah will lead you out"* (Mic. 2:13a RSV/TLB). The Hebrew word for "breaker" is *parats,* and it means "to break down, to destroy and to scatter and disperse hostile forces."[9] The Lord prophesies through Micah that God's "Ruler in Israel" shall come, and Bethlehem Ephrathah "will be the birthplace of My King" (Mic. 5:2 NASB/TLB). Jesus is the Breaker. He goes before us. He storms the gates of our prisons and breaks open the bars holding us captive and makes a way out. We are free to come home.

The Amplified Bible calls the Breaker "the Messiah" (literally "the Anointed One"). The Breaker—a/k/a the Messiah, a/k/a the Anointed One—comes to lavish His Breaker anointing upon us. The very next line of scripture tells us, *"They **break out** (same word, "parats"); the people will **break through** the gates and leave the city where they were held captive"* (Mic. 2:13b NASB/NCV; emphasis and note in parenthesis mine). The same Breaker anointing empowers us, and just as our Messiah, we break out of any spiritual prison holding us captive. The Lord says, *"I will open the way for you to return. I will march in front of you.* ***You will break through*** *the city gates and go free. I am your King. I will pass through the gates in front of you. I will lead the way"* (NIRV; emphasis mine)! The Lord Jesus, our Messiah, sets us free with His Breaker anointing. The Breaker anointing covers us and we "break out" of any strongholds of sorcery that would try to hold us in bondage. It's "the anointing that breaks the yoke" (Isa. 10:27 KJV).

Jesus, the Breaker, has come and given us His two-fold breaker anointing.

The Lord does two things through the power of His Breaker anointing: He transforms us into His Wild Ox and into His Roaring Lion. As His Wild Ox, we shatter the power of sorcery; as His Roaring Lion, we scatter seduction.

Joseph, the Wild Ox of God

Just as we learned the Lord changed Habakkuk into His Mighty Stag to defeat and tread down the high places of violence; we must grasp the revelation of the Lord changing us into His Wild Ox in the spiritual realm, to deal with and defeat the attacks of sorcery. There's nothing to fear because the Lord our King goes before us. Like soldiers who follow their commander-in-chief, we simply look to our victorious Warrior King to lead the way. Before we jump into the fray, let's study an example in the Bible of one who possessed this anointing of the Wild Ox. Our example is Joseph.

Before he died, Moses declared over Joseph, *"He is a* ***young ox*** *in strength and splendor. His power is like the horns of a* ***wild***

ox. *With them he will butt and push all the nations together even to the ends of the earth"* (Deut. 33:17 BBE/TLB/NLT/AAT/Dar/YLT/WEB; emphasis mine).

When we examine the life and heart of Joseph, first and foremost we see a man who knew that his father, Jacob, loved him unwaveringly and unconditionally. The Bible tells us that Jacob loved Joseph more than any of his other sons, because Joseph was born to him late in his life (Gen. 37:3). Because Joseph knew the love of his father was steadfast, he was always secure, always at peace, always able to calmly overcome the obstacles life threw his way – and they were many.

This revelation is paramount for us today. To truly be God's Wild Ox we cannot have an orphan spirit of rejection. We must have the "spirit of adoption" living and working within us. In Jesus we have been adopted into the family of God and can cry out "Daddy!" to the King of heaven (Rom. 8:15). The spiritual revelation of the Father God's indisputable, eternal love for us must be firmly anchored deep in our hearts. Then we are at peace. Then we will have a wild heart and be a Wild Ox for God.

Examine the Wild Ox heart of Joseph revealed through the many trials he faced. No matter what came his way, he was calm and peaceful:

- His brothers hated him: "That's okay, my Father loves me."
- His brothers wanted to kill him: "That's okay, my Father loves me."
- His brothers sold him as a slave: "That's okay, my Father loves me."

- He was falsely accused of attempted rape: "That's okay, my Father loves me."
- He was falsely accused of being a sex offender and imprisoned: "That's okay, my Father loves me."
- He was forgotten for two years while in prison by the cupbearer: "That's okay, my Father loves me."
- He rejected the chance to punish and take revenge on his brothers because he knew his Father loved him and them.

The picture of Joseph we find in scripture is of a wild heart beating in the breast of a Wild Ox of God. A Wild Ox is one who knows the love of his Father, and as a result, has the calm courage and strength to love people. To love those who have mistreated us and treat them as the Father loves and treats them.

Before we ever go into battle against sorcery and seduction, we must know the heart of our Father God. This beautiful heart of love is part of our training and preparation to be God's warriors. With the revelation of God's heart and how much He loves us, we can see more clearly the lies and deception of the evil one. The Father's heart is being revealed to His children around the globe. This move of God is being documented worldwide[10] as believers everywhere are beginning to reach out with God's true heart of love to their neighbors. Without God's heart, we are not equipped to be part of the army of God. Without His heart of love, we will do much damage to God's children. Until we have the full revelation of God's love, the Lord won't let us dispatch these war songs. Understanding God's love for *all* of His creation is fundamental to our warfare.

The Breaker Anointing of God's Wild Ox

Now that we have an example and a better understanding of what it means to have the heart of God's Wild Ox, let's get ready to deploy the power of our God. The Lord, through the prophet Micah, asks Israel, *"Why do you cry out so loudly? Isn't the king in you?"* (Mic. 4:9a CEB). He is asking them, "Don't you have the Lord as your King dwelling among you? You should be shouting the victory, not crying out in agony." Of course, God knows the answer: They're crying because they have left the Lord for false gods. They have turned from His love and lost His presence.

Through Micah's question, God is reminding His people, Israel, of an ancient promise, and at the same time, revealing to them the source of their current sorrows. We read about this promise in the book of Numbers, when Balak, the king of Moab, tried to get Balaam, a prophet of the false god Baal, to curse the children of Israel. Instead of curses the Lord causes Balaam to release His blessings and promises upon Israel. One such promise is that the King of Glory would dwell among them, and that they will shout the victory. The Lord spoke this blessing upon Israel through Balaam:

> *"There is no idolatry in Jacob; no false god is seen in Israel: The Lord their God is with them, and they hear the shout of victory of their King, the shout of the King is in them!"* (Num. 23:21 WYC/NIRV).

During Micah's day, Israel had turned to idols and false gods, and in doing so, had lost their victory shout. During this specific time of Moses, the King of Glory was able to dwell among Israel, and they couldn't help but shout His victory. We find out why they shout in the next verse. They shout because:

> *"God, Who brought them out of Egypt, gives them **the horns and the strength of a wild ox!**"* (Num. 23:22 CJB/AAT/BBE; emphasis mine).

God delivers us out of the world with the strength of a wild ox. With Him in our midst, we become strong, just like Him, just like His Wild Ox.[11] This revelation is so important that later the Lord had Balaam repeat this promise to Israel: *"God brought them out of Egypt; **they have the strength of a wild ox**. They devour hostile nations and break their bones in pieces; with their arrows they pierce them"* (Num. 24:8 NET; emphasis mine). Twice the Lord has spoken this promise over Israel, that they will be His Wild Ox. When God repeats something to us it *"means that the matter is determined and established by God, and God will bring it quickly to pass"* (Gen. 41:32 NASB/NKJV). The blessing of being God's Wild Ox is a very important promise for us to claim today because God is determined to bring this anointing into our lives.

When we submit to God's Breaker anointing and are given "the horns and the strength of the wild ox" of Numbers 23, something incredible happens in the realm of our invisible warfare. In Numbers 23:23 we are given a promise that is so beautiful and powerful we need to read it in many translations:

> *"**No evil power has effect against Jacob**, no secret arts against Israel"* (BBE).

*"**No one can put a spell on Ya'akov (Jacob)**; no magic will work against Isra'el"* (CJB).

"No spell can curse the descendants of Jacob. No magic can harm the people of Israel" (GOD'S WORD).

"No magic spells can bind Jacob; no incantations can hold back Israel" (MSG).

*"For **there is no sorcery against Jacob**, neither is there any divination against Israel"* (NKJV/KJV).

Evil spells, incantations, magic, sorcery, none of it can touch God's Wild Ox. Let the power of that promise soak in for a moment, and then put those words into a war song and sing them as you go into battle. When we sing God's word in His war songs, we release the power of the Holy Spirit. He is with us as we sing and go forth in the power of God's Wild Ox. He drives away any attack of sorcery. As a result, no one can put a curse on us. All magical spells fall to the ground. This is the anointing we need today.

No curse, no magic spell can harm Gods' wild ox.

If you still need some convincing that God has called us to be His Wild Ox, take a look at what the Lord says about this same subject to Micah. The Lord gives Israel—ergo, us—a very specific command in dealing with this onslaught of sorcery. First, we must repent and turn away from any idolatry or any use of sorcery or divination. Like the children of Israel, *"We will follow the Lord our God forever and ever, even though all the nations around us worship idols"* (Mic. 4:5 TLB)! Then the Lord will say to us:

> *"**Arise and thresh,** oh, daughter of Zion, people of Zion, **get up and crush your (demonic) enemies.** I will make you like a **threshing ox**. I will give you **iron horns and bronze hoofs,** so you will crush many nations. You will dedicate their plunder to Yahweh and their wealth to the Master of all the earth"* (Mic. 4:13a NIRV/KJV/ISR/JB; emphasis and note in parenthesis mine).

When we turn away from our false gods and return to the Lord, He changes us, just as He did with Habakkuk. The Wild Ox of God has the power to shatter the spirit of sorcery over our land. And as Habakkuk, who was able to bend a bow of bronze, we now become as strong as His Wild Ox with bronze hoofs and iron horns. The Lord doesn't give us regular hooves; He gives us hooves of bronze.[12] He gives us exactly what we need to completely crush the head of sorcery. As we praise Him, we arise. As we worship Him, we thresh and shatter divination and sorcery.

Arise and thresh, wild ox of God, and crush your demonic enemies!

ALL I CAN DO IS BLESS THEM

This anointing of God's Wild Ox was apparent even to Israel's enemies. Just look at what Balak said when he saw the people of Israel coming:

> *"And Balak, the son of Zippor, saw all that Israel had done to the Amorites. And Moab was exceedingly afraid of the people because they were many, and Moab was in dread because of the children of Israel. The Moabites were sick with fear at the sight of them, and Moab said to the elders of Midian, 'Now this company is licking up all that is around us,*

> ***as an ox*** *licks up the grass of the field, this mob will eat us* ***like an ox eats grass"*** (Num. 22:2-4 KJV/ISR/ TLB; emphasis mine)!

Our enemies see this anointing of God's Wild Ox upon us, and they are "sick with fear." You have to just love it when the demons are "in dread" and "sick with fear" at the power of our God. (Sounds like another song for us to sing against the spirit of sorcery).

As we saw earlier, when Balak tells Balaam to curse Israel, Balaam is completely powerless to obey. He tells the Moabite king "All I can do is bless them!" This is a powerful revelation and warrants a closer look. Balaam, who was supposedly a mighty prophet of Baal, can only say the words the God of Israel puts in his mouth (Num. 23:12). To better understand the significance of this scripture, you need to understand that Balaam was a prophet for hire (Jude 1:11).

In other words, he performed his sorcery for money. Here, Balaam is trying to curse Israel; trying to "use sorcery" against them (Num. 24:1 ISR). He is a greedy man and his lust for money drives him to do evil. Balaam knows the king is rich and desperate – a promising combination for one of Balaam's profession and character. He wants to curse Israel so he can collect his hefty fee and be on his way, but he cannot do it. All Balaam can do is bless them. Moses tells us:

> *"But the Lord your God refused to listen to Balaam, and* ***changed the curse to a blessing, for the Lord your God loves you"*** (Deut. 23:5 NET; see also Joshua 24:9-10 and Nehemiah 13:2; emphasis mine).

Stand on this wonderful promise: Even when our enemy tries to use magic and sorcery to curse us, those curses will fail and fall to the ground. God stalwartly refuses to listen. And then, because of His great love for us, He turns those curses into blessings.

No one can curse Gods' wild ox: God will change their curses to blessings!

Be like Joseph, who fully comprehended the unconditional, unwavering love of his father, and therefore, was able to receive the call of God to be His Wild Ox (Deut. 33:17). Just as Joseph, we will stand and give the word of the Lord to the kings and leaders of this world, and as God's voice on earth, we will speak His revelation and guidance even during years of famine. The magicians and sorcerers of this world can only stand by in silence.

The principle of reaping and sowing (Gal. 6:7) is nowhere more applicable than in the context of practicing sorcery. If you participate in sorcery and sow curses, have no doubt, curses you will reap. Balak is a perfect example of this. Balaam repeatedly warned Balak what the Lord had said concerning Israel: *"Blessed is everyone who blesses you, and cursed is everyone who curses you"* (Num. 24:9b NRSV). Balak did not heed God's warning, and as a result, the nation of Moab became subject to a curse. Balaam declares to Balak:

> *"I will let you know what this people [Israel] will do to your people [Moab] in the latter days…I see in the future of Israel, far down the distant trail, there shall come a Star out of Jacob, and a Scepter shall rise out of Israel; One who will lay low the chiefs of Moab, who shall bring devastation on the skulls of all the sons of strife and tumult"* (Num. 24:14, 17 Amp/TLB/ASV/ NEB/JB/Knox).

This Breaker anointing of God's Wild Ox is for us today. We need this anointing to shatter the shackles of sorcery and set God's children free from "all the sons of strife and tumult." Through Micah, the Lord urges us to remember what Balaam spoke concerning Israel when Balak wanted him to curse them:

> *"I brought you up from the land of Egypt and from the house of bondage; I ransomed you from slavery; I sent before you Moses, Aaron and Miriam. My people,* ***I urge you, remember*** *what King Balak of Moab devised, and* ***what Balaam the son of Beor answered him;*** *(also the events) from Acacia to Gilgal, so that you may fully understand and know the righteous deeds of Jehovah, in order* ***that you may know the triumph of the Lord, that you may be sure that the Lord is strong to save"*** (Mic. 6:5 NCV/NEB/Phi; emphasis mine).

This is our song of deliverance and triumph that the Lord brought us out of bondage and made us strong to conquer strongholds and high places. It is our song of remembrance and thanksgiving that the Lord has given us His Breaker anointing and that no curse can harm us. As we sing God's word in praise to Him, He descends in power and shatters the demon of sorcery. He sets His children free.

Newsflash: God Loves Witches and Warlocks

When we think about defeating sorcery in our land, we usually think about helping those who are being oppressed by people wielding this demonic power. We tend to steer clear of anyone who is participating in sorcery. But we have it backwards. It is the witches and warlocks who the Lord is addressing here! The witches and warlocks are His people. God is addressing the children of Israel, not some foreigner. The Israelites, God's chosen people, are the ones who are using this spirit of sorcery and manipulation. They are the ones the Lord is coming after to set free. Yes, the Lord desires to set free those who are oppressed by this spirit, but here in Micah, His focus is on the sorcerers themselves. It is the so-called witches and warlocks that the Lord wants us to go after in His love. These sadly mistaken sorcerers think they command and control demons, when in reality they are under that demon's control. They are the most enslaved people in the world. If anyone needs God's love, it's them.

Micah and Nahum are God's love letters to all the witches and wizards. These prophecies reveal God's love reaching out to them. The Lord is warning them and wooing them: "Jesus, the Breaker, is coming! Return now to Me, your loving Father, while you still have time. Jesus is coming to shatter the power of that demonic stronghold, and He is setting My children free. Return to your Father". There is no defense against the love and mercy of God and there is no excuse for us to not share that love and mercy. Imagine this scenario: You walk into the local palm reader's shop and ask if *you* can read *her* palm. You don't really "read her palm"; instead, you take her hand and pray for her, that she receive the unconditional love of our Abba, Father God. This is the heart of God.

Micah and Nahum are God's love letters to all witches and warlocks.

Think about it. Jesus says, *"The Most High is kind to the ungrateful and the wicked"* (Luke 6:35 JB). Let's have a heart like our Father.

LORD, SHINE AND EXPOSE THE DARKNESS

Finally, as the Lord shines His glory upon the earth, His light will expose these deeds of darkness. He declares to Nineveh that He will expose her to the people of the world, and they will see what this demon of sorcery really looks like:

> *"I'll strip you of your seductive silk robes and* ***expose you*** *on the world stage.* ***I'll let the nations get their fill of the ugly truth of who you really are and have been all along.*** *I will cover you with filth, dog dung and* ***show the world how vile you really are.*** *All who see you will shrink back in horror. They will gag and say, 'Nineveh's a pigsty:* ***What on earth did we ever see in her?*** *Who would give her a second look? Ugh! Who will want to comfort you?'"* (Nah. 3; 5-7 MSG/NLT/GNB/NIV; emphasis mine).

Although this verse is ninety-nine percent disgusting and discouraging, the last eight words are a message of hope. *"Where can I find anyone to comfort you"* (Nah. 3:7b NIV)? Glory to God, they will find comfort in the Lord and in us.

The word for comfort is *nacham* and means "to comfort and console" or "to grieve, to pity, to be comforted."[13] The name Nahum actually comes from this same root word and means "comfort."[14] The entire book of Nahum is the story and a reflection of God's Great Comforter, the Holy Spirit, the One whom the Lord has sent to comfort us. As we sing God's word, the veil of darkness is torn away and those ensnared by sorcery are free and can return to the

Lord. Then they can receive the wonderful comfort of His Holy Spirit. Digging a little deeper, the word for "comfort" comes from the Latin word *"confortare,"* which means to "strengthen greatly; to make strong." The Latin base word is *"fortis"* from which get our words "fort and fortress," meaning "a place of strength."[15] Wow! God's Holy Ghost Comforter makes us Army of God strong. That's true comfort.

As we sing God's word, sing with faith. Sing and believe for the Breaker anointing to fall and the power of the Lord to be released. Like a Wild Ox, the Lord crushes the enemy under our feet. Let's move into this Wild Ox anointing, as we stand on this precious promise of God's protection, as we sing and shout the victory.

Oh, Lord, let those practicing sorcery feel Your power. Let them repent and return to You. Lord, we don't look at the deeds of darkness, but we focus on Your holy light. As we sing Your word against these forces, let the power of Your light shine out. Your light drives back the darkness every time. Let Your light shine, oh, Lord and tear back this seductive screen. Let us see what sorcery and seduction really look like in the spirit: She's covered in dung and stinks. Give us Your eyes. At Your revelation all will shrink back from such an ugly, stinking spirit. And Lord, send Your Comforter. Let Your Holy Spirit comfort and console those You set free from the bondage of sorcery. Let this Holy Comforter strengthen Your people so they can shine the light of Your love, mercy, and hope into the darkness of demonic control.

Lord, cause us to be a channel of your love and Holy Ghost comfort to those bound by sorcery.

Silence the songs of witchcraft with God's songs of war!

ENDNOTES:

1. Retrieved at: http://www.blueletterbible.org/lang/lexicon.cfm?Strongs=H3785&t=KJV.
2. Seekins, pp. 10-11.
3. Webster's Dictionary 1828 Hardcover Edition.
4. Ibid.
5. Ibid.
6. Retrieved at: http://www.blueletterbible.org/lang/lexicon.cfm?Strongs=H3784&t=KJV.
7. *Belial* is the transliteration of the Hebrew word *Beliya'al*. Retreived at: http://www.blueletterbible.org/lang/lexicon/lexicon.cfm?Strongs=H1100&t=KJV.
8. This goes hand in hand with the beautiful promise given by Isaiah: *"How beautiful on the mountains are the feet of those who bring good news, who proclaim peace, who bring good tidings, who proclaim salvation. Who say to Zion, 'Your God reigns!'"* (Isa. 52:7 TNIV). The gospel of the kingdom releases the reign of our King. These are the very same promises that Paul quotes in Romans 10:13-15, to describe a preacher of the Gospel of Jesus.
9. Retrieved at: http://www.blueletterbible.org/lang/lexicon/lexicon.cfm?Strongs=H6555&t=KJV.
10. Retrieved at http://www.wpfilm.com/about/
11. Some translations say that it is the Lord Who delivers Israel as a Wild Ox, while other versions say that Israel becomes strong as a Wild Ox. Who has this strength of a Wild Ox? Which one is it: A) God, B) His people, or C) both? The answer is C. Both A and B are correct. The Lord comes in the power of a Wild Ox. He gives that anointing to us, and we receive the power of God's Wild Ox.
12. There is a whole study to be delved into on what bronze represents in Scripture. Bronze is produced when just the right amount of copper and tin are combined. In the Bible, copper represents the nature of God; tin represents the nature of man. When there is the correct combination of tin and copper, bronze is the result. Bronze represents judgment and is God's weapon of choice against the evil one. Bronze is just the

right mixture of the heart of God working hand in hand with the heart of a man or woman to bring about His will and His kingdom upon the earth. Note: When John saw the glorified Jesus, he saw that *"His feet gleamed like **burnished bronze**"* (Rev. 1:15a TLB emphasis mine).

13. Retrieved at: http://www.blueletterbible.org/lang/lexicon/lexicon.cfm?strongs=H5162&t=KJV&page=4.
14. Retrieved at: http://www.blueletterbible.org/lang/lexicon/lexicon.cfm?strongs=H5151&t=KJV.
15. Retrieved at http://www.merriam-webster.com/dictionary/comfort.

CHAPTER TWELVE

God's Breaker Anointing-2

God's Roaring Lion Scatters Seduction

"The remnant of Israel will go out among the nations and be as strong as a lion. Like a young lion loose among the nations. The nations will be helpless like sheep before her."
—Mic. 5:8 NLT/Phi/Mof/TLB

Jesus Reveals a Tactic of the Wicked, Worthless One

Here's one last note about Balaam. When Balaam realized he could not curse Israel because of the Lord's protection, he changed the tactics of his attack. Jesus tells us that Balaam later, *"taught Balak how to* ***entice the Israelites into sin*** *by persuading them to eat food sacrificed to idols and* ***to practice sexual immorality****"* (Rev. 2:14 TNIV/GNB; emphasis mine). When Balaam saw his words fall powerless to the ground, and his curses turned into blessings by the Lord; he stopped using sorcery on Israel and started using seduction. The devil will do the same. If one tactic doesn't work, he will move to another. If he can't lure us with blatant sorcery, he'll entice us with subtle, sensual seduction. Either way, he is defeated in Jesus.

The High Triumph of the Breaker Anointing

The second part of the two-fold Breaker anointing we began in the previous chapter, is the anointing to break the grasp of the spirit of seduction through God's Roaring Lion. These seducing spirits with their weapons of sexual addictions are infecting and destroying millions. Many who are reading this right now have been or still are enslaved to some manifestation of sexual addiction. Good news: The Lord has come to set us all free. As we study God's victory over sexual seduction and draw His triumph into our hearts, He will heal us, forgive us, give us grace to walk with Him, and perhaps best of all, empower us to go out and set others free. It is our privilege, our call to do so.

In Micah 5:8 (previously) we are given another word from the Lord to put to music as a war song. In this verse, Micah is reminding Israel of the promise the Lord gave to Balaam: *"See,* ***Israel comes up like a she-lion****, lifting himself up like a lion: he will take no rest till he has made a meal of those he has overcome"* (Num. 23:24 BBE emphasis mine). Micah repeats Balaam's prophecy to them: *"The remnant of Israel will go out among the nations and be as strong as a lion, like a young lion loose among the sheep"* (Mic. 5:8 NLT). Twice this promise of becoming "as strong as a lion, like a young lion," is declared over God's people, which means it **is established by God**, and **He will bring it to pass in our lives.** During our praise and worship, God's people release the roar of the Lion of God. We sing and become not only God's Wild Ox but also God's Roaring Lion, able to tear asunder the demonic forces of seduction.

The Lord goes on to declare that as we go forth with this Lion power from on High, *"Your hands shall be lifted up over your adversaries, and* ***all*** *your enemies shall be cut off"* (Mic. 5:9 RSV, emphasis mine)! The Old English style found in Knox is beautiful: *"High triumph thou shalt have over thy enemies; perish all that bear thee ill-will!"*

High triumph you shall have over your enemies!

In the Lord, we don't experience just any old mediocre triumph; we experience "high triumph." It's this kind of high triumph over our adversary that makes you dance and shout at the top of your lungs about the victory of God. With the power of God's Roaring Lion, *all* our enemies will be destroyed. Not one of them is exempt, particularly not seduction. Anything and everything holding you in bondage are broken by the power of the Lord.

This problem of seduction, both sexual and spiritual, is tearing apart the hearts and homes in our nation. Many are so ensnared to their sexual appetites that they have become addicted to them, like a drug. Their addiction drives them to use and abuse others. There are more than 40 million people in America who go to one of the 4.2 million pornographic websites every day.[1] Many honestly can't change their behavior. Many who want to break free don't have the power to do so.[2] We must sing God's prophetic songs in faith and release the roar of His Lion from on high over our land to set His people free from the death grip of sexual seduction. Let us manifest God's true love to the world and expose the cheap counterfeit of the evil one.

The Lord has a precise word weapon to launch against this seducing spirit. Worship leaders and pastors in particular need to catch a'hold of God's revelation about how to defeat this attack of sexual seduction coming against our homes, our churches, our cities, and our country because the roar of God's Lion is released in our praise and worship. As we sing the specific word weapons—that is, the Lord's "It is written"—against this attack of sexual seduction, we will see it defeated.

As soon as they started praising, the Lord attacked their adversaries.

Just as David's singing over King Saul ushered in a "new life" and Saul became "refreshed and well" as the "evil spirit would leave him" (1 Sam. 16:23 BBE/NKJV), or when the Israelites went out to attack their enemies, setting musicians out in front of the army, *"as soon as they started shouting and praising, the Lord suddenly attacked"* their enemies (2 Chron. 20:22 MSG/NKJV), so too will our specific roar of praise conquer the spirit of seduction.

A Spirit of Seduction is Loose in America

Sorcery and seduction often go hand in hand. What is distinctive about seduction is that it attempts to control and manipulate people by using enticing bait. Peter warns us of the danger of people operating in a seducing spirit:

> *"For they mouth empty, boastful words, and by appealing to the fleshly desires, with lustful desires* ***as their bait****, they lure back into sin, they get them* ***into their power,*** *those who have just escaped such wicked living, those who are most susceptible to their brand of* ***seduction.****"* (2 Pet. 2:18 NIV/NLT/BBE/MSG; emphasis mine).

The Greek word Peter uses here for seduction is *deleazo*, and it means "to catch by bait, to allure, entice, and deceive."[3] The evil one seduces us by using sex, power, and/or money as his bait. Just like everything else associated with satan, the promises are empty lies. His purpose is always to enslave and control. Don't be like a mindless fish and only see the nice, big, juicy bait but fail to notice the wicked hook inside. The enemy wants to set that deadly barb deep within the souls of those he can entice into his deadly net of seduction.

What makes matters worse is that the enemy's control over those poor netted souls increases. Many of those who start out enslaved to pornography find that after a time merely viewing sexual acts is not enough to satisfy their appetites. They move from seeing to doing,[4] and may shift into the more violent sexual expressions of rape, sexual abuse, and child molestation.[5] Sexual addiction has risen to epidemic proportions. It is estimated that between three and five percent of people in America—more than a million people—have some type of sexual addiction.[6] This demonic epidemic must be stopped. A flood of God's true love is the cure for this plague.

Paul warns us of this problem of things going from bad to worse: *"But evil men and* ***seducers*** *will go from bad to worse, using deceit and themselves overcome by deceit"* (2 Tim. 3:13 KJV/NRSV/BBE; emphasis mine). *"They're as deceived as the people they lead astray"* (MSG). The Greek word used here for seducers is *goes* and means a "wailer" or a "howler."[7] It refers to a wizard, sorcerer, or enchanter because they would wail or howl their incantations.[8] Paul tells us that none have been inoculated from the allure of sin,[9] but he offers believers hope in the love and mercy of Jesus. *"There was a time when some of you were just like that, but now your sins have been washed away, and you have been set apart for God. You have been made right with God because of what the Lord Jesus Christ and the Spirit of our God have done for you"* (1 Cor. 6:11 NLT).

The Heart of Hosea, the Roaring Lion

The roar of God's Lion is His weapon of choice[10] to break the hold of this spirit of seduction over His children. Just as it is in the natural, when the enemy comes in with a tank, we pick up that weapon specifically designed to destroy tanks. When seduction attacks, we respond with the roar of God. In the last chapter we studied the heart of Joseph as an example of God's Wild Ox. In the life and heart of the prophet Hosea we see an example of the Lord's Roaring Lion.

Hosea is a love story. The entire account of Hosea's life reflects the depth of God's love for us. During the days of Hosea, the children of Israel had turned their backs on the Lord and were running after false gods to be their "lovers" (Hos. 2:1-7). Hosea loves a woman named Gomer and woos her and takes her for his wife. The problem is that Gomer is an adulteress (Hos. 1:2), and after they are married, she is still running after other lovers. As a matter of fact, at least one (and quite probably two) of their three children are not fathered by Hosea (Hos. 1:9). Even worse, Gomer leaves Hosea with their three children and runs after other men. It doesn't matter: Hosea doesn't give up on her. He goes after her and wins her back.

The heart of Hosea is a beautiful revelation of God's heart of love for us. Like Gomer, Israel runs after other false gods. Like Hosea, the Lord goes after Israel, His wife, and woos her back to Himself (Hos. 2:14-23). He doesn't stop until He wins her heart and brings her back to His home. We, as Gomer, run after and give our affections to other "gods." These false gods can be anything or anyone we have placed in our hearts instead of the Lord. We are seduced away from our True Love and become subject to seduction. It doesn't matter. No matter what we are doing, how far we have run, the love of the Lord causes Him to come after us. He won't quit; His heart won't let Him. As our Great Lover, He will not stop until He has wooed us back and made us His bride.

As our great Lover, the Lord does not stop until He woos our heart back to Himself.

No matter what we've done, we can start all over again, fresh and innocent as a little child. Concerning Israel, the Lord asks Hosea, *"How long until **they attain innocence?**"* (Hos. 8:5b NKJV; emphasis mine). No matter what we have done, in the blood of Jesus, we can be made innocent again. God is asking His people to turn away from their false gods and come home. All they have to do is return to the Father and be washed and "make themselves clean" (BBE). The Hebrew word for attain is *yakol*[11] and means "to be made able, to overcome, to have power." When we return to the Lord, He gives us the ability to recapture our innocence. The word for innocence is *niqqayown*[12] and means to be pure, to be free from guilt, to be free from punishment. It literally means "the life that comes after that life has been nailed." [13] In other words, as we pick up our cross and are crucified in Christ, new life comes forth (Gal. 2:20, 5:24 & Rom. 6:6). We are forgiven and made pure and righteous in the blood of the Lamb. No longer guilty, we are free from fear because we have been made free of any punishment. Jesus took all our sins and nailed them to the cross.

In Jesus we can return to innocence, all debts cancelled, all sins forgiven.

ENSLAVED BY A SPIRIT OF WHOREDOM

One of the most disconcerting verses in the Bible is found in Hosea. It is when the Lord addresses this problem of sexual and spiritual seduction in His people. Most people don't know what kind of danger they are in when they submit to a seducing spirit. The Lord says,

> *"I have known Ephraim, and Israel is not hidden from Me. For now, oh, Ephraim, you have whored, Israel is defiled.* ***Their deeds do not allow them to turn back to their God****. It is their deeds that block their pathway back to God, for a harlot-spirit possesses them, and they do not know the Lord.* ***The spirit of fertility rites and temple prostitution in front of Baal has so implanted itself in their hearts that they can't let go. Idolatry has such***

> ***a hold on them that they no longer acknowledge Me as their God.*** *For the spirit of whoring is among them, and they've (forgotten) Jehovah!"* (Hos. 5:3-4 ISR/Phi/Mof/AEB/CW; emphasis mine).

Ephraim is in grave danger. The spirit of whoredom (i.e., adultery, seduction) has them so bound that they are actually unable to return to the Lord. We see this same bondage everywhere in our nation today. Millions of men and women are enslaved to sexual immorality. It's not just in the world. It has pervaded the church and even the homes of God's children. Men and women are bound by pornography and sexual sins, and they can't seem to break free—even though they desperately want to. There are 12-Step programs and psychological treatments of varying kinds for these souls trapped in satan's snare of seduction. As helpful as these programs are, most times they are not enough to pry apart the steel jaws of this trap. To be completely free requires the power of our God provided through His weaponry wielded by His children. Our prophetic songs of worship releasing the roar of God's Lion will blast down the spiritual barricades of seduction and allow them to run freely into the arms of the One who lovingly calls them to liberty.

The snare of seduction is so strong, that it can only be broken by the grace and power of our God.

We must cry out and entreat the mercy of our God to change the hearts of those who have forgotten Him, who have, through their own deeds, built the walls that now separate them from their loving Father. As the Apostle Paul tells us, it is the spirit of grace at work in our hearts that changes us so we want to do His will. His spirit of grace makes us willing and able (Phil. 2:13). It's all by the grace and mercy of our God. He gives us the *desire* to obey Him, to want to do His will, and then He gives us the *power* to obey, so we are able to do His will. Talk about having nothing to boast about. None of this is in our power. It all flows from the grace of God through Jesus Christ.

After we have read one of the most perplexing and downright frightening verses in the Bible, now we can look at one of the most marvelous and encouraging words in the Bible. Listen to the cry of the Father's heart over His children, who at this time were slaves to a seductive spirit of whoredom.

> *"The Lord says, 'When Israel was a child, I loved him and called him out of Egypt as My son. I was the One Who taught Israel to walk. I took My people up in My arms, I drew them to Me with affection and love.* ***I picked them up and held them to My cheek:*** *I bent down to them and fed them"* (Hos. 11:1-4 GNT; emphasis mine).

What a beautiful expression and revelation of God's love! The Lord continues to love us and reach out to us. We are His children and He will always be our Father. He has always cared for us, and He will continue to care. This same cry of God's heart is going out over America and the world today:

> *"**How can I give you up**, Ephraim (America)? How can I hand you over, Israel (My church)? **How can I abandon you and turn you over to your enemies?** Could I ever destroy you as I did Admah? Or treat you as I did Zeboim? **No! My heart will not let Me do it! My love for you is too strong. I will not execute My fierce anger**; I will not again destroy Ephraim; for I am God and not man, the*

> *Holy One in your midst, and I will not come in wrath, and I will not come with terror" (Hos.* 11:8-9 ISR/GNT/ NKJV/ NRSV/CW; parentheticals and emphasis mine).

Please understand. I am not saying that America is Ephraim, and I am not saying that the church is Israel. I am simply adding emphasis to this verse to show how it relates to us today, and our problem with seduction. The love of God is just as strong for all nations as it is for Ephraim and Israel.

The love of the Lord for us is too strong. He won't give up on us, no matter what we have done. His heart won't let Him do anything but come down and set us free. Read this word again and again—then sing it in praise back to our Father to destroy the demonic stronghold of seduction.

God says He will not destroy Israel. He will not come to them in wrath and terror. He does come in wrath and terror, but God's wrath and terror are not directed against His children. The wrath and terror of the Lord are released against His adversary.

> *"My people will follow Me,* ***when I roar like a lion at their enemies,*** *when He roars, and His cry will be loud.* ***Oh, how I will roar!*** *Then His children will come trembling to Him from the west, and I will settle them in their own homes. This is the very word of the Lord"* (Hos. 11:10 NEB/NIRV/GNT/ BBE/TLB; emphasis mine).

This is the "very word of the Lord." This word that says that when the roar of God's Lion (i.e., His children transformed through praise and faith) resounds, then His power is released, the strongholds are broken, and the captives are set free from their adversary. When the Lion roars, God's children return to Him "trembling" because they realize that but for the grace of their God, they would have been enslaved forever. Sing these words for the deliverance of our nation, the church, and our homes. Let the roar of the Lion of Judah (praise) sound forth and shatter that seducing spirit holding them back from returning to their Father.

The Hebrew word for roar is *sha'ag*.[14] It literally means "to lift up the power that destroys."[15] The Lord roars declaring His power to destroy anything that is coming against His children. God's voice shatters anything holding us captive. Let the majestic voice of the Lord roar (Psalm 29).

When God roars, the chains of seduction are shattered. The demons flee and we are free to come home to Papa!

Now obviously, we aren't going to go around roaring like a lion. The roar of the lion is not the sound made by the *panthera leo*. The roar of the Lion is what happens when we sing praises to our Father. As we praise, prophesy, and preach, we trust Him to release His roar in the Spirit. It's the same principle discussed earlier challenging worship leaders to bring worshipers to a point of praise where we can hear the voice of Jesus joining us in praising the Father (Heb. 2:11-12). Just as David, singing before King Saul to drive away the tormenting spirits, or King Jehoshaphat and his troop of worshipers going out into battle before the army, we must step out in faith and release the roar of the Lord in the Spirit against this seducing spirit. As the roar of the Lion from Zion reverberates, God's people are set free. Not only are they set free, God then takes them back to "their own homes," back to His Promised Land.

This "very word of the Lord" is for us, now, **today**, before it is too late. We must confess and stand on this promise for our nation. If the Lord does not act, if He does not roar, we are doomed. Sing God's word and release God's Lion.

Lord, roar from the heavens! Release Your roar in our praise and worship. Let us see the chains of seduction broken, and the demons flee in terror from Your awesome power.

We cry out,
"Roar, Lion from Zion, roar!"

ENDNOTES:

1. Retrieved at http://www.thedailybeast.com/newsweek/2011/11/27/the-sex-addiction-epidemic.html. "Sex addiction" remains a controversial designation—often dismissed as a myth or providing talk-show punch lines thanks to high-profile lotharios such as Dominique Strauss-Kahn and Tiger Woods. But compulsive sexual behavior, also called hypersexual disorder, can systematically destroy a person's life much as addictions to alcohol or drugs can. And it's affecting an increasing number of Americans, say psychiatrists and addiction experts. "It's a national epidemic," says Steven Luff, coauthor of *Pure Eyes: A Man's Guide to Sexual Integrity* and leader of the X3LA sexual-addiction recovery groups in Hollywood.

   Reliable figures for the number of diagnosed sex addicts are difficult to come by, but the Society for the Advancement of Sexual Health, an education and sex-addiction treatment organization, estimates that between 3 and 5 percent of the U.S. population—or more than 9 million people—could meet the criteria for addiction. Some 1,500 sex therapists treating compulsive behavior are practicing today, up from fewer than 100 a decade ago, say several researchers and clinicians, while dozens of rehabilitation centers now advertise treatment programs, up from just five or six in the same period. The demographics are changing, too. "Where it used to be 40- to 50-year-old men seeking treatment, now there are more females, adolescents, and senior citizens," says Tami VerHelst, vice president of the International Institute for Trauma and Addiction Professionals. Now, Grandfathers are getting caught with porn on their computers by grandkids, and grandkids sexting at 12.

In fact, some of the growth has been fueled by the digital revolution, which has revved up America's carnal metabolism. Where previous generations had to risk public embarrassment at dirty bookstores and X-rated movie theaters, the Web has made pornography accessible, free, and anonymous. An estimated 40 million people a day in the U.S. log on to some 4.2 million pornographic websites, according to the Internet Filter Software Review. And though watching porn isn't the same as seeking out real live sex, experts say the former can be a kind of gateway drug to the latter.

"Not everyone who looks at a nude image is going to become a sex addict. But the constant exposure is going to trigger people who are susceptible," says Dr. David Sack, chief executive of Los Angeles's Promises Treatment Centers.

2. Retrieved at: http://psychcentral.com/lib/2006/what-is-sexual-addiction/. "Sexual addiction is best described as a progressive intimacy disorder characterized by compulsive sexual thoughts and acts. Like all addictions, its negative impact on the addict and on family members increases as the disorder progresses. Over time, the addict usually has to intensify the addictive behavior to achieve the same results.

   For some sex addicts, behavior does not progress beyond compulsive masturbation or the extensive use of pornography or phone or computer sex services. For others, addiction can involve illegal activities such as exhibitionism, voyeurism, obscene phone calls, child molestation or rape. Sex addicts do not necessarily become sex offenders. Moreover, not all sex offenders are sex addicts. Roughly 55 percent of convicted sex offenders can be considered sex addicts. About 71 percent of child molesters are sex addicts. For many, their problems are so severe that imprisonment is the only way to ensure society's safety against them.

   Society has accepted that sex offenders act not for sexual gratification, but rather out of a disturbed need for power, dominance, control or revenge, or a perverted expression of anger. More recently, however, an awareness of brain changes and brain reward associated with sexual behavior has led us to understand that there are also powerful sexual drives that motivate sex offenses.

   The National Council on Sexual Addiction and Compulsivity has defined sexual addiction as "engaging in persistent and escalating patterns of sexual behavior acted out despite increasing negative consequences to self and others." In other words, a sex addict will continue to engage in certain sexual behaviors despite facing potential health risks, financial problems, shattered relationships or even arrest.

The Diagnostic and Statistical Manual of Psychiatric Disorders, Volume Four describes sex addiction, under the category "Sexual Disorders Not Otherwise Specified," as "distress about a pattern of repeated sexual relationships involving a succession of lovers who are experienced by the individual only as things to be used." According to the manual, sex addiction also involves "compulsive searching for multiple partners, compulsive fixation on an unattainable partner, compulsive masturbation, compulsive love relationships and compulsive sexuality in a relationship."

Increasing sexual provocation in our society has spawned an increase in the number of individuals engaging in a variety of unusual or illicit sexual practices, such as phone sex, the use of escort services and computer pornography. More of these individuals and their partners are seeking help. The same compulsive behavior that characterizes other addictions also is typical of sex addiction. But these other addictions, including drug, alcohol and gambling dependency, involve substances or activities with no necessary relationship to our survival. For example, we can live normal and happy lives without ever gambling, taking illicit drugs or drinking alcohol. Even the most genetically vulnerable person will function well without ever being exposed to, or provoked by, these addictive activities.

3. Retrieved at: http://www.blueletterbible.org/lang/lexicon.cfm?Strongs=G1185&t=KJV.
4. Retrieved at http://psychcentral.com/lib/2006/what-is-sexual-addiction.
5. Ibid.
6. Retrieved at http://www.thedailybeast.com/newsweek/2011/11/27/the-sex-addiction-epidemic.html.
7. Retrieved at http://classic.net.bible.org/strong.php?id=1114e.
8. Retrieved at http://www.blueletterbible.org/lang/lexicon/lexicon.cfm?Strongs=G1114&t=KJV.
9. Paul gives us a list of individuals who, if they don't repent, will not see God's kingdom. He tells us that *"fornicators, idolaters, adulterers, male prostitutes, sodomites, thieves, greedy, drunkards, robbers – none of these will inherit the kingdom of God"* (1 Cor. 6:9-10 NRSV). Thank Jesus for the next verse: *"And such **were** some of you!"* (1 Cor. 6:11 NKJV). No matter what we have done, we can be "washed clean," we can be "made holy to God," and we can be *"made right with God in the name of the Lord Jesus Christ and in the Spirit of our God"* (1 Cor. 6:11 CEB). One translation says we've been *"given a fresh start in Jesus"* (MSG). Now is the time for that fresh start in Jesus. Once we were some of them, right there in the midst of that mess, but now by the blood of Jesus we can become like an innocent child again.
10. For whatever reason, the Lord has chosen His roar to be His weapon to release His power in the Spirit that defeats seduction. Just as the Lord

chose the sound of His shofar (the war horn) and the shout of His war cry to tear down the walls of Jericho (Josh. 6:1-20), He has chosen His Lion's roar to confront, defeat, and drive out that spirit of seduction. The roar of His Lion is one of His war cries, so as we shout this specific war cry, the specific walls of seduction must fall. We may never understand all of this, but the lack of our understanding will not stop us from moving out in faith and using this weapon. It's just like a computer, I may never fully understand how it works, but that won't stop me from using one.

11. Retrieved at: http://www.blueletterbible.org/lang/lexicon.cfm?Strongs=H3201&t=KJV.
12. Retrieved at: http://www.blueletterbible.org/lang/lexicon.cfm?Strongs=H5356&t=KJV.
13. Seekins, pp. 10-11.
14. Retrieved at http://www.blueletterbible.org/lang/lexicon/lexicon.cfm?Strongs=H7580&t=KJV.
15. Seekins, pp. 10-11.

CHAPTER THIRTEEN

THE ROAR OF GOD

THE SPIRIT OF PROPHECY AND THE WAR SONGS

"Everyone is terrified when a lion roars–and ordinary people become prophets when the Lord God speaks."
—Amos 3:8 CEV

THE ROAR OF GOD ACTIVATES THE SPIRIT OF PROPHECY

God's roar is His **prophetic word**: *"A Lion has roared; who will not fear? The Lord has spoken; who can but prophesy"* (Amos 3:8 CEB)? The roar of God from heaven releases the spirit of prophecy on earth. As God roars we can't help but prophecy. Since the war songs are songs of prophecy, as we **sing,** we can release the roar of God through our praise.

Since the Hebrew word for roar is *"sha'ag,"* my wife and I will sometimes just shout out the word "Sha'ag!" against whatever spirit is attacking us, our children, or our friends.

We'll wave our war flags, crack our war whips, blow the shofar, shake our tambourines, beat our war drums, shout our war cries, and let the battle begin. We'll call out "Sha'ag! Lord, release Your Lion's roar!" as we shout and drive the demonic attack away from our home and our family. Now, I don't mean we go around all day roaring like a lion and shouting Hebrew words for no reason. What I am saying is that we believe the Lord to move by His spirit as we sing His war songs of victory. It might seem odd or uncomfortable and certainly not logical, but it's the same principle as when the Lord instructed King Jehoshaphat to lead Israel into battle against her enemies with the praise team leading the way: *"The king ordered some musicians … to march ahead of the army, singing: Praise the Lord! His love is eternal"* (2 Chron. 20:21 GNB)! The praises of God went first, then the warriors came on the scene and the battle was won.

I can only imagine what King Jehoshaphat's musicians were thinking: "We're going to *sing*? What do I do with my sword? Can I hold up my shield to at least protect me from any fiery darts of the enemy?" But they stepped out in faith, out of their comfort zone, against all these logical questions and began to praise Him because *"every word of God is pure; He is a shield to those who put their trust in Him"* (Prov.30:5 NKJV). And *"When they began singing and praising,* ***the Lord suddenly attacked and set ambushes*** *against the sons of Ammon, Moab, and Mount Seir, who had come up against Judah; and caused them to start fighting among themselves. The men of Ammon and Moab started fighting the men from Edom and slaughtered them. Then*

As soon as they began singing and praising, the Lord suddenly attacked their enemies.

they turned on each other with a savage fury" (2 Chron. 20:22-23 NASB/NLT/CW; emphasis mine).

When Israel looked at their enemies, *"They were all lying on the ground dead. Not one had escaped"* (2 Chron. 20:24 GNB). When we step out of our comfort zone in faith, our praise and worship will release the sudden attack and ambush of the Lord against our adversaries. Notice in the verse above that the ambush of the Lord caused His adversaries to fight among themselves. It doesn't say that Israel ambushed them and defeated them. It says that when the praises of the Lord went forth, the Lord ambushed those who were out to destroy His children, causing them to utterly abolish each other. All that was left for Jehoshaphat's army to do was move in and collect the spoils of the battle. 2 Chronicles 20:25 says the riches and jewels were *"more than they could carry away: and they were three days in gathering of the spoil, it was so much."* That's a sample of the power of the roar of God's Lion.

We must sing for the presence and the power of our God to come and break this hold of seduction on our land. Just as Joshua and the children of Israel shouted and the walls of Jericho fell, we must shout and sing these words and see those spiritual walls fall down. Through Micah, the Lord promises to *"tear down your walls and demolish all your strongholds"* of seduction (Mic. 5:11 NLT/NKJV). The Lord will come down, and He *"will smash your carved and cast gods and chop down your phallic posts. No more taking control of the world, worshipping what you do or make"* (Mic. 5:13 MSG). The Lord says He will *"pull up your scared poles from among you and destroy your enemies. I will pull out your poles dedicated to the goddess Asherah and destroy the cities where your idol temples stand. I'll root out your sacred sex-and-power centers and destroy the God-defiant"* (Mic. 5:14 CJB/CW/NLT/MSG).[1]

GOD'S TAUNT AGAINST THE ONCE-MIGHTY LION

Nahum tells us that the Lord has His Lion roar a "Taunt against the Once-Mighty Lion" (Subtitle in NET Bible). The Lion from Zion roars His taunt against the spirits of sorcery and seduction operating in Nineveh:

"Where now is that great Nineveh, lion of the nations, full of fight and boldness, the cave where the lion cubs lurked, even the old lion walked, and the lion's whelp, and no one made them afraid? O Nineveh, once mighty lion! You crushed your enemies to feed your children and your wives. You filled your city and homes with captured goods and slaves. ***Behold I am against you! I am your Enemy! says the Lord of Hosts. Never again will you bring back slaves*** *from conquered nations; you will no longer prey upon the land; I will take away everything that you took from others. 'Lion Country' will be strewn with carcasses. The voice of your she-lions will be stopped forever; never again will you rule the earth"* (Nah. 2:11-13 NET/GNT/KJV/TLB/BBE/MSG; emphasis mine).

God declares that Nineveh, the very embodiment of sorcery and seduction, will never again enslave His people. Once called the "lion of the nations" she is now called the "once-mighty lion." Nineveh is mighty no more. The so-called "lion country" will be covered with dead bodies. Her rebellion has made her an enemy of the Lord. The voices of her she-lions will be stopped forever. The Lord roars *"I am against you! I am your Enemy!"* Wow! What a roar! In the NET Bible, the subtitle for this section is the "Battle Cry of the Divine Warrior." The Lord knows how to knock out this lion.

God's Taunt is His War Song

Combining God's taunts against this demon in Nahum 2:11-13 and Micah 5:11-14 can be made into a war song. We can sing these word weapons against the spirit of sexual and spiritual seduction:

1. God is your enemy, your Oppressor. He is against you. With His mighty roar He breaks your chains of bondage. He tears down the walls of your stronghold. He smashes every idol and vile image.
2. He will cut up your phallic poles and sex worship.
3. Never again will you enslave the nations with your seduction. Never again will you control the world.
4. God takes back everything you have plundered from His people.
5. God silences your sensual, alluring voice forever!

With His battle cry and war songs, we break the power of this seducing spirit. Sing, as did the Psalmist, *"God, break their teeth in their mouths! Yahweh, wrench out the fangs of these savage lions"* (Ps. 58:6 JB)!

Behold, He Who Scatters is Coming

In Micah's prophecy we learned about the Breaker, the one who is coming who will shatter all the power of the evil one. Now in Nahum we read about "He who scatters." It is part of God's taunt song against those spirits in Nineveh. The Amplified Bible introduces "He who scatters" with the preface *"Then the prophet Nahum* ***sarcastically*** *addresses his* *message to Nineveh"* (Nah 1:15b Amp). Nahum mockingly sings to Nineveh that *"He who scatters has come up before your face. Man the fort! Watch the road"* (Nah. 1:15b-2:1a Amp/NKJV)! Nahum sings to those spirits in Nineveh that no matter what you do, you won't be able to stop the One whom God is calling to come and scatter you. We must sing these same words against our demonic oppressors: "Watch out prince of darkness! 'He who scatters' is coming!"

Watch out prince of darkness, He who scatters is coming.

The Hebrew word used here for scatter is *puwts* or *pus* and means "to break or dash to pieces, to disperse or scatter." [2] It's the same word used when the Ark, the war chariot of God, was brought up before Israel. In preparation for war, the Israelites would bring up the Ark of the Covenant and sing this victory song, praising God as their Divine Warrior.[3] They would sing, *"Rise up, oh, Lord! And let Your enemies be scattered and those who hate You run for their lives before You"* (Num. 10:35 NASB/JB; emphasis mine)!

Puwts is the same word David used as he rejoiced in Psalm 68. *"God is [already] beginning to arise, and His enemies to scatter; let them also who hate Him flee before Him"* (Ps. 68:1 Amp)! The Good News Bible entitles this psalm "A National Song of Triumph." Here are just a few of the beautiful promises of protection and victory we find in this song of triumph:

- David encourages us to *"let the righteous be glad–let them shout for joy at the presence of God"* (Ps. 68:3 KJV/Sept) because God is *a "Father of the fatherless and Protector of widows"* (Ps. 68:5a RSV);

- *"God gives the lonely a permanent home"* (Ps. 68:6a JB);
- *"God will shatter the heads of His enemies"* (Ps. 68:21a RSV);
- for God *"has ascended on high, You have emerged victorious, You have taken captivity captive, and received men as gifts, even with the rebellious there is a dwelling for Jehovah God!"* (Ps. 68:18 KJV/NAB/RSV).

It's no wonder David tells us to rejoice in the Lord.

Build a Road for the Lord and Release His Army of Women Warriors

In Psalm 68, David tells us it's time to build a road. He exhorts us to, *"Sing unto Yahweh, **play music to His name, build a road** for the Rider of the Clouds, rejoice in Yahweh, exult at His coming"* (Psa. 68:4 JB; emphasis mine). Our praise and worship builds a road for the Rider of the Clouds to come down and lead His army. And this is a very special army.

We've already determined that men are not the only ones who fall prey to the spirit of seduction; women are also susceptible. But glory to God, women are also warriors who can be victorious in this battle. In Psalm 68, David tells us that great are the women warriors of God's army who get to proclaim this good news: *"The Lord gave the word: **the women that published the glad tidings, are a vast army"*** (Ps. 68:11 KJV/TLB/NAB/ASV; emphasis mine)! The Lord has His army of men ***and*** **women**, and both have the Breaker anointing of the hooves of the Wild Ox to ***shatter*** sorcery, and the roar of God's Lion to ***scatter*** seduction.

In Ephesians 4:8, the Apostle Paul quotes David from Psalm 68, the "National Song of Triumph," and relates the scripture directly to Jesus' ascension, arising victoriously and taking "captivity captive," which brings us to the beautiful, loving conclusion of the matter.

What the War Songs Are All About

As we sing, our enemies *"will come from their fortresses, trembling and afraid.* ***They will turn in fear to the Lord our God"*** (Mic. 7:17 GNB; emphasis mine). That is what the war songs of God are all about. Those who were once God's enemies will come out of their strongholds of sorcery and seduction and return to Him. With David we can rejoice and say, *"The nations around us have lost heart. They come out of their fortresses to ask for peace"* (Ps. 18:45 CW). They will come in fear, but the Lord will soon turn their fear into love and rejoicing, because they will see the wonderful love of their Father.

> *"There is no other God like You, oh, Lord; You forgive the sins of Your people. You do not stay angry forever, but You take pleasure in showing us Your constant love. You will be merciful to us once again. You will trample our sins underfoot and send them to the bottom of the sea!"* (Mic. 7:18-19 GNB).

The beautiful love of God! He tramples our sins *not us* under His foot. All our sins of sorcery and seduction are thrown into the sea. The Lord loves all of us, including those using sorcery and seduction. Those who abandon their demonic activities and return to their Father are given a simple instruction from Micah on how now to live: ***"And what does the Lord require of you? But to do justly, to love mercy, and to walk in humble fellowship with your God"*** (Mic. 6:8 NKJV/GNB, emphasis mine).

Jesus and Nineveh

God has a calling and a future for the people of Nineveh. If there is a calling and a future full of hope for her, there is a calling and future for all who have been enslaved to sorcery and seduction. Listen to this promise, the vision that the Lord has for Assyria, which includes Nineveh, because she is the capital. The prophet Isaiah tells us that a day is coming when:

> *"On that day there will be a highway out of Egypt to Assyria, and Assyria will come into Egypt, and Egypt will come into Assyria. No longer rivals. The Egyptians and Assyrians will worship God together. And Israel will be their ally; at that time Israel, Assyria, and Egypt will join together, which will be a blessing in the heart of the earth. The Lord of hosts, Who rules over all, will bless those three nations. He will say, ' Blessed be Egypt My people!... Blessed be Assyria, the work of My hands!... Blessed be Israel, My inheritance!'"* (Isa. 19:23-25 BBE/NCV/NLT/MSG/YLT/NIRV).

Twice in the Gospels Jesus addresses Nineveh. He had this to say about her: *"The people of Nineveh will rise up at the judgment with this generation and condemn it, because they were turned from their sins at the preaching of Jonah and now a greater than Jonah is here"* (Matt. 12:41 NRSV/BBE; see also Luke 11:32). Notice of all the things about Nineveh that Jesus could talk about, He chose to talk about the "repenting Nineveh" not the "rebelling Nineveh." You see, Jesus knew the promise in Isaiah. He knew that just as Nineveh repented at the preaching of Jonah, that now a "greater than Jonah" has come and they will repent again.

This beautiful promise from the Lord in Isaiah Chapter Nineteen is that someday in the future, Nineveh will repent as the messengers stand on the mountain tops and proclaim the Good News. Someday in the future the people of Assyria, which include the people of Nineveh its capital, will repent and be the work of God's hands. Someday Egypt and Israel will join Assyria and be a blessing to the whole world.

This is a wonderful word from the Lord and we will cover it in more detail later in the chapter on Israel, God's Soaring Eagles. But I want to take this beautiful promise and apply it to our adversaries of sorcery and seduction. Both Assyria and Egypt in the Word of God are representations of our enemies of sorcery and seduction. The first mention of sorcery is in reference to the magicians and sorcerers of Egypt who could turn their staffs into serpents (Ex. 7:11). As for Assyria she represents people enslaved to seduction.

We've just finished studying about the seductress operating in Nineveh her capital of Assyria. So by faith I take this promise in Isaiah 29:23-25 and apply it to those enslaved to sorcery and seduction. That one day those walking in seduction (Egypt) will return to the Lord and be called *"God's people."* And those operating in sorcery (Assyria) will be called by the Lord *"the work of My hands."* Then God's people (Israel) will be called by God, *"My inheritance!"* Together these born again believers will be God's blessing to the whole earth.

They are *"no longer rivals,"* they become allies in the world. I would venture there are not many of God's people who are singing this song from God's word to bless God's people, and the sorcerers and the sexual seducers of this world. We'll sing this promise until we are all united in Him. Yet this is what the heart of God is after. Let us sing God's prophetic songs over them and see it come to pass. As God's people, we must receive the Lord's vision for us, the sorcerers and seducers. What a day that will be! That day is coming, and we can have a part in bringing it to earth, if we so desire.

Oh, Lord, thank You for giving us the desire to do Your will. Thank You for giving us the power to once again attain innocence and start fresh. Thank You for pursuing us with your unfailing love. Father, guard us from the schemes of the wicked one. Give us Your clear eyes of discernment to see any demonic traps set before us. Roar, oh Mighty Lion, roar! Release Your roar against the principalities and powers in high places, terrify them. Together all nations will worship the Lord our God! Oh, Lion of Zion, release the sha'ag, the roar of Your Spirit of prophecy over our land! Roar!

Rise up women of God!
Preach the Good News of Jesus.
Become warriors in God's vast army!

ENDNOTES:

1. The major demon that Nineveh worshipped was the goddess Asherah. The false goddess was the goddess of fertility. The way she was worshipped was the men would go in and have sex with her temple prostitutes. Talk about a sex-and-power center! This 'sex worship' was supposed to ensure them of prosperity in their homes and on their crops and livestock. There were figures of lions on her gates and statutes of lions around her temple. The lion was her symbol. She was a cruel and heartless goddess and this cruel nature came out through the people she enslaved. The goddess represented the worst in seduction and sexual perversion. The Asherah poles were phallic symbols of a penis stuck up into the sky. Like mailboxes, every home had one stuck up somewhere in their yard. These people desperately needed the Lord's forgiveness, deliverance and salvation!
2. Retrieved at: http://www.blueletterbible.org/lang/lexicon.cfm?Strongs=H6327&t=KJV.
3. The Jewish people saw the Ark of the Covenant as God's war chariot. He would ride in it before the children of Israel before they went into battle.

ZECHARIAH

GOD'S WAR SONG TO DEFEAT THE ANTICHRIST

CHAPTER FOURTEEN

14

GOD'S WAR HORSE

WARFARE—WORSHIP AND THE MANIFESTATION OF GOD'S WAR HORSE

"The people of Judah are Mine, and I, the Lord Almighty will care for My flock, and make them strong and glorious. I will transform My flock into My majestic War Horse; that I will ride into battle!"

—Zech. 10:3b GNT/NCV/NLT/NASB/CJB/REB/Knox

As we sing the war songs of God, He changes us. Whether it's into the anointing of His Mighty Stag against demonic violence, His Wild Ox against sorcery, or His Roaring Lion against spiritual and sexual seduction, we are all changed. As we come into His presence with praise and worship we are transformed. No matter what is going on around us, God's word contains His transforming power, and He transforms us into His specific weapon to handle the specific warfare we are facing. In the battle to destroy the one-world government, the anti-Christ system called Babylon, our Commander-in-Chief rides into the fight on His majestic War Horse. We, His people, are transformed into a special type of warrior as we enter into His warfare worship to destroy the strongholds in our land.

SING THE WAR SONG OF GOD'S WAR HORSE

(Zech. 9:1-11:3)

The Lord gives the prophet Zechariah two war songs to deliver to the people of Israel. In this chapter we'll study the first war song about God's majestic War Horse (Zech. 9:1-11:3). And in the next chapter we'll look at the second war song which releases the revelation to Israel, God's Soaring Eagle, that Jesus is their Messiah (Zech. 12:1-14:21).

This first prophecy is another burden, another war song from the Lord (Zech. 9:1). Here the Lord declares His word against three nations who have been oppressing Israel. Those countries are 1) Syria, with its cities of Hadrach and Damascus (9:1-2a); 2) Phoenicia, with its cities of Tyre and Sidon (9:2b-4); and 3) Philistia, with its cities of Ashkelon, Gaza, Ekron, and Ashdod (Zech. 9:5-7). At one time all of these cities had been under the rule of Kings David and Solomon, but by the time of Zechariah, they had broken away from Israel's authority. Now the Lord wants them back.

These three nations that were a source of conflict for Israel during Zechariah's day, are still an area of conflict today. Now is the time to sing the war songs of God over these Middle East nations. Now is the time for their repentance, deliverance, and return to the Lord.

SING THE WAR SONG OF GOD'S MERCY AND TRANSFORMING POWER

(Zech.9:1-8)

We'll just look at the Lord's burden for the people of Philistia. It is **not to judge them but to heal them.** This beautiful war song is an expression of God's wonderful heart of forgiveness and restoration. Read these words slowly and hear the heart of our Father.

> *"I will cut off the pride of the Philistines. I will take away their abominable religious practices; drinking blood, eating blood-filled sacrifices. They will no longer eat meat with blood in it. Then those who survive will* ***become a community of believers*** *in our God, They* ***will worship our God****. They* ***will be adopted*** *and become chieftains,* ***leaders as a family in Judah****. And the Philistines of Ekron will join My people, just like the Jebusites once did.* ***So the Philistines will become a part of Israel!"*** (Zech. 9:6b-7 NASB/NET/NCV/NLT/HNV/NIRV; emphasis mine)/

Here we see the magnificent results of the war songs of our God on Philistia. The Lord promises that, *"He will* ***transform those who turn to Him*** *and take away their diet of meat and blood and other abominable things they eat"* (Zech. 9:7a CW; emphasis mine). The Philistines, a nation given over to demonic worship and rituals of literally drinking the blood of their sacrifices, the age old enemies of Israel, will one day become a part of God's family of praise (Judah). They will be "adopted" by God and "become a community of believers." Not just members, they'll be leaders, "governor(s)" (KJV) and "dukes" (WYC) in the family of God. The Philistines, *"will belong to Him and share in the leadership of Judah. They will inter-marry with the Jews and become as much a part of His people as the Jebusites did"* (Zech. 9:7b TLB/CW). Sing these words declaring the love and mercy of God over modern-day Palestine and see this wonderful transformation of the Philistines by God's mercy be released over them.

Sing God's war songs and transform demon worshippers into leaders of God worshippers!

GOD, THE GREAT TRANSFORMER

This revelation of God's love and forgiveness towards the Philistines is a hint to us of God's glorious transforming power that is coming to His children. If God desires to transform our enemies, such as the ungodly Philistines, into leaders in His family of praise, how much more will He desire to change us, His children? God the Great Transformer quickly forgives and forgets our sins. He quickly changes, restores, and fortifies us. For the final battle for creation, God will transform His people into His Holy Ghost warriors. This transformation takes place through our engaging in warfare worship.

Specific instructions on engaging in true warfare worship are found in the ninth chapter of Zechariah. In this crucial chapter, God reveals to us His ten components of warfare worship that we must master in order to evoke the manifestation of His warriors and vanquish satan once and for all. These elements are covered in detail in the other books in the *"God's Heart of War Series."* They are the war song, the war dance, the war cry, the Warrior King, the war bow and arrows, the war sword, the war horn, the war sling, the war wine, and the war flags.

Here is a brief summary of these nine spiritual weapons out of God's arsenal:

> ***"Rejoice*** **(the War Dance)** *greatly; exceedingly, oh, daughter of Zion! Make full out joy!"* (Zech. 9:9a NIV/YLT/WYC).
>
> *"**Shout*** **(the War Cry)** *with gladness; shout aloud in joy and in triumph, oh, daughter of Jerusalem! Raise the roof!"* (Zech. 9:9a NASB/MSG/NRSV/NCV/JB).
>
> *"**Behold your King is coming*** **(the Warrior King)** *to you; He is just and endowed with salvation. He is righteous and victorious. He has overcome, a good King Who makes all things right. Humble and mounted on a donkey, even on a colt, the foal of a donkey"* (Zech. 9:9 NASB/NET/MSG/BBE; emphasis mine).
>
> *"**Judah is now My weapon, the bow I'll pull, and Ephraim is My arrow*** **(the War Bow and Arrows)***! The sons of Zion are **My sword*** **(the War Sword)***, and like a Warrior, I will brandish it against the Greeks. I mean to make you like the sword of a hero, and I will wield you like a warrior's sword against the sons of Greece" (Zech. 9:13 NLT/MSG/JB/NRSV; emphasis mine). "I will rise up and rouse the sons of Zion against the sons of Greece; I will use the men of Zion like a **sword**, to fight the men of Greece"* (Zech. 9:13b NIV/GNT).
>
> *"And the **Lord God will sound the war-horn*** **(the War Horn)***, Adonai ELOHIM will blow the shofar, **God will blast the ram's horn**, the Lord God shall sing in a trumpet. He will march out against His enemies like a*

> *whirlwind out of the southern desert"* (Zech. 9:14b BBE/CJB/NIV/MSG/GNT/WYC/NLT; emphasis mine).
>
> *"The Lord Almighty will protect his people, and* ***they will subdue their enemies with sling stones*** **(the War Sling)**. *"And they will prevail and overcome with sling stones. They will destroy and subdue their enemies with sling stones, crushing underfoot the armed men, and* ***make them subject with the stones of a sling"*** (Zech. 9:15a BBE/NET/NIV/NLT/WYC; emphasis mine).
>
> *They will shout in battle as though roaring drunk with* ***wine*** **(the War Wine),** *shedding the blood of their enemies"* (Zech.9:15a NLT/NEB; emphasis mine).
>
> *"The Lord their God will save them on that day, as the flock of His people. For they shall be like the jewels of a crown,* ***lifted like a banner, an ensign upon His land (the War Flags)"*** (Zech. 9:16 NKJV/KJV; emphasis mine).

As I said all nine of these spiritual weapons from God's arsenal are covered in detail in the other books of the *God's Heart of War Series*. I want to mention a few of them briefly. The rest of these spiritual war weapons are briefly covered in the Endnotes of this chapter for those who would like to read more about them.[1]

The War Dance

(Zech. 9:9a)

God has something specific in mind when He tells us to "rejoice." The word used here by Zechariah is a word we studied earlier, the Hebrew word *giyl, which* means "to go in a circle, to leap for joy and to dance."[2] This circular dance is one of the war dances of God, and it goes great with the war songs of God. Putting the war song and the war dance together makes a perfect weapon.

This Hebrew word for rejoicing is the same word David uses in the Psalms when he tells us to rejoice in the Lord (See Psalms 9, 16, 31, and 35, to list a few). Rejoicing is not just about being happy and joyful. It's an instruction from the Lord to perform specific actions such as leaping, twirling, going in circles, skipping, and dancing. When God calls us to rejoice, that specifically means He wants us to dance. God wants us to dance because He knows it releases His power in the Spirit (see Chapter 18 for a short list of the benefits of dancing before the Lord).

The War Cry

(Zech. 9:9a)

Next the Lord instructs us to shout His war cry. The Lord tells us to shout, but this is not just any old shout, it's not just any old yell. This is the war cry of God we're told to shout. The Hebrew word used here for shout is *ruwa*. It means "to shout a war cry, to sound the signal for war." [3] It's the same Hebrew word used by Joshua when he told Israel to shout as they encircled the city of Jericho. When they shouted, the walls of that city came crashing down (Josh. 6:20).

There are many different war cries in the Bible besides *ruwa*. Another war cry is *kumah or koom,* which means "to arise," and it is used to call out to the Lord to rise up as a warrior and attack. *Kumah* is a military term that sounds the attack of the Lord as He rises from the Ark of the Covenant. The Ark was God's war chariot that He rode in going before the army of Israel as they went into battle. Listen to the war cry of Moses:

"And whenever the Ark set out, Moses would cry, 'Arise, oh, Lord, and let Your enemies be scattered! ***Let those who hate You run for their lives before You'"*** (Num.10:35 NLT/JB/NASB; emphasis mine)!

Let us shout the war cry, mix our faith with the word, see the Lord rise up, and watch His (and our) enemies scatter. The praise and worship leaders in our churches need to teach God's people about the atomic power of God's word. As we praise God in unity of faith, as we sing and shout, our adversary and all his minions have to run for their lives.

We don't run from Babylon; we attack it!

Notice the glory and power of our God! He rises up and all His enemies scatter. Too many believers have it backwards. They have the devil and his antichrist rising up and God's people scatter (or rapture) out of here. No, we don't scatter from Babylon we attack it!

Some would say the Lord tells us to, "Flee from Babylon. Run for your lives" (Jer. 51:6 NIV)! Yes, of course, but read the rest of the verse. We leave because we don't want to be a slave to that kingdom of darkness and its sins any longer. We don't want to reap its coming destruction. But we never flee in terror from it. My Bible says that we're to resist the devil and **he flees from us** (Jam. 4:7). In fact we leave Babylon rejoicing, shouting and singing in victory. God says, "Be free from your captivity! **Leave Babylon with the sound of joyful shouting, singing as you go, with the sound of song make it clear, give the news**, let the word go out to the end of the earth: say, The LORD has redeemed His servants" (Isa. 48:20 NLT/NASB/BBE; emphasis mine). We leave to get out of Babylon's clutches, so we can turn around and attack that demonic stronghold in the power of our God (See Jer. 50-51). This war song of Zechariah prophecies the coming of God's special elite soldiers, who will take on and destroy this one-world government.

The Arrival of the Warrior King

(Zech. 9:9b-12)

As we obey in faith to sing the war songs, shout the war cries, and dance the war dances of the Lord, something marvelous happens: Jesus shows up. He can't help it. He wants to be there in the fray with His brother and sister warriors. By our singing, shouting, and dancing, just as David we're preparing the Ark for the very presence of the Lord to come into our midst.

"Jesus," we cry out, "Come into our midst as our Warrior King!" And when He comes, He does something remarkable. He destroys all the worldly weapons and declares His peace (Zech. 9:10). All natural weapons will be destroyed by Him. God says there will be *"no more chariots in Ephraim, no more war horses in Jerusalem, no more swords and spears, bows and arrows,* ***I will destroy all the weapons used in battle,*** *and He shall* ***command peace to the nations"*** (Zech. 9:10a MSG/NLT/NRSV; emphasis mine).

As we read on in Zechariah, we find God brings these very same weapons back; however, this time the weapons that He restores are His spiritual weapons. The Lord takes away the weapons of the natural world so we can only use His weapons in the Spirit. Only by His weapons can we usher in His dominion and kingdom. In His presence we will no longer rely on the arm of the flesh but on His holy arm of the Spirit. Only by His Holy Ghost weapons will we be able to bring His Holy Ghost peace to the earth.

The War Sword

(Zech. 9:13b)

Sometimes God needs us to do some warfare that is "up close and personal." This face-to-face combat is where His war sword comes into play. The Lord says: "**From now on people are My swords"** (MSG). The Lord desires to use His people as His weapons.

The sword of the Lord represents His word (Eph. 6:17 and Heb. 4:12). Here are a few examples of what happens when God uses His sword:

- By the sword of the Lord, God destroyed Pharaoh and the Egyptian army (Ex. 15:1-10).
- By the sword of the Lord, God rendered vengeance against His adversaries (Deut. 32:34-43).
- By the sword of the Lord, God will kill Leviathan, the dragon (Isa. 27:1-2).
- By the sword of the Lord, Jesus will fight against the people in Pergamum who served satan (Rev. 2:12-17).
- By the sword of the Lord, Jesus will destroy those who follow and worship the beast and false prophet (Rev. 19:21).

The Sword of the Lord is Used to Destroy the Sex Trade

In this chapter of Zechariah, the Lord's sword also has another very specific purpose. It manifests in the "sons of Zion" to destroy the lies of the "sons of Greece." Greece is not the people of Greece, but it symbolizes the demonic spirit operating over that nation. Greece, also known by its older name Javan, is linked with the two evil nations of Tubal and Meshech in human trafficking and slavery: *"Greece, Tubal, and Meshech did business with you; they* ***traded human beings*** *and articles of bronze for your wares;* ***they supplied you with slaves****"* (Ezek.27:13 TNIV/AAT; emphasis mine). Greece, a/k/a Javan, represents the demonic spirit involved with human trafficking, the perverted sex trade of young boys and girls that is so prevalent in our nation and around the world.

Through the prophet Joel the Lord declared His judgment against this perverted spirit that would cause an individual to throw *"dice for My people and used them for barter. They would trade a boy for a whore and sell a girl for a bottle of wine when they wanted a drink. They put a boy child in the bordello* [French word for brothel, a house devoted to prostitution] *and sold a young girl for wine"* (Joel 3:3 MSG/WYC; words in parenthesis mine). It was the nation of Philistia that *"****sold the children*** *of Judah and the children of Jerusalem* ***as slaves to the Greeks****, so that you could*

Sons of Zion, rise up as the sword in God's hand and destroy the chains of slavery of the sex trade in our land.

send them far away from their land" (Joel 3:6 KJV/Mof/NCV; emphasis mine). This perverted sex trade and slavery is prevalent all over the world and flourishing in America. Anyone who knows someone who has been abused by this demon of slavery knows how wicked and vile this spirit is. It must and will be stopped by people who submit to God to be used as His sword. Let us be the sharp sword in His hand that easily severs these chains of bondage.

THE WAR HORN

(Zech. 9:13b)

Jesus in the midst of our praise and worship is not finished. Next He picks up the war horn and sounds His shofar! Nothing can withstand the sound, when Jesus blows the *shofar* of God. In the Wycliffe translation this verse says "the Lord God shall sing" through His *shofar*. You can bet He is singing a war song.

God sounds His war horn as He marches out against His enemies. If the huge, fortified walls of the stronghold of Jericho fell at the sound of natural war horns sounded by humans, imagine the massive demonic walls that fall at the sound of Jesus' war horn. When the Lord blows the *shofar*, the devastation and mass chaos that will take place in the kingdom of darkness is nothing short of epic.

No demonic wall can withstand the power of God, when Jesus sounds the shofar!

A few things that happen when God's people blow the war horn are

- With Joshua, the walls of Jericho fell (Josh. 6:20-25).
- With Gideon, the enemy forces fled and were defeated (Jud.7:19-25).
- With Israel, they will be freed from Assyria and Egypt and are able to worship the Lord (Isa. 27:13 TLB).
- With the Lord, He ascends His throne and reigns over the earth, when the ram's horn is sounded (Ps. 47:5-9 NET).

These all are Old Testament examples of the power of the war horn sounded by man. They must pale in comparison to the atom-bomb power of the trumpets and war horns sounded in the New Testament, under the new covenant, by God's sanctified soldiers and his army of angels. And when the Son of Man sounds His war horn, the effects will be multiplied ten-thousand-fold.

The Lord Has Not Called Us to Be His Sheep Forever

The Lord is our Shepherd (Psa. 23:1), and we are the sheep of His pasture (Psa. 100:3), but He has not called us to be sheep forever. Just as Jesus told His disciples, "I do not call you servants any longer … but I have called you My friends" (John 15:15 Amp). God wants something else besides a bunch of sheep. It's nice being God's sheep, but God needs something else when He goes to war. Zechariah reveals to us that as we enter into spiritual warfare and utilize all nine of God's spiritual weapons something glorious happens to us in the Spirit. Just as Jesus wants friends not servants, the Lord wants something else besides sheep.

The War Horse of God

(Zech. 10:3b)

Chapter 10 of Zechariah brings to culmination the faithful acts of our warfare worship. After we sing the war songs, dance the war dance, and shout the war cry, Jesus our War King arrives. Then Jesus takes us up and uses us as His war bow and arrows and as His sword to strike His enemies. He then sounds the war horn and releases the power of God crashing down any barriers set up against us. We sling the rock, the name of Jesus, from His war sling at the giants standing against us, we get drunk on His war wine, and we signal God's commands with His war flags. That pretty well sums up where we are so far. Now God has one additional mighty thing to do:

> *"The people of Judah are Mine, and I, the Lord Almighty will care for My flock, and make them strong and glorious;* ***I will transform My flock into My majestic War Horse that*** *I will ride into battle!"* (Zech. 10:3b GNT/NCV/NLT/NASB/CJB/REB/Knox).

In our warfare worship the Lord transforms us from His sheep into His majestic war horse that He rides into the battle. Our Father does not want us to be sheep forever, because in a time of war, Jesus does not ride in on a sheep but on a war horse (Rev. 19:11). The Lord rides into battle mounted on

His war horse, with those ready to fight by His side. And "the armies of heaven followed Him, riding on white horses" (Rev. 19:14a). Fellow warriors, we don't have to wait around for the end of the world for Jesus to show up in His glory and power. We need His glory and power now!

Sheep of God ... it is time to be transformed into the war horses of God!

Here are just a few things that happen to us when we are changed into God's War Horse through the warfare worship in the war song of Zechariah:

- As God's war horse we are now able to "contend or race with horses" (Jer. 12:5 NKJV/NLT).
- As God's war horse we "laugh at fear" (Job 39:22 NET).
- As God's war horse we run towards conflict not away from it. The war horse is created for spiritual warfare (Job 39:19-25).

In the natural realm war horses were trained for the utter chaos of battle. One translation describes a war horse this way: *"**He goes out to meet the shock of battle.** Fear cannot daunt him, nor the sword drive him back"* (Job 39:21-22 Knox; emphasis mine). Just as the natural war horse is trained for combat, God's war horse is trained for spiritual warfare. Our God is looking for some war horses to ride into battle.

The war horses of God laugh and race toward the sounds of spiritual battle.

WAR HORSES ARE LEADERS RAISED UP FOR THE ARMY OF GOD

The Lord shows us that this anointing of the war horse is the anointing for leadership:

> *"From him shall come the cornerstone, from him the tent peg, from him the battle bow, from him every ruler, all of them together. From Judah will come rulers, leaders, commanders to govern My people"* (Zech. 10:4 ESV/GNT/NCV/NASB/MSG).

Under the anointing of the war horse, which is birthed out of our warfare of praise and worship, the Lord will raise up leaders from His people. They will be leaders in every facet of life:

- the Cornerstone for the building of His Church;
- the Tent Peg for the tent of our Homes;
- the Battle Bow for our Military; and
- the Rulers for our Marketplace and Civil Government.

Once we've been transformed into the war horse of God, we are now ready to lead the fight. As a War Horse of God, fear has been driven out of our lives. God declares to Job about His War Horse, *"He laughs at fear,* ***afraid of nothing****"* (Job 39:22 NIV; emphasis mine).

The next two verses in Zechariah's war song don't require much commentary:

> *"Together they will be like warriors, mighty men, heroes, treading down their enemies in the mire of the battlefield,*

> *crushing down their haters into the earth. They will fight and make war because the Lord is with them. They'll confound and put to rout even those on horseback. I shall give triumph to the house of Judah and victory to the house of Joseph.* ***I'll put muscle on the people of Judah,*** *and I will be the Savior to the children of Joseph.* ***I shall restore them in My compassion,*** *in My tender love for them, and they will be as though I had never cast them off. They'll get a fresh start, as if nothing had ever happened, for I am the Lord their God, and I shall graciously answer them"* (Zech. 10:5-6 ASV/YLT/BBE/MSG/WYC/NIRV; emphasis mine).

What a powerful promise and war song! God puts muscle on us and makes us mighty warriors and heroes in the Spirit. We'll crush the evil one under our feet, and be triumphant against the spiritual principalities and powers in high places set against us because the Lord is with us. We will be restored to the Lord as if nothing ever happened. He will hear us when we call, and with grace He will answer our prayers.

God puts muscle on the people who praise Him.

A Double Blessing for the Drunken Warriors

God promises warrior *parents* a double blessing. As we fight off the oppression of the evil one, we win the hearts of our sons and daughters at the same time. As we lead the way, our children are drawn to us and to the Lord.

> *"The people of Ephraim will become like mighty men, strong like soldiers.* ***Their hearts will be happy as if they were drinking wine. Their children will see it and rejoice and be filled with joy****. Their children will get in on it, too—oh, let them feel blessed by God! I will make their hearts glad and they shall rejoice in the Lord"* (Zech. 10:7 NIRV/NCV/ASV/NRSV; emphasis mine).

Your children will see you standing in the battle, full of joy from God's Holy Ghost wine, and they will rejoice and exult in the Father God with you. The word for rejoice used here is the same word we studied earlier. It is *giyl*, the Hebrew word for leaping and dancing. Our children will not only be glad, but they will dance with us before the Lord as we go into battle as His "drunken warriors."

> No matter where we are, God will care for and protect us and our children.

As if this wasn't blessing enough, God then adds another promise, one that we must stand on for the future of our homes, our church, and our country. He tells us that no matter where we are, God will care for and protect us ***and our children:***

> *"Even though I scattered them to the far corners of the earth,* ***they'll remember Me*** *in the faraway place. They'll keep the story alive in their children,* ***and they will come back****"* (Zech. 10:9b MSG; emphasis mine).

We and our children will be rescued and delivered from the captivity of any demonic stronghold or family curse. We'll inherit the Promised Land set apart for us and our children. We'll be so blessed there won't be enough room to contain it all (Zech. 10:10 TLB). And we will be imbued with God's strength, power, and authority:

> *"**I will make My people strong in My power**, and they will go wherever they wish by My name and authority. I, the Lord, have spoken!:* (Zech. 10:12 NLT/NRSV).

What else can we say but, "Yes, Lord!"

The War Horses of God Proclaim the Fall of Babylon

(Isa. 21:1-10)

As I was reading another burden, another war song of God against Babylon (Isa. 21:1), I received a word from the Lord: "When the War Horses begin to appear, know that the fall of Babylon is near." For a better understanding of this word, we need to look at this war song the Lord gave, to the prophet Isaiah:

> *"Meanwhile, the Lord said to me, 'Put a watchman on the city wall to shout out what he sees. When he sees riders, **horsemen in pairs,** riders on donkeys, riders on camels, let him listen diligently, very diligently, let him give special attention, tell him to keep his ear to the ground, and note every whisper, every rumor. Then he cried as a lion, I stand continually on the watchtower in the daytime; I have sat at my post every night. Now behold, here comes a troop of riders, **horsemen in pairs**.' And one said, '**Fallen, fallen is Babylon**; and all the images of her gods are shattered on the ground. Dear Israel, you've been through a lot, you've been put through the mill. The good news I get from God-of-Angel-Armies, the God of Israel, I now pass on to you"* (Isa.21:16 NLT/NRSV/BBE/MSG/NKJV/NASB; emphasis mine).

This prophecy in the natural realm is talking about the physical armies that came and destroyed Babylon in 689 BC and 539 BC. But many years later the apostle John hears the angels in heaven cry out this same prophetic word against spiritual Babylon and her downfall (Rev. 14:8 & 18:2). This glorious promise and war song in Isaiah 21 is not just about natural Babylon.

When we see the riders on the War Horses of God begin to appear we are to pay very close attention. They are one of the indicators that the end of Babylon, the one-world government ruled by the antichrist, is near. When War Horses begin to appear it indicates that the Lord is producing His warriors, who are trained and battle-ready to take on and destroy Babylon. God has not called us to fear Babylon; He has called us to destroy it.[4]

The Bible says that the Holy Spirit in me is greater than the devil in someone else. The apostle John tells us, *"This is the* ***spirit of the antichrist,*** *of which you have heard that is coming, and now is already* ***in the world.*** *You are from God,* ***little children, and have overcome them;*** *because greater is He who is in you than he who is in the world.* (1 John 4:3b-4 NASB). Who is he "who in the world," that John says we have to overcome? John tells us in the verse before this one. He says, he is "the spirit of the antichrist … (who) is already in the world." That spirit in the world is the spirit of the antichrist, and we have overcome him. Another translation puts it more clearly, ***"You have defeated them; because God's Spirit, Who is in you, is greater than the devil, who is in the world"*** (NCV). Let me repeat that. The Word of God says that, greater is He (the Spirit of Christ)

When the war horses appear, you know the fall of Babylon is near!

in me than he (the spirit of the antichrist) that is in the world. That means that no group of people full of the devil or the antichrist spirit can conquer a group of people full of the Holy Spirit of Christ. Even the "little children" have overcome this spirit of antichrist! God has not called us to flee; He's calling us to fight.

OUR PRAISE AND WORSHIP MAKES A DIFFERENCE

We don't praise and worship the Lord to feel good, and we don't praise Him because He needs the praise so He'll feel good. We praise Him because He is worthy, it makes us feel good, and because it's what we were born to do. The psalmist declares:

> *"Because of Your adversaries, You have built a fortress; You have established a stronghold from the mouths of babes against Your opponents.* ***You have taught children and babies to sing praises to You.*** *Nursing infants gurgle choruses about You; toddlers shout the song that drowns out, silences and destroys the enemy and the avenger"* (Ps.8:2 HCSB/GOD'S WORD/HNV/MSG/NRSV/WYC).

While we were still babes sucking milk, the Lord was teaching us praise, to establish a fortress, a stronghold against His enemies. Yes, our praise and worship make a difference. Never let the devil tell you otherwise. Our praise protects us and defeats him. The devil wants us to clam up, to pipe down, and to be silent. This is exactly why we can't. You see, as we praise the Father, we muzzle the evil one and we make him powerless. Our praise and declarations of God's word in faith destroys the hold of the enemy over an area. Sing, children of God, sing! Sing to set these children and all of God's creation free!

Lord, we sing against the adversary as we sing for the salvation of all. We sing that like the Philistines, even your enemies will be adopted into Your family. Thank You for giving us the songs to sing to release Your transforming power on the earth. Thank you for Your presence that surrounds and protects us. Thank You for teaching us Your warfare worship.

We worship You with our war dance and our war shout. No spirit of antichrist can stop us! The Holy Spirit of Jesus is in our midst. You use our praise as Your war bow and shoot Your arrows of glory into the camp of the wicked. Let us be the sword in Your hand to break the chains of slavery. Sound Your war horn, Jesus, and disintegrate the demonic strong-holds holding your creation captive. Lord, help us to manifest your love and character on the earth as we come fully into Your calling and destiny. Change us, Father, into your Majestic War Horse. Ride us into the battle as we laugh at fear. Let Your warrior leaders arise, destroy spiritual Babylon and bring heaven to earth. And Lord, let our children see the joy of our battle and dance with us!

Ride, War Horses, ride!
Laugh at all fear and
charge into the fight!

ENDNOTES:

1. The other spiritual weapons not covered in detail in Zechariah Nine are:

    - **The war bow and arrows (Zech. 9:13a)**

      Our praise and worship activate the power of God. He tells us "Praise (Judah) is now My weapon!" Stop and think about that for a minute. We need this revelation to go deep within our hearts: Our praise is now God's weapon. In verse 10 the Lord takes away our weapons of the flesh, of our natural man, and we're forced to use His weapons of the Spirit. Then the Lord pulls another fast one on us and tells us: "Guess what, now you're My weapons."

      God tells us that Judah, our praise, becomes a bow in His hands, and Ephraim, God's "double fruitfulness" becomes His arrows. The arrows of Ephraim that the Lord wants to shoot out all over the world are God's arrows of blessing and fruitfulness. Sometimes in our praise and worship the Lord desires for us, by faith, to be used by Him to release the arrows of His blessings and fruitfulness in the Spirit over the nations of His world.

      The bow and arrows of the Lord represent our intercessory prayer, praise, and worship. The word Judah means praise and Ephraim means double fruitfulness. So as we praise Him, we become the war bow in His hand and He releases Ephraim, the anointing of God's prosperity and blessings over the land. Let's sing and dance so we can be His bow and arrows and release His double blessings!

    - **The war sling (Zech. 9:15)**

      As we go forth under the protective covering of the Lord, He directs us to use this spiritual weapon of His war sling and let fly the rocks of the Lord into the camp of the wicked one. To understand what the war sling of God represents as a weapon in the Spirit, we need only look to one of the most well-known stories from our Sunday school days, the story of David and Goliath. The Philistine giant Goliath was taunting and scaring the heaven out of God's people, but God's anointed one, David, was coming to save the day. Goliath came with his sword, shield, and spear while David only came with his staff, stones, and sling (1 Sam. 17:40-45). We can only guess what was in David's mind as he devised his attack. Maybe he thought he could stun Goliath with one of his sling stones, and then get close enough to knock him in the head with his staff. Whatever it was, God had a better battle plan.

      David gives us the key of the war slingshot of God as he charges across the battlefield toward this formidable foe. The war sling of God is to release the name of God into our battle. David runs toward Goliath shouting, *"You attack me with a sword, and with a spear, and with a shield; but* ***I attack you in the name of the Lord*** *of heavenly forces, I'm coming in the name of ADONAI – Tzva'ot, the God of the armies of Israel, whom you have insulted"* (1 Sam. 17:45 CJB/Rhm/CEB/Mof; emphasis mine).

As David races toward Goliath, he declares that Goliath has a sword, a spear, and a shield, while David only has a sling, a sack, and five stones. You would think David would say to Goliath, "You have a sword, spear, and shield, and I have a sling, a sack, and five stones" if he was listing their respective weapons. But that's not what David said. As David rushes forward, charging Goliath, whirling his sling, he doesn't say, "I'm coming with my slingshot." No! He proclaims he's attacking Goliath **in the name of the Lord our God**, as he lets fly just one of his rocks.

Those stones in David's bag represent the name of the Lord our God, the name of Jesus. God is our Rock. One of the compound names of the Lord is "Jehovah-Sela," which means "the Lord is my rock" (Ps. 18:2). In the New Testament, the Apostle Paul refers to Jesus as the spiritual Rock from which the children of Israel drank in the desert: "For they drank of that spiritual Rock that followed them, and that Rock was Christ" (1 Cor. 10:4). As we sling the spiritual Rock – that is, God's name in the Spirit – at the evil one, we are releasing the power of the names of God as we enter the fray.

Just like David, it only takes one "stone" to fell a giant Philistine. There are approximately 50 different compound names of the Lord in the Old Testament that express His glory, nature, and power to us. (A wonderful source on the names of God is *The Names of God in Bible* by Ann Spangler. © 2011 by Baker Publishing Group.) We don't have space to adequately cover this spiritual weapon in God's arsenal, but just a few examples should be enough to explain. If we are in need, we can sling the rock of God's name Jehovah Jireh, God is my Provider (Gen. 22:14). If we are sick, we can loose the rock of God's name, Jehovah-Rophe, the Lord our Healer (Isa. 53:4-5). As we proclaim the name of the Lord against the devil, it is like hurling a huge boulder at him.

We also have the powerful name that is above all names: Jesus! The stone in the war sling of God represents the name of Jesus and "at the name of Jesus every knee shall bow – in heaven and on the earth and under the earth" (Phil 2:10 NET). That means that everyone must fall, including Goliath and any other "giants" in our lives. The war sling of God is our releasing the power of His name into a battle. The war sling releasing the name of God is the specifically designed "giant killer" weapon in God's arsenal. All giants fall at the name of Jesus! Release the name of the Lord our God as a rock into the camp of the enemy and watch those giants run for cover.

- **The war wine (Zech. 9:15b)**

  The second half of this verse is even more difficult to translate than the first half. Close examination of the verse reveals that the focus is on God's warriors behaving as though they were drunk. Before warriors go into a battle, it's good strategy to be prepared, to be stirred up, and to be inoculated. In Zechariah 9:15b, we are told that the soldiers of God "shall be inebriated as it were with wine" (DRB). This inebriation comes not from the "fruit of the vine"; it comes from the new wine of the Spirit with which God satiates us before the battle.

  There are many stories of armies in the past where the leaders would provide drugs or some form of stimulant or hallucinogen to their soldiers before they went into battle. The warriors would take something to get them fired up before charging into the fight, or they would use some form of drug to dull any pain from any possible wounds they may incur in the conflict.

  One interesting example is seen in the origins of the word "*assassin*." It "is a word which entered the languages of Europe during the Crusades, when the members of a certain Mohammedan sect, having vowed the killing of Christian leaders, made use of the narcotic hashish to work themselves into a state of frenzy sufficient for the dangerous task. *Assassin* (Arabic, hashshashin) consequently first meant "eater of hashish," then a special group of "hashish-eating terrorists," and finally any "treacherous murderer whether under the influence of drugs or not" (Taken From: Ayers, D. M., *English Words from Latin and Greek Elements.* Tucson, AZ: The University of Arizona Press, 1986, p. 83).

  Other examples of the use of drugs prior to battle have happened throughout history in all areas of the world:

  - To treat pain Native American warriors would chew the bark from willow trees, (Retrieved at: http://www.mountainroseherbs.com/learn/white_willow.php). Because the active ingredient in the bark is salicylic acid or aspirin. (Bellis, M., The History of Aspirin, retrieved at http://inventors.about.com/library/inventors/blaspirin.htm).

  - New research has shown that Zulu warriors used a cannabis-based snuff, known for its hallucinogenic properties, as well as a codeine type pain killer found in the bulb of a flower in the Amaryllis family during the famous "Day of the Zulu" battle of 1879. (From *Secrets of the Dead: The*

Day of the Zulu, Retrieved at: http://www.pbs.org/wnet/secrets/previous_seasons/case_zulu/clues.html).

- The Masai warriors of East Africa also would take cannabis in advance of battle (Booth, M. Cannabis: A History (New York, NY: Picador St. Martin's Press, 2005), p. 56).
- Viking "berserkers" were known to eat drugged food or drink contaminated alcohol before their famous wild ravages (at http://www.wordiq.com/definition/Berserker_%28viking%29).

These are some potent drugs, but none of these worldly counterfeits can equal the war wine of God.

The war wine of God is not a fermented grape juice that temporarily dulls your senses and inhibitions. The war wine is the new wine we now have by the blood of Jesus. It's the wine of the joy of the Lord. We experience God's presence in our midst. On the day of Pentecost when the 120 disciples first received God's new wine – His baptism in the Holy Spirit – the people observing them thought them drunk on wine (Acts 2:13). Peter explains, "These men are not drunk" on wine, but that this is a fulfillment of the promise made by God through the prophet Joel that the Lord would pour out His Spirit upon all flesh (Acts 2:15-21 NET).

Proverbs warns us about getting drunk with wine and alcohol. How wine can cause us to become so drunk, we don't even feel the beatings and hits if we get in a fight (Prov. 23:29-35). Guess what, the new war wine of the Lord is just like that in the Spirit! When we are drunk on God's new wine we don't feel a thing when the evil one tries to attack us with his false accusations and lies. We just laugh and want another drink of God's wine!

It's good to be inebriated with the new wine of the Lord before we go into battle. When we are filled to overflowing, completely quenched in the Spirit, the "beatings" of the enemy, i.e., his lies and false accusations, have no impact. You just keep on advancing the attack. "Drunk" on God's war wine, your joy turns to laughter at the enemy's puny attacks. The pain he intends to inflict is completely allayed by the war wine of God.

- **The war flag (Zech. 9:16)**

In most translations the Hebrew word for banner or ensign is translated "sparkle." The word is nacac, and its exact meaning is uncertain. It could mean "to sparkle" or it could mean "to be conspicuous as a signal through the idea of a flag fluttering in the wind, to raise up a beacon or to lift up as an ensign." That is why different Bible versions translate it differently. In the context of battle in Zechariah Chapter Nine, it makes sense that nacac is referring to a flag, a banner, or an ensign being lifted up for all to see. In a war we need war flags which make more sense than jewels sparkling.

War flags are a vital weapon in warfare. Battlegrounds are places of chaos and commotion. The general can't simply yell orders to the men on the front line and expect them to comprehend. Amid all the noise and confusion of war, war flags are used to clearly communicate the orders of the commanders to the soldiers engaged in the fight. They signal the moves and direct the strategies of an army. They can be seen from far off and their meaning is clear and concise. The war flags dictate the who, the when, the where, and the how the soldiers are to obey in a skirmish. The specific function of an Ensign is to direct the military band on what tunes to play. Doesn't that sound applicable to our study of God's war songs? Without the war flags, warriors would be confused, disoriented, and uncertain in the midst of a battle. The war flags keep the troops organized, focused, and confident of their mission.

2. Retrieved at: http://www.blueletterbible.org/lang/lexicon.cfm?Strongs=H1523&t=KJV.
3. Retrieved at: http://www.blueletterbible.org/lang/lexicon.cfm?Strongs=H7321&t=KJV.
4. I have dedicated Book 7 of the *God's Heart of War* Series to the War Horses of God. In that book I go into greater detail about this glorious revelation.

CHAPTER FIFTEEN

GOD'S REVELATION TO ISRAEL

"I will fill David's family and the people living in Jerusalem with a spirit of kindness and mercy. They will look to Me. I am the One they have pierced. They will sob over Me as someone sobs over the death of their only firstborn son who has died. They will be full of sorrow over Me, just like someone who is full of sorrow over the death of their firstborn son"
—Zech. 12:10 ERV/NIRV

THE WAR SONG OF GOD FOR ISRAEL

(Zech. 12:1-14:21)

The final chapters of Zechariah are God's war song for Israel. This war song is not sung to defeat a demonic foe, although that is the ultimate outcome. This burden (Zech. 12:1) is sung over the nation of Israel to bless her, give her God's peace and raise her up to new heights of power that she has never experienced. We sing to release her into her full calling from the Lord and restore her into her full position and glory as the chosen people of God.

ISRAEL, GOD'S WARRIOR

The nation of Israel has had more influence on the history of the world than any other people. Some may argue that the societies that gave us the great pyramids of Egypt, the Great Wall of China, the Greek and Roman Empires or the Mayan Empire of South America were great nations. As great as those nations may have been, their influence has not shaped the political, geographical, social, and spiritual history of the world in any way even close to how the nation of Israel has and continues to do. Of course, we know the reason for this: The people of Israel, the Jewish race, have been chosen by Jehovah God Almighty to fulfill His divine plan of salvation and ultimately bless the entire world.

> *"Now the Lord had said to Abram: 'Get out of your country, from your family and from your father's house, to a land that I will show you. I will make you a great nation; I will bless you and make your name great; and you shall be a blessing. I will bless those who bless you, and I will curse him who curses you; and* ***in you all the families of the earth shall be blessed'"*** (Gen. 12:1-3 NKJV emphasis mine).

It's only because of the New Covenant God gave us in Jesus that we can know and be a part of what God is doing in the world; that we can have hope in the promises He made to the nation of Israel; that we can partake in the blessings He promised His people. The Apostle Paul reminds us that before Christ, the Gentiles–that is, everyone who is not a Jew–were outside these rich blessings of God.

> *"You (Gentiles) were excluded from God's people, Israel, and you did not know the promises God had made to them. You knew nothing of that rich history of God's covenants and promises in Israel. You lived in this world without God and without hope.* ***You didn't have a clue about what God was doing in the world at large****"* (Eph.2:12 NLT/MSG; emphasis mine).

The people of Israel are called by God. Their name Israel means "the Prince or Warrior of God."[1] As God's warriors they are to lead the way in releasing His blessings over the world. Israel as a nation is called to be priests to the world. As God's people they are to minister and pray for the nations. The Hebrew word that means to minister or to serve is *sha-rat* and means "to be a Prince, a Warrior of the Cross or Covenant."[2] The Jewish people are still called to be God's Warrior prince and priest to the nations.

ISRAEL, GOD'S SOARING EAGLE

Another word that has the Hebrew word *sar* (prince) as its root is the word for "eagle," which means "the living warrior or prince" or "the warrior or prince who brings life."[3] Both words "Israel and "eagle" have *sar* as their root word, they are related. We see that Israel is called to be God's soaring eagles. They are His warriors to set the captive nations free and serve them by bringing them to God.

From the beginning of the covenant God made with Israel, there has been a connection between this nation and the eagle. Scripture is chock-full of these Israel/eagle references. A few are:

- **Exodus 19:4:** The Lord reminds them of His power over Pharaoh and how He delivered them. *"You yourselves have seen what I did to the Egyptians, how* ***I bore you on eagle's wings*** *and brought you to Myself"* (NASB; emphasis mine).

- **Deuteronomy 32:11:** The Lord refers to Israel as His eaglets. ***"As an eagle, teaching her young*** *to make their flight, He spread abroad His wings and He took them, He bore them on His strong feathers"* (BBE/Amp; emphasis mine).

- **Psalm 103:5:** As David recounts the blessings of the Lord, the psalmist reminds us that God *"satisfies your years with good things, so that your* ***youth is renewed like the eagle's*** *[strong, overcoming, soaring]!"* (NASB/Amp; emphasis mine).

- **Isaiah 40:31:** *"Those who wait upon God get fresh strength.* ***They spread their wings and soar like eagles****; they run and don't get tired; they walk and do not become weary"* (MSG/NASB; emphasis mine).

- **2 Samuel 1:23:** Israel had two great warriors, Jonathan and his father, Saul. When David heard of their death, he *"chanted this dirge … they were* ***swifter than eagles,*** *they were stronger than lions…Alas for the mighty heroes fallen in… battle"* (2 Sam. 1:17, 23 & 25 KJV/Rhm/Mof; emphasis mine).

As the eagle of the Lord, Israel was called to manifest His power, His glory, and His blessings to all nations. For hundreds of years Israel fulfilled this calling of the eagle and reflected the glory of God to the world. Then came the day of the Messenger of the Covenant, Jesus, and they stumbled on the Stone that became the chief cornerstone (Luke 20:17; Acts 4:11). But because of the nature of our Father, even their temporary rejection of Jesus as their Messiah brought blessings to the world.

Israel is God's soaring eagle.

A DAY IS COMING

When Israel rejected Jesus the first time He came, Paul tells us it resulted in God's salvation poured out upon the rest of the world:

> *"So I'm asking you, they haven't stumbled so that they've fallen permanently, have they? Heaven forbid! Quite the contrary. It is* ***by means of their stumbling that deliverance and salvation have come to the Gentiles,*** *in order to provoke them to jealousy"* (Rom.11:11 CEB/CJB; emphasis mine).

Paul explains that for a season the Jewish people will have a veil over their hearts and minds. He says, *"Yes, even today when they read Moses writings, their hearts are covered with that veil, and they do not understand"* (2 Cor. 3:15 NLT). We are no different than the Jewish people. Everyone has a veil over their hearts and minds (2 Cor. 4:3-6). It is only removed by Jesus. That veil *"has not been removed, because only by believing in Christ is it taken away"* (2 Cor. 3:14b NLT/NIV). But a day is coming when that veil shall be removed!

IF Israel's rejection of Jesus in the past set off an outpouring of God's salvation for the whole world, THEN we know their acceptance of the Messiah in time to come will set off an explosion of His resurrection life and power unlike anything we can imagine.

> *"If Israel's rejection means that the world has been brought back to God, that God offered salvation to the rest of the world, all other people were changed from God's enemies into His friends,* ***their (i.e. Israel) recovery is going to set off something even better: mass homecoming!*** *So what will happen when they are accepted?* ***It will be life for those who were dead!****"* (Rom. 11:15 GNT/GOD'S WORD/NIRV/MSG; emphasis mine).

The branches of a tree or vine are where leaves, flowers, or fruit are produced. The root is what gives the branches life. Jesus is the root (Isa. 11:10), and the people of Israel are the natural branches. For a season, the natural branches have been cut off from the root, and we Gentiles, the wild branches, have been grafted in. The tree has grown and the grafted-in branches have produced fruit, but the root is still very Jesus and still very Jewish. However, a day is coming when the Jews, the natural branches, will be grafted back into God's tree as well (Romans 11:17-24). If we, as the wild branches, can experience such great power and blessings in this day, when Israel is grafted back in, the power and blessings will be nothing short of supernatural.

ISRAEL, GOD'S FIRE

Woe to the spirits of darkness! When the church begins to rise up and sing the war song of Zechariah over Israel, her eyes will be opened. She will be grafted into full fellowship with the Father, and a nuclear spiritual firefight as has never been witnessed will be loosed on satan and his minions. Zechariah tells us in the last days the Lord will make Israel His unquenchable fire on the earth:

> *"On that day,* ***I will make the clans of Judah unstoppable against their enemies,*** *at that time I will make the leaders of Judah* ***like a fire burning in a forest. They will destroy their enemies like fire burning straw.*** *They will destroy the enemy around them, and the people in Jerusalem will again be able to sit back and relax, safe and secure, bustling with citizens"* (Zech. 12:6 ERV/ Voice; emphasis mine).

As the Fire of the Lord, Israel will clean and purge the spirits of everyone around them. The people of God will calmly sit back and relax; in His presence and by His protection they will be safe and secure.

Israel's acceptance of Jesus will be like the resurrection of the dead!

ISRAEL'S WEAKEST BECOME AS MIGHTY AS DAVID

Zechariah informs us that the Lord is not finished infusing Israel with His power. As God's chosen warrior, Israel is imbued with God's incomparable power. At her recognition of Jesus as the Messiah, this power will be revealed to all nations. The Lord will be their shield, and at the same time, make the weakest among them as mighty as David. Standing united, they will be like God, like the Angel of the Lord. Imagine thousands of men and women, anointed like David, running around with their spiritual slingshots in hand, looking for a demonic giant to slaughter.

> *"On that day, the Lord will fight for, defend (and) shield those who live in Jerusalem, so that the weakest,* ***the feeblest among them will be mighty like David, and the house of David will be like God,*** *like the Angel of the Lord marched before them, at their head in battle"* (Zech. 12:8 NET/NIV/NLV/NLT/Knox/Voice; emphasis mine).

FOR NOW AND ALWAYS

There has been a glorious call on the Jewish nation since their inception and that call remains just as powerful today. God's call on them has never been changed or taken away. Paul tells us this beautiful promise from God concerning His gifts and His calling is "irrevocable."

> *"God's gifts and God's call are under full warranty – never canceled, never rescinded."* (Rom. 11:29 MSG).
>
> and
>
> *"For God's gifts and His call are irrevocable. [He never withdraws them when once they are given, and* ***He does not change His mind*** *about those to whom He gives His grace or to whom He sends His call]" (*Rom. 11:29 Amp; emphasis mine).

These statements, just like the entirety of Romans Chapter 11, are all about the call of God upon Israel. When that irrevocable call is finally fulfilled—and it will be—watch out! The power and the glory of God are on the way. The call of the Lord is to manifest His power and glory on the nation of Israel in ways never before seen. The weakest will be strong like David, taking on the giants in the land,

and together the house of David will look like God, like the Angel of the Lord on the earth. This is the reason we sing the war song over Israel. We sing for the full release of God's gifts and calling on her to release the full power of God in the earth.

The Spirit of Grace and Prayer

As we sing the word of the Lord over Israel, the Lord removes the veil from their hearts and pours out His Spirit of power and revelation upon them. He opens a fountain for their uncleanness and refreshing and destroys the demonic forces of religion and legalism once and for all.

> *"I will pour out on the house of David and on the inhabitants of Jerusalem, the Spirit of grace and prayer so that they will look on Me whom they have pierced; and they will mourn for Him as one mourns for an only son. They will grieve bitterly for Him as for a firstborn son who has died"* (Zech. 12:10 NASB/NLT).

> *In that day a fountain shall be opened for the house of David and for the inhabitants of Jerusalem, for sin and uncleanness" (Zech. 13:1 NKJV).*

At the release of this outpouring of God's Spirit, all demonic idols and unclean spirits will be destroyed.

> *"'It shall be in that day,' says the Lord of hosts, 'that I will cut off the names of the idols from the land, and they shall no longer be remembered. I will also do away with their prophets and **those evil spirits that control them**. I will get rid of the spirit that put lies in their mouths, and **I will take away their desire to worship idols'"*** (Zech. 13:2 NJKV/ CEV/GNT/NIRV/ Voice; emphasis mine).

What a glorious day! Warriors of God, it is our responsibility to sing aloud this war song to release God's glory over Israel, to sing this promise from God's word for them to receive the revelation that Jesus is the Messiah. When they receive this revelation of Jesus, the demons might as well run on to hell and get it over with. There will be no stopping the chosen people of God.

Sing over Israel, see the eagle of God fly!

"Then the Lord will march out against the godless nations and ***attack those nations like a Warrior fighting in battle****, as He has fought in times past.* ***It will be a real battle****"* (Zech. 14:3 NLT/MSG/ERV/CEV; emphasis mine).

A WAR SONG FOR THE MIDDLE EAST

There are other war songs in the Bible that we must sing directly to Israel. One such war song is found in Isaiah Chapter 19. It is a war song that releases God's glorious healing and restoration power over Israel, Assyria, and Egypt. As we have read, when Israel turns to Jesus, the weakest shall be like David and a group of them will be like God on the earth. Israel will lead the charge against the demonic hosts set against God's people, and there will be peace. The Lord tells us, *"When the ways of people please the LORD, He makes even their enemies live at peace with them"* (Prov. 16:7 NLT). This is exactly what happens with the two ages-long enemies of Israel. Assyria and Egypt have been at war with Israel throughout her lifetime. One day these peoples will be reconciled. One day they will become allies together in the Lord.

Isaiah declares, *"The burden against Egypt. Behold, the Lord is riding on a swift cloud and comes to Egypt; the idols of Egypt will tremble at His presence, and the heart of the Egyptians will melt within them"* (Isaiah 19:1 NRSV/NKJV). The Lord will come and judge Egypt, but the outcome will be His glory upon Egypt, Assyria, and Israel.

> *"On that Day, Egyptians will be like hysterical schoolgirls, screaming at the upraised fist of the Lord Almighty. Little Judah will strike terror in Egyptians! Say, 'Judah' to an Egyptian and see panic. For the* ***Lord Almighty has laid out His plans*** *against them. In that day five of Egypt's cities will follow the Lord Almighty. They will even begin to speak the Hebrew language of faith and promise to follow God-of-the-Angel-Armies. One of these cities will be honored with the title 'City of the Sun'"* (Isaiah19:16-18 MSG/NLT; emphasis mine).

These three nations will come together and worship the Lord. They will be a blessing to the whole world and reap the blessings of God Almighty.

> *"In that day there will be a highway from Egypt to Assyria, and the Assyrians will go to Egypt, and the Egyptians will go to Assyria. The Egyptians and Assyrians* ***will have peace and will worship God together.*** *In that day Israel shall be the third with Egypt and with Assyria and will be joined together [in a Messianic league] a whole-earth blessing, the hub of proper worship in the heart of the earth. The Lord Who rules over all will bless these three nations. He will say, 'Let the Egyptians be blessed. They are My people. Let the Assyrians be blessed. My hands created them. And let the Israelites be blessed. They are My very own people, My*

inheritance. You are all blessed'" (Isa. 19:23-25 EXB/Knox/Amp/NCV/Voice/YLT/NIRV/ESV).

SING THE WAR SONGS OF GOD OVER ISRAEL AND THE MIDDLE EAST

Do you want to pray for the peace of Israel? Singing war songs is one of the best ways to do it. This is the ultimate goal and culmination of the war songs of God: For His church to battle against evil on all fronts and to sing over Israel and usher in her revelation that Jesus is the Messiah. Sing, church, as you've never sung before:

- Sing over Israel that they will be God's Warrior on the earth and destroy the works of the wicked one.
- Sing that they will rise up and soar as the Eagle of the Lord, manifesting His glory and power.
- Sing over Israel to be the Fire of God, consuming His enemies and purging His world of evil.
- Sing over Israel the anointing of God so the weakest will be like David and the house of David like God.
- Sing for the Lord to pour out His Spirit of grace and prayer over Israel so they will see Jesus as their Messiah and mourn for Him as the firstborn son, the One Who was pierced for them.

- Sing for the Lord to open up His fountain for cleansing of our sins.
- Sing for the Lord to cut off all the names of the idols, the false gods, the demons in the land.
- Sing that Assyria and Egypt will join Israel in worship of the Father.
- Sing for these three age-old enemies to become allies and a blessing to all the earth.

There are not adequate words to express how glorious the day will be when the revelation of Jesus comes to Israel and the reconciliation and salvation of her enemies are fulfilled. In the meantime, we *must* find the words to sing to and for Israel to remove the veil covering their minds, to saturate their hearts with the spirit of grace and supplication, to open their eyes to Jesus as their Messiah, their King, and receive a deeper revelation of their Father God.

Sing for God's peace to fall on the Middle East!

This is our responsibility, church. This is our calling. This is our destiny. Sing, church! Sing!

Oh, Lord, pour out Your Spirit of revelation upon Your people, Jews and Gentiles alike. Let us all see the revelation of Your Son. As we receive the beautiful picture of Your love and mercy, as we repent and cry out to You, open Your fountain of healing and cleansing for us. Father, take away the veil that covers the hearts and minds of Your chosen people that they may be grafted back into Your life and assume their role as Your warrior, Your soaring eagle in the earth. Make Israel mighty to defeat the powers of darkness. Pour out your spirit of grace on Israel, Assyria,

and Egypt, so that they may realize the joy of knowing you as "Abba", so that Your word will be fulfilled that You will bless them and the whole world through them.

Sing for God's peace
to fall on the Middle East!

ENDNOTES:

1. Seekins, p. 186.
2. Ibid.
3. Seekins p. 162.

MALACHI

GOD'S WAR SONG TO DEFEAT COVENANT-BREAKING

CHAPTER SIXTEEN

CALLED TO RESTORE

GOD'S PRIESTS ARE CALLED TO RESTORE HIS COVENANTS

"'You priests have left God's paths. Your instructions have caused many to stumble into sin. You have corrupted the covenant I made with the Levites,' says the Lord of Heaven's Armies. Are we not all children of the same Father? Are we not all created by the same God? Then why do we betray each other, violating the covenant of our ancestors? Judah has been unfaithful, and a detestable thing has been done in Israel and in Jerusalem. The men of Judah have defiled the Lord's beloved sanctuary by marrying women who worship idols"
—Mal. 2:8, 10-11 NLT

Our nation, our churches, and our homes are in serious trouble. All around we see the devastating effects of hatred and envy fueled by the demonic spirits of strife, discord, and division. Our nation is torn apart with covetousness and disunion that is raging between the different socio-economic levels of the "haves" and the "have-nots." There is tension and open hatred between racial and ethnic groups. Even in the church, which is supposed to be the very source of love and unity, we see petty religious in-fighting and church splits. Looking into our homes, we see nearly half of our marriages ending in divorce.[1] We need God's help and healing, and we need Him **now**. This is the day God is revealing to us how His war songs heal our broken covenants, crush our enemies under our feet, and reverse the curses on our land. We must move forward in faith and regain the territory that has been stolen. Take heart; God has our back. (Isa. 52:12, 58:8 RSV).

God sent Jesus to make us one in His love (John 17:20-23). The very foundation of our union and fellowship with the Lord is in the blood covenant of His Son, Jesus. As believers, we stand or fall dependent upon our covenant fellowship with the Father. Our nation stands or falls contingent upon us obeying the laws of love in God's commands and covenants with our fellow men and women. Likewise, our homes will stand or fall dependent upon our faithfulness to the marriage covenant with our spouse.

Half of you reading this may have experienced the pain of a divorce, or you may be in the process of divorce right now. Some of you are in a church caught in the midst of bitter disagreements to the point that church members are going their separate ways. Still others of you may be facing jealousy, divisiveness, and strife at your job that are creating unbearable stress and threatening your livelihood, or worse yet, your health. And how many of us know, sadly, that there are areas of our very towns where we can't safely travel if we are of a different ethnic or racial group than those who predominantly live there?

Of all the problems facing the United States today, this problem of strife and division ranks close to the top. The spirit of division is nothing to be trifled with. This same spirit of division was able to invade the very throne room of heaven and rend one-third of the angels from God's army as they followed lucifer in his pride and rebellion (Rev. 12:4).

This spirit of division even struck the throne of heaven, when lucifer rebelled and tore one third of the angels from the army of heaven.

We must face and destroy this spiritual attack of strife and divisiveness. Our nation faces many difficult issues, and if we don't walk in unity and face our problems together, we're doomed to failure before we begin. As the saying goes, "United we stand; divided we fall." There is no greater unity than when God's children sing with one accord the word of the Lord, releasing His power and blessings on the earth.

Believers: God's New Testament Priests

The word of God given to the prophet Malachi pertained to the same divisive spirit that invaded God's very throne room and that attacks us on every front today. Malachi's words, his war songs, were directed to the priests of his day, and that involves you and me. Remember, in God's New Covenant we are all priests unto the Lord. The apostle Peter tells us, *"God is building you, as living stones, into His spiritual temple. What's more, **you are God's holy priests**"* (1 Pet. 2:5a NLT; emphasis mine). Further, the apostle John tells us,

"You made them a Kingdom, ***priests for our God****, priest-kings to rule over the earth"* (Rev. 5:10 MSG; emphasis mine).

Every time Malachi mentions "priest" just replace it with the New Testament word "believer." Better yet, insert your name there. This word is for all believers, to all of us walking with the Lord. For a season, we Gentiles are called to be God's priests on the earth until such time as the children of Israel return to Him and are grafted back into the family tree of God (Rom. 11:24).

The book of Malachi starts, *"The burden of the word of the Lord to Israel by Malachi"* (Mal. 1:1 NKJV). It is another burden (*massa*), another war song from the Lord, a song to sing and declare God's doom and destruction over these spiritual forces of dissension and division. The first two chapters of the book are sad to read because of the plight of Israel The subjects Malachi addresses are:

- Chapter 1—Israel dishonors the Lord and His name;
- Chapter 2—the three broken covenants: man with God, man with man, and man with woman;
- Chapter 3—the war songs to restore each of the broken covenants;
- Chapter 4—the war songs repeated with additional ammunition from the Lord to restore the three broken covenants.

Malachi Chapter 1: God's Message of Covenant Love

In the first words of Malachi, the Lord reminds Israel of His covenant love for them. *"I have loved you, says the Lord"* (Mal. 1:2a CEB). The problem, as usual, was not that God had broken covenant with Israel, but rather that Israel was not walking in covenant love with the Lord. They were not honoring God as their Father, and they were not respecting Him as their Master. They were dishonoring His name in their very worship. (Mal. 1:6). It was so abysmal that the Lord desired that someone would close the doors of the temple so no one could enter (Mal. 1:10). That is how repulsive their worship had become to Him.

When the priests dishonored the Lord's name and turned their back to Him, they walked out from under the shield of God's protection and blessings and right under a curse. What they did not only affected them, but also those around them, including their children (Mal. 2:2-3). Today, as God's priests of the New Covenant these responsibilities, blessings and curses apply to us as well.

God's Covenant Love Restores All Relationships

God's love is expressed to us by His covenant and can restore all of our broken relationships. The New Covenant love of Jesus holds us together and protects us. As we return to the Lord and walk in fellowship with Him in the cool of the day, once again the paradise of Eden is restored on earth. Under His New Covenant, wrought through the blood of Jesus, the Lord affirms the three areas in which His church and children are to operate. Not surprisingly, they are the relationships of 1) man with God, 2) man with man, and 3) man with woman. Just as the three areas of covenant have not changed since the days of Malachi, neither has the assault launched by our adversary.

The sole purpose of our adversary's attacks on these divine covenants is to destroy the work of God's love and harmony, but these covenant breaking demons of strife and division will not succeed. God is calling us to return to Him, sing His war songs, and annihilate these demonic spirits. As they are conquered by the power of God, the Lord will replace demonic jealousy, strife, and division with His divine love, grace, and unity.

Our only hope is the covenant love of the Father and His Son, Jesus, that can heal the division in our world.

This message of covenant love is vital for us today. It is the *now* word of the Lord. God is calling us to return to Him in covenant love so we can have fellowship with Him and with one another. The covenant love of God and Jesus is the only hope for our world. Without it there is only selfishness, division, chaos, and ultimately death.

OUR ONLY HOPE FOR PEACE AND UNITY

If the love of God is in our hearts, it will be manifested by our love for each other. Jesus said, *"Your love for one another will prove to the world that you are My disciples. By this all men will know; it will be clear to all men that you are My disciples, if you have love one for another"* (John 13:35 NLT/NASB/BBE). God's love in action in our lives is the true sign to the world that we are His. It was the love of God that first healed our hearts (1 John 4:19), and now it's the love of God that holds our hearts together. It's the love of God that holds our marriages together. Only the love of God can hold our country and all the nations of this world together.

The love of God releases His heaven on earth. Without it, we'll continue to have hell on earth. This is the call from our Father God to us His children: *"I love you, says Adonai; I have always loved you"* (Mal. 1:2a CJB/GNT). The Lord tells His children He has always *"dealt lovingly with you"* (Knox). The name Malachi means "My messenger."[2] We, as God's messengers, His modern-day priests, must manifest and proclaim this message of God's covenant love to the world. It's the love of Jesus that is our only hope.

MALACHI CHAPTER 2: THREE BROKEN COVENANTS

As God's priests in the Old Testament turned away from the Lord and broke covenant with Him, all of their other covenants were affected and broken. When God's covenants are broken, discord and disunion follow. The same causes and effects are true today. The spirit of division is destroying the harmony and unity of God's creation. This is happening not only in America. It's rampant around the globe. If we're seeing the same effect, chances are the cause is also the same, that is, we, as God's priests, have turned from Him. It's time to seek the Lord.

I. The Covenant with Levi:
Man with God (Mal. 2:1-9)

The first covenant God mentions is the most important. It is His covenant with Levi. The Lord made a covenant with the tribe of Levi to establish them as His priests. They were called to stand in the gap and intercede for the people of Israel (Deut. 21:5). God's covenant *"with Levi was to give him life and peace"* (Mal. 2:5a Amp). As the Levites walked with the Lord they *"made many turn from iniquity"* (Mal. 2:6b CEB). The Knox translation here is beautiful: *"From no other lips men will expect true guidance"* (Mal. 2:7b). "True guidance" comes from the lips of those who speak God's word. No matter what your I.Q. or how many college degrees you have, true guidance resides in the Spirit of the Lord.

This word from Malachi applies to all believers today. When this priestly covenant is fulfilled, all heaven floods the earth, but when this priestly covenant is broken, all hell breaks loose. When we turn our backs to the Lord and His life full of blessings, the only thing we can possibly face is an existence filled with curses and death. There is not a third option with the Lord. There is no neutral ground. Jesus said, *"This is war, and* ***there is no neutral ground****. If you're not on My side, you're the enemy; if you're not helping, you're making things worse"* (Luke 11:23 MSG; emphasis mine). There is a war going on, and it's time for us to pick our side.

If we walk away from the Lord, we walk out from under the fortress of His spiritual protection. We are no longer covered by His shield. We become easy targets for curses to fall on us and our offspring (Mal. 2:3). One translation states, the Lord *"will scatter your blessing, and it shall not be among you"* and the other, *"the curse will extend to your children"* (NETS and MSG, respectively). When God's people do not walk in covenant fellowship with Him, the whole world is affected.

This priestly covenant is vital because it affects all the other covenants. Without our covenant bond with Father God, all our other covenants fall apart. Without His covenant love in us, it's impossible for us to "keep covenant" with anyone. Walking with the Lord is a dance filled life with immeasurable blessings and joy, but if we turn our backs to Him, it becomes a death march of curses and sorrow. Now is the time for us to turn to the Lord and reverse this curse on us, on our homes, and on our nation.

Walking with the Lord is a dance of immeasurable joy.

That We Become One

At the last supper, the night before Jesus went to the cross, He prayed what is called His "High Priestly Prayer" (John 17:1-12, Subtitle in NASB). He prayed to the Father that we become one just as He is one with the Father. This was the work that Jesus was sent to finish upon the earth (John 17:4). The Son of God came that we may have eternal life. Eternal life is when we know the Father (John 17:3). As we walk in love and unity with Him, we'll walk in love and unity with each other. When we are *"made perfectly one, then the world will know"* that Jesus is the Son of God (John 17:23b CEB).

It's no wonder the evil one lets loose this divisive spirit upon the earth. He does not want us to walk in God's love and unity, and this spirit of division is one of the most powerful weapons in his armory at separating us from our

Father and then from one another. Our adversary is doing all he can to prevent the love, peace, and unity of God from filling the world. He is doing all he can to undo the work and unity of Jesus.

The enemy wants to stop this revelation from reaching the nations: That Jesus is the Son of God, and as God's Son, Jesus, in His New Covenant, restores us all to the heart of the Father. When all are restored to the heart of the Father, our adversary is defeated and the love of God floods the earth. Of all the prayers that have ever been prayed, we can know most assuredly that the Father is answering the prayer of His Son Jesus. Let's make it our goal to be a part of God's answer to that prayer.

The Father is going to answer His Son's prayer that we are made one.

Our mission, should we decide to accept it, is to walk in this message of God's covenant love. The revelation of God's love is released through us as His priests and we reconcile the world to the Father. As His children, our call is to bring all His creation into His kingdom of light. As we have been forgiven, we forgive others. As His priests we release His love, life, blessings, and truth to the nations.

2. The Covenant of the Fathers:
Man with Man (Mal. 2:10-12)

The second broken covenant is the relationship of mankind with their fellow man. Malachi cries out, *"Are we not all children of the same Father? Are we not all created by the same God? And yet we are faithless to each other, violating the covenant of our fathers?"* (Mal.2:10b NLT/TLB). Prior to Malachi's time,

God had established several covenants with His children: The covenants with Adam, Noah, Abraham, Moses and David. While Malachi is referencing all of them when he tells Israel they are *"violating the covenant of our fathers,"* his focus in this heart cry was on God's covenant with Noah.

The reason I say it is God's covenant with Noah, is because this is the covenant James refers to when he settled the dispute in Jerusalem. When James stood and gave his advice, all the Jews knew he was referring to the covenant and laws of Noah (Acts 15:13-29).[3] God's covenant with Noah also included the seed for the establishment of court systems and for our civil government (Gen. 9:5-6). This covenant was established by the Lord after the flood because of the violence of man toward his fellowman. This covenant was God's instruction manual on how to handle any future violence. Later, through Moses, the Lord would add more instructions (i.e., the Ten Commandments) to His covenants to show us how to live in Godly love with one another.

During the days of Malachi, God's people were destroying this covenant of peace, this covenant of their ancestors, by not abiding by His laws of love. They were dealing falsely with each other. God's people were *"breaking faith with one another, cheating each other; (they would all) despise his brother and break our promises to one another"* (Mal. 2:10 NIV/CEB/DRB/GNT; words in parenthesis mine). As *The Message Bible* puts it, ***"Why can't we get along? Why do we desecrate the covenant of our ancestors that binds us together?"***

The ultimate expression of Israel breaking this covenant of their fathers was manifested when the single men of Israel began to marry *"women who worship foreign gods"* (Mal. 2:11 GNT). The results were devastating. When the single men of Israel married women who worshipped demons, they were breaking God's instruction to be holy and separate unto Him. The Jews were to be a light to the world and draw the nations unto God.

The men of Malachi's day had it backwards. Instead of bringing men and women into the kingdom of God, they were leaving God and following after the false gods, the demons, of their neighbors. Paul sums it up well when he asks, *"How can Christ get along with the devil? How can the house of God get along with false gods? Do not be joined to them. I will be a Father to you. You will be My sons and daughters"* (2 Cor. 6:15-18 NLV). It's hard to have a peaceful home when one spouse worships demons.

The Example of King Solomon

To many it may seem an Israelite's marriage to a non-Israelite (or a Christian's marriage to a non-believer) is not such a big deal. After all, how does an Israelite marrying a woman who worships a false god affect this covenant of their fathers; how does it affect his nation? Here's how: when anyone, whether it's a man or woman, marries someone who worships false gods, that person will begin to follow those false gods (1 Kings 11:2). A perfect example of why this is a "big deal" in God's eyes can be seen in the life of King Solomon. *"Now King Solomon was a lover of women; (he) was obsessed with many foreign women"* (1 Kings 11:1 Mof/MSG).

In King Solomon's life we can see clearly the terrible devastation that follows when one marries someone who worships a false god. In direct defiance to God's word and warning that these women who worship false gods would steal Solomon's heart, he married them anyway (1 Kings

11:1-4). That was his first mistake, but he didn't stop there. Solomon did not marry women of holiness but women who worshipped "false gods," or to use the more precise term, demons. These wives stole Solomon's heart away from loving the Lord to the point he actually began to worship their demons as well (1 Kings 11:3-4). Not only did Solomon turn his heart from following the Lord, he built temples so his wives could worship their demons of Ashtoreth, Chemosh, and Molech (1 Kings 11:7, 33 NLT).[4]

The result of Solomon's rebellion opened the door to division, unlike any experienced before him. As the king, his sin resulted in one of the worst events in Israel's history when the nation was literally torn in two (1 Kings 11:11-13). As a result of King Solomon not keeping *"the covenant rules"* of the Lord (1Kings 11:10 NET), the nation of Israel was split into two distinct nations. This same spirit of division is released when we do not walk in the *"covenant of our fathers"* with the Lord.

We are seeing history repeat itself as nations are ripped asunder, if not in geographic terms, then in cultural, religious, and socio-economic terms. You and I, as the Lord's present day priests, are called to walk in His covenants. We must walk in them, if we want to restore His covenants in our nation and destroy the division we see all around us.

3. The Covenant of Marriage:

Man with Woman (Mal. 2:13-16)

The last covenant mentioned is the covenant of marriage. This spirit of division was attacking the homes of God's people. Not only were the single men marrying daughters who worshipped demons, but even the married men were now divorcing their godly Jewish wives so they could marry ungodly ones.

Malachi declares against the people of Israel, *"**Here's another thing you do:** you weep and moan, drowning the Lord's altar with tears, but He still refuses to look at the offering or receive favorably a gift from you. You cry out, 'Why doesn't the Lord, accept my worship?'"* (Mal. 2:13-14a REB/NLT; emphasis mine). Israel was so blind to their rebellion they couldn't comprehend why the Lord had turned His back on them. No wonder the Lord was rejecting their tear covered offerings; they were still in denial of their sin and rebellion.

Half of the marriages in America are ending in divorce, but research has shown that couples who practice their common faith have a more stable marriage relationship than those who don't. "People who reported that they never attended church were two to three times more likely to divorce than were people who reported attending church at least once a week."[5] God hates divorce because it is a vicious act of cruelty: *"**'I hate divorce'**, says the God of Israel. God-of-the-Angel-Armies says, **'I hate the violent dismembering of the 'one flesh' of marriage.'** "If a man divorces his wife', says the Lord God of Israel, **'he overwhelms her with cruelty'**"* (Mal. 2:16 MSG/REB; emphasis mine). God hates divorce. It's a cruel act of violence.

Research from the eighty-year study by *The Longevity Project* has shown that the effect of divorce is more detrimental to the children involved than the death of one of their parents. "Children from divorced families died almost five years earlier on average than children from intact families. Parental divorce, not parental death, was the risk. In fact, parental divorce during childhood was the single strongest social predictor of early death, many years into the future."[6] In other words, children are more capable of handling the death of a parent than they are of handling the divorce of their parents.

Take heart! If you have suffered through a divorce, the Lord is more than able to heal the hurt, pain, and rejection. This same study revealed that there were many children "who experienced the divorce of their parents and went on to live long lives."[7] By the blood of Jesus, those who have experienced the divorce of parents can live a long and healthy life.

God's grace heals, covers and protects children of divorce.

God's purpose in His covenant of marriage is to reproduce *"God-like children. What does He want? Godly children from your union"* (Mal. 2:15 NLV/NLT). This is how we affect not only our home but our nation. When homes are divided between worshipping the Lord and a false god, the children are divided and confused as well. They must decide who they will worship. Knowing this, it's easy to see why the evil one hates godly homes; they produce godly citizens. He has launched a concentrated crusade to destroy them.

God's Healing and Restoration After Divorce

To the suffering soul who has been cruelly torn apart by the unfaithfulness of your spouse, you can be healed and live again in joy and victory. You can, by God's grace, forgive and release that spouse from the injustices violently perpetrated against your mind and emotions and upon the hearts and minds of your children.

As you continually choose to forgive, you are keeping the enemy from placing you in the iron grip of unforgiveness and bitterness. You will rise above the horrible emotional storm unleashed against you. You will rise as a flame of fire in God's mercy soaring above your enemies in the spirit world. As you choose God's way of forgiveness, you will complete the healing process from your pain and grief.

When you choose to cry out your pain to the Lord, He will restore you and set you free. As you trust in Him, He will heal your emotional paralysis, free you from crippling bitterness, and enable you to move forward with Him in peace once more. As you praise Him in the midst of your hurts, He exchanges your sorrow with His joy. As you dance in faith before the Lord, you will tread upon your enemy and the pain your enemy tries to bring your way will be nothing but dust under your feet.

> *By the loving touch of Jesus, there is healing, comfort, and dancing for you.*

Jesus will draw near to you as you draw near to Him. Healing is for you. Comfort is for you. Dancing is for you.

To the one who was the covenant breaker, you too can be healed and restored. The love of God fully satisfies. Allow His forgiveness to cover you and begin to let Him remove and replace your human selfish love with His divine love. You were created for Him. His love will forgive, heal, restore, and rebuild you as well. The curse can be broken off of you and off of your children.

Everywhere Jesus went He released His forgiveness, love, and healing. He loved and forgave the woman at the well who had five husbands (John 4:4-42), and He loved and forgave the woman who was taken in adultery (John 8:1-11). This is the heart of grace and forgiveness of our God. Take this revelation, receive it deep into your soul, know that you have been forgiven, and move on in the grace of our God. Then as His priest, proclaim this forgiveness and healing of Jesus to the world.

The Spirit of Division

This same divisive spirit of covenant breaking which Malachi bemoans is at work today to destroy not only our homes and our country but our world. His attack of strife and division are seen by the wars raging in our homes to the wars raging among the nations (Jam. 4:1 NKJV). This demon uses any real or imagined inequities and differences to his advantage to drive and keep God's creation apart.

Jesus came to earth to break down all the man-made and demon-inspired walls of separation and restore unity within God's family. Paul tells us concerning Jesus, *"For He is [Himself] our peace—our bond of unity and harmony. He has made us both [Jew and Gentile] one [body], and* ***has broken down (destroyed, abolished) the hostile dividing wall we used to keep each other at a distance. He stopped the fighting between them by His death on the cross"*** (Eph. 2:14-15a Amp/MSG/NLV; emphasis mine). The Lord Jesus has come to demolish all these walls of separation and bring us back together in peace. This is the Good News of the New Covenant in Jesus.

There is a demon of strife and division whose goal is to destroy the Lord's covenant of harmony and unity. James tells us that this spirit wants everything to *"fall apart"* and everyone to be *"at each other's throats"* (Jam. 3:16 MSG). It is only in God's peace that we have peace with one another. James goes on to say, there are peacemakers who, *"will plant seeds of peace and reap a harvest of good things"* (Jam. 3:18 NLT). And when *"the God of peace"* arrives, satan is crushed under our feet (Rom. 16:20 Amp). There is not a better definition of peace than a picture of us by "the grace of our Lord Jesus Christ" walking on the head of the evil one.

Exactly how we are to do this is covered in the next two chapters of Malachi. In Malachi 3 and 4 God gives us His specific war songs to defeat this demonic spirit of division. As God's modern-day priests we are called to proclaim the message of His covenant, to stand in the gap, to sing His war songs and drive the hostile spirit of division away from God's children and out of our world. It's time to go to war!

Lord, cause us to release the healing of Your love and unity to this hate-and-division-filled world. Lead us to sing, shout, and blow our trumpets until the walls of racism, sexism, and materialism crumble, just like the walls of Jericho. Through human eyes, these walls seem formidable, but they will come down in Jesus' name. You've given us the power to demolish these walls, and the responsibility as His priests to do it. We'll sing and see true unity restored, by the blood of the Lamb.

Sing, shout, and blow your tumpets
until the walls of racism, sexism,
and materialism crumble!

ENDNOTES:

1. Guerrero, L. K., Anderson, P. A. & Afifi, W. A., *Close Encounters, Communication in Relationships, 3rd Edition.* 2011. SAGE Publications. Thousand Oaks, CA. p. 205.
2. See footnote to Mal. 1:1, the *New English Translation Bible.*
3. During the days of Noah, the earth had become so evil that the Lord had to destroy it. Only Noah found favor in the eyes of the Lord (Gen. 6:8). God started all over again with Noah and his family, and reestablished His covenant with him. Since the flood, we can all trace our ancestors back to Noah. We all fall under one of the three races from one of the three sons of Noah. (An excellent resource for this concept is *Noah's Three Sons: Human History in Three Dimensions* by Arthur C. Custance. © 1975 by the Zondervan Corporation.)

   We are all under the covenant of Noah, and we are all related as brothers and sisters coming from not only from Adam but also from the family of Noah. The Hebrew word for brother was also a term referring to nations that had formed a treaty or oath with each other. One example was the covenant that King Solomon and King Hiram of Lebanon made together (1 Kings 5:12). The Lord later judged Tyre when they broke this treaty. Tyre did not "remember their brotherly covenant" (Amp). The Lord called it their "Covenant of Brotherhood" (Amos 1:9 NKJV and NASB).

   One of the purposes of God's Covenant with Noah was to address man's relationship to man. Before the flood, the earth had been filled with so much evil and violence that there was no cure other than to destroy it and start over. To prevent this violence from recurring, the Lord addressed it by instructing mankind, through Noah, to establish a court system based upon on His laws. This is what the prohibition against murder in Genesis 9:5-6 is about. Here in Genesis chapter 9, in just a few words is our judicial system in seed form. Our government and court systems were further developed by the laws of the Lord that came through Moses. These laws instruct us on how to relate to one another, how to love our neighbor.

   In the Talmud the Jewish people had seven laws attributed to God's covenant with Noah. The Talmud (literally "to teach or instruct") is a collection of Rabbinic discussions on the Torah, the laws in the Old Testament, and on Jewish traditions, philosophy, and history. The covenant of Noah contained the seven laws of Noah also called the Noahide Laws. The seven laws were:

   1. Prohibition against idolatry
   2. Prohibition against murder
   3. Prohibition against theft

4. Prohibition against sexual immorality
5. Prohibition against blasphemy
6. Prohibition against eating flesh with blood in it
7. Establishing courts of law

Retrieved at: http://en.wikipedia.org/wiki/Noahide_laws.

The Jews believed these seven Noahide laws were for the Gentiles – because all of us come from the sons of Noah – while the Ten Commandments and other Old Testament laws were for the Jews.

4. It's interesting to note that the Lord lists three specific demons that Solomon worshiped, and as a result three specific adversaries (literally the Hebrew word satan) were raised up against Solomon: Hadad, Rezon, and Jeroboam (1Kings 11:14-42). Solomon's rebellion opened the door for these three spiritual adversaries to attack him and God's people. It is important to know the meanings of their names, and what they represent as our oppressors in the spiritual realm.

    1. Hadad means "mighty" and is the name of an ancient Semitic storm god. It comes from the root word "Adad" which means, "I shall move softly, I shall love".
    2. Rezon means "prince" and he "abhorred Israel" (1Kings 11:25 NASB). He hated (NLT) the children of Israel, he loathed (NET), despised (NRSV) and was cruel (BBE) to them.
    3. Jeroboam, son of Nebat, rebelled against the king (i.e. Solomon). Jeroboam means "The people will contend or strive against".

When we put all their names together we see that as a result of Solomon's sin and rebellion his adversaries were able to rise up against him and the nation of Israel. First, the enemy comes in softly and stealthy. With his "love" he woos you away from the Lord. Then once enslaved you are subjected to his cruelty and hatred. Last, the people who you are to lead rise up, fight, strive, and contend against you, to the point that your nation (or your home) is torn apart.

5. Guerrero p. 244.
6. Friedman, H. S. and Martin, L. R. *The Longevity Project*. A Plume Book. 2012. New York, N.Y. pg. 80.
7. *Longevity Project*, p. 85.

CHAPTER SEVENTEEN

The Great Reconciler

God Reconciles the Three Broken Covenants

"Bring all the tithes into the storehouse so there will be enough food in My temple. I will pour out a blessing so great you won't have enough room to take it in! Let Me prove it to you! I will rebuke the devourer for your sakes, nor shall the vine miscarry, abort or cast her fruit before the time in the field, says the Lord of hosts. You'll be voted 'Happiest Nation.' You'll experience what it's like to be a country of grace"
—Mal.3:10-12 NLT/YLT/NKJV/CEB/KJV/MSG

And the Answer Is ...

The first two chapters of Malachi are hard to read because they are an indictment against God's people for their transgression of broken covenants. The last two chapters of Malachi are a lot better, because they give us God's answers to exterminate this toxic demon of covenant breaking. The answers found in His war songs to sing over our church, our country, and our casa to tear down the walls of separation are His fire and soap to restore the covenant of man with God, His boundaries of love to rectify the covenant of man with man, and the tithes and offerings to heal the covenant of man with woman.

The War Song of God's Messenger for the Priestly Covenant

(MAL. 3:1-4)

"I am about to send My Messenger to clear a path before Me. Suddenly the Lord Whom you seek will come to His temple, even ***the Messenger of the Covenant****, in whom you delight. For He is like the metal-tester's* ***fire and laundry soap.*** *He will take His seat, testing and cleaning the sons of Levi,* ***burning away the evil*** *from them as from gold and silver, so that they may make offerings to the Lord in righteousness.* ***He will have a people who will offer Him pure hearts and a right spirit. This is what pleases the Lord.*** *These were the kinds of offerings the people of Judah and Jerusalem brought to Him in years gone by."*

—Mal.3:1-3 BBE/ARTB/REB/NKJV/BBE/CW; emphasis mine

This is the beautiful promise from the Father of sending His Messenger of the Covenant, Jesus, who will heal and restore all of our broken covenants. In the New Covenant of Jesus old things will pass away, and He will establish God's new things that will endure forever. This is the good news of Malachi: God's Messenger is the **Messenger of the Covenant**, and He's coming to straighten the broken covenants. The rough places made smooth and the crooked places made straight. When the Messenger comes, He brings two things with Him, fire and soap.

Most believers cringe or cry out "Oh, no, not that!" at the mere mention of God's fire. As one having firsthand experience with God's fire, I sympathize, but that's because we don't readily see the beauty of God's fire. When the gold or silver smith subjects his metal to the fire, does he think the metal is going to be destroyed? No. He knows the only things destroyed by the fire are any impurities that would weaken the metal. The metal comes out of the fire purified and stronger. (It's interesting to note that the Hebrew word for sword is *"chrev"* and literally means to be "greatly refined" [i.e. the best metal] or "great burning."[1] There are no swords of the Lord in His army without the fire of the Lord). Likewise, when you fill the washing machine with hot, soapy water and immerse your best (albeit soiled and stained) work shirt, do you think the soap is going to destroy the shirt? No. You know the only things destroyed by the soap are the dirt, grime, and sweat. Once that shirt goes through the washing machine, it comes out fresh, clean-smelling, like new again.

Without the fire of the Lord, there can be no sword of the Lord!

We need the fire of God to purify us, to burn out all the evil impurities, and we need His Holy Spirit soap to wash us as we daily walk in the world. We are totally clean and made completely righteous by the finished work of Jesus on the cross and by the washing of His blood; however, we need to be washed on a regular basis from the stains of the world. Jesus revealed this truth when He washed the disciples' feet. *"Jesus said to him, 'He who is bathed has need only to have his feet washed and* ***then he is clean all over: so now you're clean'"*** (John 13:10a NKJV/NLT/MSG; emphasis mine).

The War Song

There will be more word weapons for the war songs against division in the next chapter. But for now, here are a few verses to put to the music for a war song, as the Lord restores man's covenant with Him:

1. Come Lord Jesus, as the Messenger of the Covenant and heal our broken relationship with You and the Father. Come to Your temple and restore Your covenant, heal us and heal our land.

2. Lord, bring Your soap and fire, make us clean, pure and innocent again, inside and out.

3. Now that we're clean, as Your priests, we can offer up holy sacrifices of praise and worship that please and honor You. You hear our clean sacrifices and release Your blessings and protection on our homes and nation.

4. Now we can stand in the gap in His righteousness and in God's power drive off that covenant breaking demon.

We need to seek rather than shrink from the fire of God. We need to ask for a heaping scoop God's Holy Ghost laundry soap. We need to cry out in supplication not in terror for God to send His fire and His soap to purify our hearts and scrub us clean so that our priestly covenant is restored. Once we are restored and in right relationship with the Lord, we can boldly take our place in God's holy army, full of His authority and drive away the forces of division. O Lord, how we need Your soap and fire!

The War Song of God's Ordinances of Love for Our Neighbor

(Mal. 3:5-7a)

This war song addresses the divisions in our country that are the result of the broken *"covenant of our fathers."* Malachi declares to Israel that the breaking of the covenant of their fathers with their neighbors had loosed consequences upon their land. The Lord says,

> *"I will come as a Judge and appear before you in court, quick to testify against sorcerers, adulterers, and perjurers, against those who cheat the hired laborer of his wages, who wrong the widow and the fatherless, who thrust the foreigner aside and in this way show they do not fear Me, or* ***appreciate My covenant****"* (Mal.3:5 REB/NET/Mof/CW; emphasis mine).

The Hebrew view of a judge in this verse is different than our view today. The word for judge is *"dan"* and literally means "the door to life."[2] The judge did not come to condemn but was the protector and defender of the people. That is why they stood at the city gates (Prov. 31:23), they were there to judge and keep out any evil. Jesus is truly our Judge, our Defender, and our Doorway into life.

We saw how when King Solomon married women who worshipped false gods, he ended up not only permitting this demon worship by his wives, but he actually facilitated their demon-worship by building temples for them. The result was an excess of uncleanness and sin let loose by Solomon, as the king, over all the people of Israel. Similarly, in Malachi's day as the result of the men marrying these women of foreign gods, this breaking of God's "covenant of the fathers" released all types of ungodly behavior in their nation, and their homes were being divided.

You see, when one spouse or parent worships the Lord and the other spouse or parent worships a demon, the home and the children are bombarded by chaos and confusion. It's no wonder this disunity released the seven consequences listed above in Malachi 3:5. It's past time to restore God's covenant relationships, tear down the walls of separation, and bring God's healing and wholeness to the world.

The cure for this infection of strife and contention is the glorious ordinances (i.e., the boundaries of love) of the Lord. He declares to Israel:

> *"I, the Lord, do not change.* ***That is why the descendants of Jacob have not been destroyed.*** *Like many of your ancestors, you have turned against Me. From the days of your fathers* ***you have turned aside from My ordinances,*** *and have not kept them.* ***Return to Me and I will return to you"*** (Mal. 3:6-7a CW/HNV; emphasis mine).

There it is, in black and white. There is the basis for the song to sing to release God's ordinances of love and restore the covenant of man with man. We must return to the Lord and follow His ways, His ordinances of love. This verse may not seem like much at first glance, but as we study it more closely, we see it is a fire bomb of power and revelation for us to drop directly on the adversary.

The Hebrew word used here for ordinances [or statutes (RSV) or laws (NEB)] is *"choq"* and basically means a "limit or boundary."[3] The Hebrew word picture of this literally means "the fence that surrounds."[4] The spiritual principle of this word picture is that we are protected by God's "fence that surrounds" us as we walk in His ways of love.

There is so much misunderstanding among God's people concerning the laws, instructions, and ordinances of the Lord in the Old Testament. To attempt to cover this subject is beyond the scope of this book. Basically the laws and instructions of the Old Testament never did, and never will, bring salvation. Paul said, *"I am not one of those who treat the grace of God as meaningless.* ***For if we could be saved by keeping the law, then Christ died in vain****"* (Gal.2:21 NLT/NKJV; emphasis mine). Jesus did not die in vain; by His blood the whole world can receive His salvation (John 3:16-18). God's laws—or a better term would be instructions—of love do not save us. They are simply His road directions to guide His children, both the saved and the unsaved, on how to live together and walk on our road of life.

God's Old Testament instructions show the world how to live; they teach them how to walk until they come to Jesus. Paul explained it this way, He says, *"****The law was our guardian and teacher*** *to lead us until Christ came. So now through faith in Christ, we are made right with God. The Law was like those Greek tutors, with which you are familiar, who escorted children to school* ***and protect them from danger*** *or distraction, making sure the children will really get to the place they set out for"* (Gal. 3:24 NLT/MSG; emphasis mine). God's instructions and laws are like a guardian, like a fence, it protects the unsaved people in the world if they obey them. The law is like a teacher who shows the world how they should live and act on God's created planet ... until they come to Jesus.

Our salvation is not by the works of the law. It is only by faith in God's gift of grace manifested in the shed blood of Jesus (Eph. 2:5-8). Jesus says that we, as God's children of His New Covenant, should not only obey these rules of the Old Testament, but we are called to walk and live even beyond them (Matt. 5:17-48).

Here are a few blessings we can sing as we obey God's ordinances, as we walk behind His strong fence that surrounds and protects us from the enemy, as we recognize and live within His boundaries of love. As we walk in His ***choq***:

- **We are protected from disease for God is our Healer:**

  "And He said, 'if you listen carefully to the voice of the Lord your God and do what is right in His sight, obeying His commands and laws (**choq**)*,* ***then I will not put on you any of the diseases*** *that I brought upon the Egyptians;* ***for I am the Lord Who heals you****'"* (Ex.15:26 NLT/BBE; emphasis mine).

- **We live to a ripe old age in the Promised Land:**

  "Keep His decrees (**choq**) *and commands, which I am giving you today,* ***that it may go well with you and your children*** *after you, and* ***that you may live long*** *on the land which the Lord your God is giving you for all time."* (Deut.4:40 NIV/NASB; emphasis mine).

- **His ordinances become our songs:**

  "I set Your instructions (*choq*) ***to music and I sing them*** *as I walk this pilgrim way"* (Ps.119:54 MSG; emphasis mine).

- **The earth is filled with God's love and mercy:**

  *"**The earth, oh, Lord, is full of Your steadfast love and mercy**: teach me Your statutes (**choq**)" (Ps.119:64 NRSV/NKJV; emphasis mine).*

It is the Lord's desire to put His Spirit within us so that we will obey and walk in His ordinances. The Lord promises in His New Covenant to come that, *"I will give you a new heart and put a new spirit within you. I will take away your heart of stone and **give you hearts of compassion and obedience.** I will put My Spirit into your hearts and **He will enable you to keep My commands (choq)** and help you to carefully guard My law. Then you will live in the land I gave to your fathers; **you will be My people, and I will be your God**"* (Ezek.36:26-28 CW/NET; emphasis mine). We can't even walk in His ways until the Lord gives us a new heart. God saves us first and gives us a new heart; THEN we are able to follow His instructions and "walk in them" (Eph. 2:10).

The answer for our country and for the world is to follow the example of the Psalmist and sing the release of God's love over our nation as we keep His ordinances. I am not referring to legalism or the works of the law. God's ordinances are His boundaries for love. Love does have boundaries, you know. For example, you're called to honor and love your parents, but you should never marry your father or your mother (1 Cor. 5:1-5). Likewise, you're called to love your neighbor, but you don't commit adultery with them, and you certainly don't divorce your godly spouse just because you think you love someone else. God's limits and boundaries protect and guide our love. They make a beautiful fence for our protection.

GOD'S TEN COMMANDMENTS OF HIS COVENANT LOVE

These love ordinances have nothing to do with attaining our salvation. There never has been and there will never be a law that can save us. Let me repeat that: there is no law we can obey to bring us salvation. Our salvation is only by faith in the grace of God manifested in the shed blood of Jesus (Acts 15:11). We have read earlier what Paul said, but it is worth repeating. He declares, *"I am not one of those who treat the grace of God as meaningless.* ***For if we could be saved by keeping the law, then Christ died in vain"*** (Gal.2:21 NLT/NKJV; emphasis mine). Jesus did not die in vain; by Him the whole world can receive His salvation (John 3:16-18). God's laws of love do not save us; they are simply His directions to guide us.

When we operate in God's love we fulfill God's law: *"Owe no one anything, except to love one another, for* ***the one who loves his neighbor has fulfilled the law"*** (Rom. 13:8 NET; emphasis mine). To obey God's "covenant of the fathers" is to love our neighbors: *"Therefore, love is the fulfillment of the law"* (Rom. 13:10b NET). God doesn't want legalism in our life; He wants love.

LOVE GOD

All of this simply means that the Ten Commandments—literally the ten "words"—are God's ten words of love for us. Jesus revealed this truth when He declared that the greatest commandment was to, *"Love the Lord your God with all your heart, and with all your soul, and with all your mind, and with all your strength"* (Mark 12:30 NASB). We love God by following the instructions of the first four "words" (a/k/a first four commandments). We love God with all our heart by having no other gods before us (Ex. 20:3). We love Him with our soul by not making any graven images (Ex. 20:4-6). We love Him with all our mind by not taking His name in vain (Ex. 20:7). We love Him with all our strength by honoring His Sabbath day of rest (Ex. 20:8-11). God shows us clearly and simply how we can practically express our love to Him without any confusion on our part.

Love Our Neighbor

Jesus said the second greatest commandment was also an instruction of love: *"And the next one is just like it. You should love and value your neighbor as much as you love and value yourself"* (Matt. 22:39 CW). Our first and closest neighbors are our father and mother. We start with loving and honoring them so we may live long in the land (Ex. 20:12). We also love our neighbors by following the rest of God's ten "words." We love our neighbors by not killing them, not stealing from them, not lying to them, not committing adultery with their spouse, and not coveting what they have (Ex. 20:12-17). This is how we fulfill the second command of Jesus. As Paul tells us, *"For the commandments, 'Do not commit adultery, do not murder, do not steal, do not covet,' (and if there is any other commandment) are summed up in this, 'Love your neighbor as yourself'"* (Rom. 13:9 NET). The last six commands show us "how" to love our neighbors.

These are the ordinances, the boundaries that we, as God's children, are to follow to show our love to our fellow men and women in our nation. It's all very plain and simple. What is also very plain and simple and has been proven repeatedly through history is that if we don't stay within these boundaries, the results are sorcerers, murderers, adulterers, liars, and cheaters who are oppressing each other.

Jesus said we are to *"love others as much as you love yourself"* (Matt. 22:39 CEV). This law to love our neighbor and the law to love God are the bases for *"all the Law of Moses and the books of the Prophets"* (Matt. 22:40 CEV). When we love we fulfill all of God's prophetic words and laws. Living in divine love by obeying God's ordinances of love is the only answer to solve the discord and division in our land and restore the covenant of man with man. Believers are called by the Lord to walk in love not only with our fellow brothers and sisters in the Lord but with the whole world. The world must see the love of the Father in our lives or they will never see Jesus.

The War Song of God to Restore Unity in the Home

(Mal.3:7b-12)

Here the Lord gives us His solutions to sing over our families being torn apart by strife, division, and divorce. It's the song of His tithes and offerings. The Lord declares,

> *"Begin by being honest. Do honest people rob God? But you rob Me day after day. You ask, 'How have we robbed You?' You are robbing Me of the offerings and of the ten percent that belongs to Me that's how. That's why your whole nation is under a curse. I challenge you to put Me to the test.* ***Bring the entire ten percent into the storehouse*** *so there will be enough food in My temple. 'If you do,' says the Lord Almighty, '****Then I will open the windows of heaven*** *for you. I will pour out a blessing so great you won't have enough room to take it in! Try it! Let Me prove it to you! Your crops*

> *will be abundant, and* ***I will rebuke the devourer*** *for your sakes, so that he will not destroy the fruit of your ground,* ***nor shall the vine miscarry, abort, or cast her fruit*** *before the time in the field,' says the Lord of hosts. Every one of every nation will talk about how I have blessed your wonderful land. You'll be voted 'Happiest Nation.' You'll experience what it's like to be* ***a country of grace.*** *I, the Lord All-Powerful, have spoken"* (Mal.3:10-12 NLT/YLT/NKJV/CEB/KJV/MSG/CEV; emphasis mine).

In case you don't know it, God doesn't need our money. He's not short on cash. He doesn't need to get it, but we definitely need to give it. When we give our tithe we are recognizing Who our Master is. The very act of giving money away frees us from any stronghold money attempts to have upon us. The act of giving our tithe results in money not lording over us, instead we lord over it. The Hebrew word for tithe (or tenth) is *asar* and literally means to "greatly recognize your Prince." In other words, "who you tithe to is your leader."[5] Our tithe (ten percent) and offerings (extra gifts given over the tithe) are usually given in the form of money. The reason for this is that our money is a reflection of our life because it takes our time and the work of our hands to produce it. By giving our money, we are giving our life to the Lord, our Prince, and giving support to His people.

The Tithe-Home Connection

There is a connection between the tithe and our home and children being protected. The Lord tells us to bring all the tithes and offerings to His house. What happens when we do this is that the Lord releases His blessings:

1. The curse over us, our children, our business and our nation is removed.

2. God opens the windows of heaven and we are blessed.

3. The devourer is rebuked for our sake off of our businesses and homes.

4. Every nation will see God's blessings on us and call us the 'Happiest nation,' a country full of God's grace.

Giving of our tithe and offerings is the divine, appointed key that unlocks heaven's windows of blessing. Our tithing breaks open the floodgate of God's goodness toward us. When we tithe we obey God's ordinance to love Him with our very life, and in so doing, we remove any hindrance, any obstacle between us and God's immeasurable blessings. Because God will not violate His own ordinances, our obedience in tithing allows Him to pour out His blessings, His "overflowing blessing" (RSV) upon us and our homes. There will be so much we "won't have room enough to take it in" (TLB). In the past where a curse had slithered in, now a flood of God's blessings washes the curse away.

As we open our pocketbooks and give our tithe, God opens up His windows and gives us His blessings.

The other great blessing is the second half of God's promise to "rebuke the devourer." God's rebuke applies to both the physical and spiritual realms. He will not only rebuke the devourer from our business and labor, He will also rebuke the devourer from our family in the Spirit. Look closely at His promise.

> *"'Your crops will be abundant, and I will rebuke the devourer for your sakes, so that he will not destroy the fruit of your ground,* ***nor shall the vine miscarry, abort or cast her fruit*** *before the time in the field,' says the Lord of hosts"* (Mal.3:11 NLT/YLT/NKJV/CEB/KJV; emphasis mine).

The Hebrew word for the phrase "cast her fruit" is *shakol,* and it means "to make childless, to kill its children, to rob of children, to show barrenness, to suffer an abortion or to miscarry." [6] The Lord is not just talking about fruitful vines in the natural here; He is also referring to our wives and our children. In the Psalms we are told that our *"wife will be like a* ***fruitful vine*** *in the very heart of your home. And look at all those children! They will sit around your table as vigorous and healthy as young olive trees"* (Ps. 128:3 NET/NKJV/NLT; emphasis is mine). The Lord is talking about protecting our family! There is no more abhorrent devourer of families than the spirit of division and divorce. That is why the tithe is so important to our families. As we return to Him with our tithes and offerings, He will protect our home, our children, and our entire family.

Research conducted on families who attend church weekly and give their entire tithe would reveal some very blessed homes.

Remember the research that showed families who attend church at least once a week are less likely to divorce? What would they find if research was conducted on families that not only attended church weekly, but also gave their entire ten percent? They would discover some very blessed homes.

Tithing and God's Richness

Tithing releases the blessings of God on our home. The word for tithe *asar* ("to greatly recognize your Prince"), is closely related to the Hebrew word for rich or prosperous. The Hebrew word for prosperous is *"asheer"* and literally means "to see the Prince."[7] As Dr. Seekins states, "We cannot recognize the Prince without giving, we cannot recognize the Prince without prospering."[8] As we tithe we prosper spiritually and financially in our home and in our business.

Jesus explains it this way, *"A curse is on you Pharisees! For you are careful to tithe your mint and rue and all manner of herbs, but you completely forget about justice and the love of God.* ***You should tithe, yes,*** *but* ***you should not leave undone*** *the more important things of the law like* ***fairness and compassion and commitment"*** (Luke 11::42 and Matt. 23:23 NLT/MSG/KJV; emphasis mine). Jesus says, yes, we should tithe, but a true tithe is not just giving our money. It is giving the more important things such as the mercy, grace, and love of God to our neighbors.

According to research in 2007, the average believer gives only 2.56 percent of their income. It is estimated that if the believers in the US gave their full ten percent over 161 billion dollars would be given![9] Can you imagine what would happen if everyone gave their full ten percent? The gates of heaven would be flung open and a tidal wave of God's blessings would cover our nation. Many government entitlement programs would be closed down overnight. We simply wouldn't need them. The church would become the true source of blessing to the world, as God intends.

Sing this war song of the blessings and power of the Lord's tithes and offerings. Sing so the children of God receive this revelation of God's blessings on our tithe that will restore the covenant of man with woman, protecting our homes and our children from the vicious spirit of division. When we fully grasp this revelation, God will pour out so much of His love that we won't be able to contain it. We'll have to keep giving the blessings away, to make room for more.

The result will be that the world will call our nation blessed and give our God glory. *"You'll be voted* ***'Happiest Nation.'*** *You'll experience what it's like to be* ***a country of grace****"* (Mal. 3:12 MSG; emphasis mine). Give to the Lord so our nation will once again be a fully blessed nation, a happy nation, because we are obeying God's grace of giving.

Open our eyes, oh, Lord, and let us see the glory of Your fire and soap. Purge out our iniquities. We sing in earnest, "Send Your Fire!" Wash us with Your Holy Ghost soap so we'll be fresh and pure again. Clean out the grime and sweat and stains of the world. Once Your cleansing is complete, then as Your priests, we can offer up acceptable, holy sacrifices to You. Then the covenant of man with God will be restored. Then we will stand in the gap for the nations to restore the covenants of man with man through Your ordinances of love and man with woman through your laws of giving. Then we will see the evil spirits of division demolished!

As we give God our tithe
He gives our homes His protection.

ENDNOTES:

1. Seekins, 210.
2. Seekins, 175.
3. Retrieved at http://classic.net.bible.org/strong.php?id=02706.
4. Seekins, pgs. 10-11.
5. Seekins, p.215.
6. Retrieved at http://classic.net.bible.org/strong.php?id=07921.
7. Seekins, p. 195.
8. Ibid.
9. http://www.sj-r.com/features/x1914253234/Study-shows-Americans-tithe-just-2-56-percent. "Are U.S. churchgoers stingy?" That's one possible conclusion from a newly updated report that shows if parishioners tithed the biblically recommended 10 percent of their income — instead of their current 2.56 percent — an extra $161 billion would be flowing to charity. The report, published by Illinois-based research firm Empty Tomb Inc., also found that congregations continue to keep more money for their own needs instead of "benevolences" beyond the four walls of a church.

   "Money is training wheels," said Sylvia Ronsvalle, executive vice president of Empty Tomb Inc. "If we're not faithful in giving, how will we see the church grow?" Ronsvalle, along with her husband, John, co-wrote the "State of Church Giving through 2007: What Are Our Christian Billionaires Thinking — Or Are They?" The annual report examines financial trends in Christian churches. The Ronsvalles found some room for optimism. Churchgoers, at 2.26 percent given to charity, outpaced the general population, which gave 1.8 percent. Nearly two-thirds of all U.S. charitable donations were funneled through churches or religious institutions."

CHAPTER EIGHTEEN

18

God's Dancing Calves

God's Dancing Calves Smash Divorce and Division

"'And you will go out and dance like calves released from the stall. On the day when I act, you will tread upon the wicked. They'll be nothing but dust under your feet,' says the Lord Almighty"

—Mal. 4:2b-3 NLV/NET/NLT/MSG

The Lord Adds to His Solutions Against Division

As the Lord concludes His prophetic word to Malachi, He repeats His solutions to the attack of division and covenant breaking. Remember, when the Lord repeats something, it is an indication that it is very important and that He is sure to bring it to pass. In the final chapter of

Malachi He adds something extra to each one of His divine solutions. His additions are:

1. He adds His **oven** to His fire and soap for His church, to heal the covenant of man with God.
2. He adds His **statutes and judgments** to His instructions for the country, to heal the covenant of man with man.
3. He adds **the coming of the spirit of Elijah** to His tithes and offerings for the home, to heal the covenant of man with woman.

To Restore the Covenant of Levi God Adds His Oven

(Mal. 4:1-3)

In Malachi 4 the Lord adds His oven to His fire and soap to rectify the broken covenant of man as God's priests. The Lord God says,

> *"The day is coming; it is burning* ***like an oven, like a furnace****, all the men of pride and all who do evil will be burned up like stubble and it shall not leave them with any roots. But to you who give worship to My name the Sun of Righteousness will rise with healing in His wings; My saving power will rise on you like the sun and bring healing like the sun's rays. You will go forth, and gambol, playing like calves released from the stall,* ***jumping, leaping and skipping: bursting with energy, you will go out and dance like calves loosed from the yoke****, free and happy, grown up, full of food"* (Mal.4:1-3 ASV/NKJV/BBE/CCB/CEB/CJB/GNT/MSG/NRSV/NLV/NLT/WYC/BBE/MLB; emphasis mine).

The Lord declared this same principle of His cleansing fire through the prophet Zechariah:

> *"I will refine the one-third like silver.* ***I will purify them with fire as men purify gold.*** *They will call on My name and I will answer them. I will say, 'These are My people,' and they will say, 'This is our God'"* (Zech.13:9 CW; emphasis mine).

Many Bible commentators say this "day of fire" refers to the "day of the Lord" at the end of time, but as most believers will attest, there can be many times of God's baptism of fire. The truth is we need many days of God's Holy Ghost fire to purge His people now, not just at the end of the world. So to complete His work of restoring the covenant of Levi, the Lord adds His Holy Ghost oven to His soap and fire. As with the fire, the oven of God is beneficial, it is not an object of terror. This kiln completes the Lord's cleansing, purifying work, preparing us to take our place as God's priests. After God's oven, we come out complete, well done.

The best picture of God's "shake and bake oven" in action is found in the story of Daniel's three friends being thrown into the fiery furnace by Nebuchadnezzar king of Babylon. What happens to them is exactly what happens to us whenever we are placed in God's oven, also known as His baptism of fire. The results of our time in the oven are:

1. Our adversaries, not us, are the ones burned up (Daniel 3:23 and 48).
2. Our bonds, not us, are destroyed (Daniel 3:92 and 94).
3. We have a great time of prayer, praise, and worship (3:24-90).
4. Jesus shows up and joins in our worship (Daniel 3:49-50, 92).

5. Rulers receive a revelation of God and His power (Daniel 3:94-96).
6. Rulers praise and proclaim the power of our God (Daniel 3:98-100).
7. We get promoted (Daniel 3:97, Dan. 3:1-100 NETS).[1]

Many of God's people are singing, "Lord send your fire!" Not many are singing, "Lord, send your oven!"

God's children have no reason to fear His oven. Quite the contrary, it's the very means by which we are set free from fear. Through the work of His oven, the power of the Lord is manifested, God is magnified, and we get promoted in His kingdom. This forge burns up any chaff (i.e. "wood, hay and stubble"; see 1 Cor. 3:12-13 KJV) in our life, to make us vessels fit for the Master's use.

To Be Blessed and Happy Means "Fire on the Head"

The Hebrew word for blessed and happy is *ashar* and literally means "fire on the head."[2] In Dr. Seekins' book he has a picture of the 120 believers in the upper room when the Holy Spirit fell and baptized them with the flames of fire on their heads (Acts 2:1-4). That is a beautiful picture of being in God's oven. Dr. Seekins states, "Fire on the head can symbolize both the presence of God or facing the uncomfortable realities of life."[3] Then again, with the fire of God on our head we're more than able to face any of the uncomfortable realities of life. Believers need to ask for God's fire to clean us up *now,* when we may face some of those "uncomfortable realities of life," rather than on the last day.

We Dance in Victory over the Wicked One

Emerging from God's oven, purified by His merciful fire, with the tethers of sin in ashes, we claim even more blessing. You see, after we go through God's oven the Lord tells us that for those *"who fear My name, the Sun of Righteousness will rise with healing in His wings"* (Mal.4:2a NLV/NLT), and that we will *"go forth and skip about, bursting with energy, free, leaping with joy and* ***dance like calves released from the stall****"* (Ma.4:2b NET/NLT/MSG/NLV; emphasis mine). In God's life-giving oven, we learn to really dance just as these three friends of Daniel were likely dancing with Jesus in their fiery oven. At the end of this chapter we cover God's revelation, that when we dance, we reverse the curses oppressing our families and our nation.

God Adds His Law and Judgments to His Ordinances

(Mal. 4:4)

Next, to restore our covenant of love with our neighbors, our fellow brothers and sisters, both the saved and the unsaved, the Lord adds His law and judgments to go with His ordinances.

> *"**Remember** the **Law** (torah) of Moses, My servant, which I commanded him in Horeb for all Israel, with the **statutes** (choq) and **judgments** (misphat) for right living. They are for all people to obey"* (Mal.4:4 NKJV/MSG/CW; emphasis mine).

In Malachi 3 the Lord mentions only His *"choq"* (His boundaries) to restore our covenant with our neighbors. Now in Malachi 4, He adds His law—the Hebrew word *'torah'*—which refers to "God's instructions, prophetic teachings, and instructions on how to live during the age of the Messiah."[4] The word *torah* is comprised of four letters. They are:

- ***"tav"*** which means "the sign, the covenant, or the cross;"
- ***"vav"*** which means "hook or nail;"
- ***"reysh"*** which means "head, man or leader;"
- ***"hey"*** which means "behold" or "what comes from,"

When we put these all together we find that *torah* means "**Behold, what comes from the man nailed to the cross.**"[5] This powerful revelation can change our whole view of God's instructions and guidance. Jesus, the Man nailed to the cross, declares the love of the Father to His children. He declares His love laws, prophesying how we are walking in love, now during the age of the Messiah.[6]

Since we are now living in the age of the Messiah; therefore, we must follow His instructions of love given to us that we find in His law, His *torah*, the "behold what comes from the man nailed to the cross." It is Christ's absolute demonstration of love we behold in the *torah*. As we follow God's glorious instructions of love in the *torah*, we reap its blessings and eternal promises. One of those promises is *"Great peace have those who love Your law (torah); and nothing causes them to stumble"* (Ps.119:165 NKJV). The fruit of loving God's *torah* is not just a little peace but a great peace, and there is *"no stumbling around in the dark for them"* (MSG).

God's Misphat Destroys Chaos

The other addition to God's *choq* and *torah* is His judgment. It is the Hebrew word *misphat* and refers to the "act of deciding a case, the process and procedures performed before the judges, the case presented for judgment, the sentence or decision of judgment, and the execution and time of the judgment."[7] Whew! That's a mouthful! Are there any lawyers in the house to explain all of that? With *misphat* we have our whole judicial system covered from beginning to end.

Looking at the Hebrew word *misphat,* we discover its importance to us in our battle with the wicked one. Every good warrior knows the importance of flanking the enemy in order to gain victory. Take a look at the word picture for *misphat. Misphat* is comprised of four Hebrew letters:

- ***"mem"*** which means "water or chaos;"[8]
- ***"sheen"*** which means "to devour or destroy;"[9]
- ***"pey"*** which means "to speak;"[10]
- ***"tet"*** which means "to surround."[11]

When we put this all together we find that God's *misphat* are the words of the Lord that when we **"speak (them) we surround and destroy chaos."** Revelation like that makes me feel like dancing! As we obey and speak these words of God (*misphat*) we destroy chaos in our land.

So in summary, the *choq* refers to the Lord's boundaries, His limits, which the Israelites crossed over when they married women who worshipped demons. These boundaries are like kindergarten rules for us to follow, as though we were little children. When our mothers would admonish us, "Don't play in the street" or "Don't talk to strangers" she was putting boundaries on our activities in love. But we are not called to stay in kindergarten forever. We are to move on to high school level, the *torah,* with God's prophetic teaching and instructions on the age of the Messiah. Even as teenagers our parents would say, "Be home by such and such a time." Those were instructions given to us, again, for our well-being.

When we leave home as adults and go to college or step into the business arena, working a job day to day, we need the *misphat,* the whole judicial system and counsel of God to come into play. We are no longer children who have to be instructed or teenagers who have to be watched over. We now are adults who must assume the responsibility for prudence, making wise choices, weighing all that we have learned from *choq* and *torah* and acting with wisdom, forethought, and determination. We have a lot to learn, church, and a long way to go.

WE NEED GOD'S HOLY GHOST LAWYERS

From a practical standpoint, God is calling for more of His children to step into the legal arena and stand up for His righteous laws of love that give godly guidance and protection for the nations. Some may believe I have gone too far here, and that I am getting too extreme with too much detail about God's laws of love. Not so. In fact, the Lord is calling many of His children to become godly lawyers and retake the judicial and civil arenas in our nation, to step into the legal arena and become lawyers, judges, mayors, governors, congressmen and women, senators, and presidents. Too long this area has been ruled by the evil one.

Some would argue and say, "We don't need the laws of the Old Testament." Then how do we respond to Paul's exhortation? In Paul's letter to the church at Corinth he exhorts us:

> *"Do you dare, when you have a dispute with another member, go to a heathen judge to arbitrate between you instead of taking the problem to fellow believers?* ***Don't you know that God's people will one day judge the world?*** *So if you are to judge the whole world, don't you think you should be able to judge the small problems within your own congregation?* ***Do you realize that someday you'll be asked to judge angels?*** *So surely you can judge the ordinary things in this life. If you have problems, why do you depend on nonmembers who know nothing about what we believe or on judges of ill repute to settle disputes for you? If you think I'm trying to shame you, you're right.* ***Surely there is at least one person in your congregation wise enough to judge such matters.*** *Why should brothers go to court to have their little differences settled by a heathen judge?"* (1Cor.6:1-6 CW/NCV; emphasis mine).

If we are to one day judge the world and the angels, what will we use as our standard to go by? I rest my case. No one is better suited to begin the restoration of the covenant of man with man than the Spirit guided believer who understands the nation's judicial system as well as God's *misphat.* One day God is going to call us to judge the world and the angels. The current-day church is ill-equipped to fulfill that portion of our destiny. An entire book could be written concerning God's laws and regulations of love. It's beyond the scope of this book to study these in detail except to stress that I am not talking about legalism or the works of the flesh and religion. I am talking about the ordinances of God's love. The laws of God that only love can fulfill. We are saved by the grace of God in the blood of Jesus. It's only after we're saved that we can obey His laws of love. It's up to God's people to restore His peace and drive chaos out of our nation. What are we waiting for?

Don't you know, one day God's people will judge the world; one day we'll be called upon to judge the angels.

A CITY ON A MOUNTAIN

Any nation that follows God's laws of love becomes a beacon of light to the other countries of the world. Jesus said, *"You are the light of the world. You cannot hide a city that is on a mountain. Men do not light a lamp and put it under a basket. They put it on a table so it gives light to all in the house. Let your light shine in front of men. Then they will see the good things you do and honor your Father Who is in heaven" (Matt.5:13-16 NLV).* This was true for Israel, who was blessed with peace as long as she followed God's love laws with each other and with the nations around her.

America, was also founded on God's love laws, and experienced God's peace and prosperity for a season. Our nation has blatantly strayed from the Lord and His ways. To restore the covenant of our fathers we must follow God's ordinances of love toward our fellow man, fix our eyes on the love of Christ demonstrated on the cross, and decree God's wisdom to surround and destroy chaos. When we do this, the Lord will cast out discord and restore His blessings of peace and unity to our land.

God Promises the Coming of Elijah

Mal. 4:5-6

Last, to restore the marriage covenant the Lord adds to the blessings of His tithes and offerings the promise of the coming of Elijah.

> *"Behold* ***I will send you Elijah the prophet*** *before the coming of the great and dreadful day of the Lord. This message will be taken to the whole world. It will knit My people together, and* ***the hearts of the fathers will turn in love to their children and the hearts of the children will turn in love to their fathers.*** *He will lead children and parents to love each other more, so that when I come, I won't bring doom to the land"* (Mal.4:5-6a KJV/CW/CEV; emphasis mine).

The spirit of Elijah is coming to restore and reconcile the hearts of parents back to their children and the hearts of children back to their parents. Elijah must come because the spirit of Elijah prepares the way for Jesus, and it is the spirit of a father's heart.

As Elijah was preparing to leave and be with the Lord, He asked his pupil, Elisha, what he desired. Elisha asked to be given a double portion of the anointing which had been imparted to Elijah (2 Kings 2:9). First, we notice that Elijah asked Elisha if he wanted anything, because Elijah wanted to bless Elisha. This is a father's heart: Elijah longed to leave a blessing, an inheritance for his son in the Spirit (Prov.

13:22). Second, he did not rebuke Elisha for what could be taken as a prideful and selfish request. It was actually neither.

Sure, from our human viewpoint, the pupil asking to be twice as great as the teacher may seem somewhat arrogant and puffed up, but before casting that judgment, we need to ask from where came such an idea. This idea came first from Elijah, who placed it in Elisha's heart while Elijah was training him. Notice that Elijah didn't discourage Elisha when he asked for this double portion. Elijah simply said that this was a hard request because, *"You have asked me for something I can't give you."* This is something *"only the Lord can give"* to you (2 Kings 2:9-10 NIRV). The spirit of Elijah is the spirit of a father's and mother's heart. Every parent's heart wants their children to be doubly blessed by God.

Jesus, of course, also has a father's heart. In fact, He has *the* Father's heart. He spoke to His followers, *"I say to you, he who believes in Me, the works that I do, he will do also; and* ***greater works than these he will do****, because I go to the Father"* (John14:12 NASB; emphasis mine). The heart of a parent wants their children to go farther, higher, and deeper in their walk with the Lord. When the Lord promised the coming of the spirit of Elijah, He was promising the coming of the spirit of a father's heart on the parents. Let's sing the war song of the Lord pouring out the spirit of Elijah's father's heart upon our homes (Mal. 4:5-6a).

The spirit of Elijah comes to prepare the way for Jesus to come into our marriage.

The covenant of marriage is restored and our children are protected by the power of God's blessings on our tithes and offerings. By giving our tithes and offerings in faith, we set in motion God's word and power to rebuke the devourer from our home. Then God sends the spirit of Elijah to unite the hearts of families and restore harmony in the home. Praise God for His grace that brings His healing touch of reconciliation to our homes. We sing our war songs in faith, releasing that divine grace that restores one home at a time, one city at a time, one state at a time, and one nation at a time, until the end of time when all people and all nations will confess that Jesus Christ is Lord, to the glory of God our Father.

MALACHI COMPLETES THE OLD TESTAMENT

In Malachi, the curse on the land brought about by the broken covenants is removed as God's children walk in His laws of love for each other. As we obey God's *torah,* (i.e., what comes from the Man nailed on the cross), His instructions of love, the dissension and division that has been plaguing the world, will be eradicated. It will all be swept away when we learn to walk by the grace of God in covenant fellowship and love with our neighbor.

As the last book in the Old Testament, Malachi ties up the Old Testament and brings it to an anticipative conclusion. What was started and lost in the garden in Genesis, we are promised in Malachi will be restored at the coming of Jesus, God's Messenger of the Covenant. The New Covenant in Jesus will restore all covenants that have been broken.

When Adam and Eve sinned, breaking man's covenant with God, the relationship they enjoyed with Him was severed. No longer would they commune with God in the garden He'd prepared specifically for them. No longer would He provide for their needs and comforts (Gen. 3:22-24). The spirit of division had entered the realm of man.

As a result of Adam and Eve's broken covenant with God, the spirit of division and strife entered their marriage covenant. Now, instead of walking in unity with each other, the curse of rebellion causes the wife to "desire" her husband. This is not a pleasurable desire. It's the Hebrew word that means to manipulate and control. As the NET Bible puts it, *"You will want to control your husband"* (Gen. 3:16). And instead of loving and serving his wife, as Jesus loves and serves His bride, the husband *"will dominate"* (MLB) or *"lord it over"* her (Gen.3:16 JB). This is the sad result of our broken relationship with the Father. Lord, send Your Messenger of the Covenant and heal our marriage relationships in Jesus.

A broken covenant with the Lord brings strife and division into our home.

Once the spirit of division had infiltrated the home, the spirit of death was not far behind. It began when Cain, their oldest son, in a fit of demonic rage and jealousy, sacrificed his younger brother, Abel. You see, Cain had given himself over to the wicked one (1 John 3:12). He was warned by God, *"Sin is a demon lurking at the door.* ***His desire is toward you****, like a crouching beast hungering for you; yet you can be its master"* (Gen.4:7 NAB/JB/KJV; emphasis mine). The Hebrew word used here for sin's desire for Cain is the same word used about Eve's desire to control Adam.

In demonic anger and jealousy, Cain *"killed his brother by severing his jugular vein"* (1 John 3:12 Wuest). Cain did not use a rock or club like some caveman to murder Abel. He slit his throat. This gory detail, left out of our Sunday school classes about this tale, is important. This is the exact method the Israelites used to sacrifice their lambs and bulls to the Lord. Cain was so demonized he was basically saying, "All right, God! You want a sacrifice of blood? Well, here he is!" and slit his brother's throat. The demonic spirits of division and violence spread from there, infecting the earth to the point that the Lord had to send a flood to stop them. Through the flood, God baptized the whole world and started over with Noah and his family.

In Genesis 3:14 (NKJV), before banishing Adam and Eve from the garden and before separating them from His presence, God cursed the serpent. *"Because you have done this, you are cursed more than all cattle, and more than every beast of the field; on your belly you shall go, and you shall eat dust all the days of your life."* So, the serpent was charged to eat dust. But wait, snakes don't eat dust. They eat small animals – mice, rats, hamsters, and the like. So what's this "dust" the Lord is talking about? We find out what was the serpent's dust food in Verse 19 when the Lord declared that Adam was now dust (Gen.3:19). When mankind does not walk with the Lord and in His ways, man becomes as dust and is open game to the serpent. Mankind has been the devil's dust food ever since the fall. But now, because of Christ, all that has changed.

EVERYBODY DANCE NOW!

Through Malachi, God tells us exactly how to defeat the serpent:.

> *"'And you will go out and* ***dance like calves released from the stall****. On the day when I act, you will tread upon the wicked. They'll be nothing but* ***dust under your feet****,'*

says the Lord Almighty" (Mal. 4:2b-3 TLB/NET/ NLT/MSG; emphasis mine).

When we sing our war songs and come out of God's oven as God's dancing calves, the tables are turned. Now, God tells us, the wicked shall be **"dust under your feet"** (Mal. 4:3 BBE). We trample on that serpent, the wicked one like frolicking calves, reversing the curse. No longer are we the dust. Instead, we are trampling the wicked one, who is nothing but dust under our feet. The hooves of God's calves leaping for joy destroy the devil and all of his works of evil.

This is fulfilled in the New Testament. Paul tells the believers in Rome, *"The God of peace* ***will soon crush satan under your feet****"* (Rom. 16:20a NLT emphasis mine). The Message Bible here says it this way: *"And before you know it,* ***the God of peace*** *will come down on satan with both feet, stomping him into the dirt.* ***Enjoy the best of Jesus!"*** (emphasis mine). Believers, let's sing the war songs of God and dance like God's bounding calves. As we dance like calves released from the Lord's wonderful oven, the God of grace crushes our enemy under our feet, and we enjoy the peace of God and the best of Jesus. So sing and dance and have the Lord God release HIs peace in our homes, in our churches, in our cities, and in our nation.

When we dance we reverse the curse over us, our homes, and our nation.

There are so many reasons for us to sing and dance:

1. When we dance the Lord releases His power through us and the wicked one is defeated (Mal.4:2-3).

2. When we dance the curse is reversed. The evil one now becomes dust and we dance on him (Mal.4:2-3).

3. When we dance religious spirits are exposed and made barren (2 Sam. 6:20-23).

4. When we dance with the high praises of God in our mouth we bind up the demonic spirits attempting to manipulate our leaders (Ps.149:1-9).

As we walk in this New Covenant of grace, we are sealed by faith in Jesus' finished work on the cross. *"Christ has truly redeemed us from the curse of the law, being made a curse for us. That the blessings of Abraham might come on the Gentiles through Jesus Christ; that we might receive the promise of the Spirit through faith"* (Gal.3:13-14 KJV). The war songs transform the atmosphere from darkness and judgment to the light and grace that enable us to walk in God's love. We sing so that others may become the adopted sons and daughters of God and join in our song and dance. It's time for us to dance! Everybody dance now!

Lord put us in Your oven! We'll come out well done as Your complete and finished work. We emerge as Your Dancing Calves trampling the evil one as dust under our feet. The curse is reversed, Your love laws are obeyed, homes are healed, the spirit of Elijah prepares the way for Jesus, Your Messenger of the covenant, Your covenants are restored, and our world becomes like Eden again. We enjoy the best of Jesus!

Everybody Dance Now!

ENDNOTES:

1. These notes are taken from the New English Translation of the Septuagint (NETS) of Daniel Chapter 3 which has 100 verses not 30. For those who do not accept the Septuagint, you can still use all of these promises, except #3. Here is a comparison of the Septuagint verses from NETS with KJV in Daniel 3:

NETS	KJV
1. 23 & 48	22
2. 92 & 94	25
3. 24-90	No Mention
4. 49-50 & 92	24-25
5. 94-96	27-28
6. 98-100	29
7. 97	30

2. Seekins, p. 150.
3. Ibid.
4. Retrieved at http://www.blueletterbible.org/lang/lexicon/lexicon.cfm?Strongs=H8451&t=KJV.
5. Seekins, p. 217.
6. In the second chapter of Daniel, we read about the coming of the Messiah as revealed in a dream to King Nebuchadnezzar: *"In your vision, Your Majesty, you saw standing before you a huge, shining statue of a man. It was a frightening sight. The head of the statue was made of fine gold. Its chest and arms were silver, its belly and thighs were bronze, its legs were iron, and its feet were a combination of iron and baked clay. As you watched, a rock was cut from a mountain, but not by human hands. It struck the feet of iron and clay, smashing them to bits. The whole statue was crushed into small pieces of iron, clay, bronze, silver, and gold. Then the wind blew them away without a trace, like chaff on a threshing floor.* ***But the rock that knocked the statue down became a great mountain that covered the whole earth"*** (Dan. 2:31-35 NLT emphasis mine).

   When Daniel interpreted Nebuchadnezzar's dream, he was prophesying the time of the Messiah, the coming of the King of the Jews. Jesus is that King, that rock cut *"without hands from a mountain. It struck the feet of iron and clay, smashing them to bits"* (Dan.2:34 KJV/NLT). Jesus, on the cross, has ushered in God's Kingdom of light and has smashed all the ungodly and Babylonian systems vying for control of the world. Jesus is the Rock that has struck the ungodly governments. At His coming *"the iron and the earth, the brass and the silver and the gold, were smashed together, and became like the chaff on the floors where grain is crushed in summer; and the wind took them away so that no sign of them was to be seen"* (Dan.2:35a KJV/BBE; emphasis mine). The powerful wind of the Spirit drives their chaff away.

When the rubbish is blown away, the kingdom of God is set up, and *"the stone which gave the image a blow* ***became a great mountain, covering all the earth"*** (Dan. 2:35b BBE). At the time of the destruction of these ungodly kingdoms, *"the God of heaven will establish a kingdom that will never be destroyed. No other people will be permitted to rule it. It will smash all the other kingdoms and put an end to them. But it will be established forever"* (Dan.2:44 GOD'S WORD).

The focus of the Lord is not on the nations represented by the head of gold, the chest of silver, etc. Ever since the Cross, God's focus has been on His kingdom. Jesus is the Rock of God. All these empires were struck by the Rock of God. Ever since then that Rock has grown into a mountain that will cover the whole earth. People who teach that a one-world government will rise and take over the world are trying to resurrect chaff. It won't happen. Daniel prophecies, "The God of heaven set up a kingdom, which shall never be destroyed; no one will ever conquer it. It will never be superseded" (Dan. 2:44 KJV/TLB/Knox). It is not the antichrist's one-world government that will cover the earth; it is the Kingdom of God and His "Rock," Jesus the Messiah. More on this is teaching is covered in the 6th Book of God's Heart of War, *The War Horses of God.*

7. Retrieved at http://www.blueletterbible.org/lang/lexicon/lexicon.cfm?Strongs=H4941&t=KJV.
8. Seekins, pp. 60-61.
9. Seekins, p. 93.
10. Seekins, p. 77.
11. Seekins, p. 45.

CONCLUSION

We Won't Stop Singing Until Every Enemy Is Made a Footstool for Jesus' Feet

So there you have some of the War Songs of God. Songs the Lord wants to sing against the devil and his host of darkness. Songs declaring their doom, defeat, and destruction by the grace and power of our God. We covered only seven of the War Songs of God in this book. There are over 20 burdens, War Songs, left for us to cover that are in the Word of God. We have only scratched the surface. My plan is to cover these other 20 burdens in the next book of the *God's Heart of War Series: The Lock and Load Prophecies of God.*

I would like to conclude with a few examples of some possible lyrics that could be put to music to make a war song. These are just the bare bones of the principles of God's truth. Ask the Lord for His help to give you what and how He wants you to sing His word-weapons. Put these prophetic words into music so the Body of Christ can sing them over the nations. See God's fire and glory fall! See all the nations dancing and rejoicing before Him. We'll not stop singing until every enemy is made a footstool for the feet of Jesus (Psa. 110:1).

AGAINST VIOLENCE
THE WAR SONGS OF HABAKKUK

As the Wild Stag of God against hamas, the demon of violence, we sing:

Justice will catch up with you,
you will be shaken, and you will tremble.

You will be the victim, no longer the victor;
you will get what you deserve.

The Holy Spirit will 'haunt' the home of the violent man
until he repents of his violence.

The foundation of your demonic house will be ruined,
your house will fall.

The voice of the Holy Ghost will be heard
and your wrong will be exposed.

You'll weary yourself in the work of the flesh.
It will all be turned into ashes.

All your work will accomplish only weariness
and produce nothing,

The Lord's glory like a flood will wash it all away,

His glory will cover the earth as the waters cover the sea.

Your sin and your wickedness will be exposed for all to see.

Shame, disgrace, and vomit will cover your so-called glory.

You will reap the violence you have sown.

You will be terrified and you will be cut down.

Anyone who follows your path of violence
will reap and be overcome with violence.

As this War Song is sung the warriors of God
will be transformed into His Wild Stag.

They shall tread and trample over all the demonic
high places of violence set before them.

They shall overcome by God's songs!

AGAINST SORCERY AND SEDUCTION THE WAR SONGS OF MICAH AND NAHUM

The two-fold Breaker Anointing against the demons of sorcery and seduction. The Breaker Anointing of God's Wild Ox and Roaring Lion is needed to drive these evil forces back to their doom and destruction.

We sing against sorcery and seduction that:

The Lord God Himself is against you.

With an overflowing flood the Lord will make an end of you.

Darkness will pursue His enemies.

God will stop you with one blow;
He won't need to strike again.

He will break your chains and set His children free.

He will bury sorcery and seduction in a
grave of manure, for they stink of sin.

The Breaker, the Messiah will come
and how glorious are the feet of those
who proclaim His coming!

Those who proclaim the gospel become part of
the burial crew who get to bury the evil one.

Belial, the wicked counselor, will never pass through
God's people again;
he is utterly annihilated.

Blessed are those who proclaim peace,
who say to Zion, 'Your God reigns!'

He will bare His holy arm and all the nations
will see the salvation of our God!

Sing to the demons, get out of here, get up
and leave, you are trespassing here.

You have befouled the land and it will vomit you out.

The Breaker is coming and He will break
open the gates of our captivity!

The two-fold Breaker anointing shall be released
and God's people will be His Wild Ox and Lion!

As His Wild Ox, no sorcery, no enchantment
shall prevail against God's children.

No witchcraft, sorcery, or curse can be placed on Jacob;
No magic shall be done against him.

The Lord shall roar from Zion
and shatter the demonic hold of seduction on his people.

They shall be set free and return to the Lord their God.

God shall cut off all the sorceries,
all the witchcraft from our land.

There will be no more soothsayers, no more magicians.

God will destroy all the Asherah poles,
all the phallic symbols from off our land.

People will come trembling out of their
demonic strongholds and return to the Lord!

The Lord says, "I am against you
spirits of sorcery and seduction."

I will expose your wickedness.
The entire world shall see how vile you are,
and I will cover you with excrement as your garment.

Silence the songs of witchcraft
by singing God's songs of war.

About God's War Horse
The War Songs of Zechariah

Sing the War Song of God
against His enemies (like the Philistines)

They repent and become leaders in His family of Praise.

Release the transforming power of our God on the earth!

Release the presence of the Lord.

He encamps around us as our Shield and Protector.

He will guard us and no oppressor
will overrun and hurt His people again.

Dance the War Dance of God
releasing His power and glory.

Shout the War Cry of God and silence the lies
and false accusations of the evil one.

Sing, shout, and dance to usher in
the Warrior King in our midst!

Come out of your waterless pit, all you prophets
and proclaim the Word of the Lord.

Shoot the War Bow and Arrows of the Lord
into the camp of the wicked,

and let His glory fly on
His arrows of fire land in their midst.

Be the Sword in His hand to break the
chains of slavery and bondage.

Destroy that spirit of sex trade in the world,
and let God's love and mercy shine.

Jesus sound Your War Horn!

Sound Your Shofar and see the walls
of those demonic strongholds fall!

Loose the War Sling of God.

Fling the Rock of God's name
into the camp of the wicked.

Declare the name of our God against all
the giants in the land and see them fall.

Drink of the War Wine of the Lord
get drunk on His Holy Spirit.

As drunken warriors, we will never feel
the blows of the evil one.

Wave His War Flags giving signals and directions
to God's warriors in the battle of warfare worship.

Wave the War Flags for God to pour out
His divine power and anointing upon His people.

When we manifest God's love and character on the
earth; we come fully into His calling and destiny.

Sing, shout and dance to usher in the War King,
and He will transform us into His War Horse.

As the War Horse of God we laugh at fear
and race towards the sounds of battle.

Jesus will ride His War Horse into
the battle, and He shall overcome.

As His War Horse we are changed into
His leaders and bring heaven on the earth.

His will is done here as it is done in heaven.

We bring heaven on earth.

As we become His Drunken Warriors,
our children will see it and dance with us!

Sing for God's War Horses to appear
and know that the fall of Babylon is near.

For Israel, God's Soaring Eagle
The War Song of Zechariah

Lord, release the revelation that Jesus is the Messiah!

Sing to Israel to become the soaring eagle and fire of God.

Sing over Israel the anointing of God
so the weakest will be like David

and the house of David like God!

The weakest will be like David and thousands of them
will cover the earth looking for giants to kill.

Sing for the Lord to pour out His Spirit of Grace
and prayer over Israel
so they will see that Jesus is the Messiah.

They will mourn for Him as the firstborn son,
Who was pierced for them.

Sing for the Lord to open up His fountain
for cleansing of our sins.

Sing for the Lord to cut off all the names of the idols,

The false gods, the demons will all fall
by the hand of the Lord.

Sing the War Song that Israel will join in worship
of the Father with Assyria and Egypt.

These three age-old enemies will become allies
and a blessing to all the earth.

Sing for God's peace
to fall on the Middle East.

AGAINST THE DEMON OF COVENANT BREAKING
THE WAR SONGS OF MALACHI

Sing the War Songs of God's Dancing Calves
against the demon of division and covenant breaking.

Sing that believers may be one,
and the world will know Jesus.

Sing for the release of God's Messenger bringing
His soap and fire to cleanse His people.

Sing for the restoration of God's statutes
to restore order in the land.

Sing for the revelation of tithing
to protect and restore our homes.

Sing for the Lord to rebuke the Devourer
and pour out His blessings on us.

There will be so many blessings we will
not be able to contain them all.

Sing for tithing to reverse the curse and
we will be called the 'Happy Nation.'

Sing for the work of God's furnace to
make us pure and complete in Him.

Sing for the anointing of the dancing calves to fall on us.

As we dance, we are treading on
the heads of our enemies.

Dance to reverse the curse,
the devil is now the dust, and we are the victors.

Everybody dance now!

Sing for the spirit of Elijah to come
and restore the hearts of our families.

Elijah makes the road smooth
and prepares the way for the Lord to appear.

Sing for the spirit of Elijah to release
a father's heart over our homes.

APPENDIX A

List of Bible Translations and Abbreviations

Throughout this book, I have used wording from many translations, combining them for clearer understanding. I have denoted all the versions used following each reference, even though it may only have been a few words. Many people paraphrase scripture, and some may criticize my approach as trying to manipulate words or make the verses say what I want them to say to back up my concepts.

Nothing could be further from the truth. I honor God's Word. I appreciate the thought and labor that has gone into each translation—knowing that every word was painstakingly considered, compared, and thoughtfully chosen. It is this respect that drives me to be so careful in citing source material. The list below is my best effort to provide accurate copyright information and give proper credit to publishers and authors alike. I invite you to look into these resources and study them for yourself. The richness of the language of the Bible is a beautiful thing!

James M. Massa
July, 2013

- **AAT – An American Translation**
  Portions of scripture taken from *The Holy Bible in the Language of Today, AN AMERICAN TRANSLATION* are marked AAT. William F. Beck. Copyright © by William F. Beck. A.J. Holman Company. Philadelphia, PA,

- **AB – Aramaic Bible**
  Portions of scripture taken from the *Aramaic Bible* are marked AB. Vic Alexander. Burbank, CA. Retrieved at: http://www.v-a.com/bible.

- **AEB – (2001 Translation) An American English Bible**
  Portions of scripture taken from *An American English Bible* are marked AEB. Jim Wheeler, Editor. Retrieved at: http://www.2001translation.com.

- **AMP – Amplifed® Bible**
  Portions of scripture taken from the *Amplifed® Bible* are marked AMP. Copyright © 1954, 1958, 1962, 1964, 1965, 1987 by The Lockman Foundation. Used by permission. www.lockman.org

- **ARTB – Ancient Roots Translinear Bible**
  Portions of scripture taken from the *Ancient Roots Translinear Bible* are marked ARTB. A. Francis Werner. Copyright © 2005, 2006. Used by permission of the author."

- **ASV – American Standard Version**
  Portions of scripture taken from the *American Standard Version* are marked ASV. This Bible is in the public domain. © 1901.

- **BBE – The Bible in Basic English**
  Portions of scripture taken from the *The Bible in Basic English* are marked BBE. C. K. Ogden. New York, NY: Cambridge University Press, (© date unavailable).

- **CAB – The Complete Apostles Bible**
  Portions of scripture taken from *The Complete Apostles Bible* are marked CAB. Paul W. Esposito; *The Complete Apostles' Bible.* Paul W. Esposito, ed. Bloomington, IL: Authorhouse, © 2005.

- **CCB – Christian Community Bible 2nd Edition**
  Portions of scripture taken from the *Christian Community Bible 2nd Edition* are marked CCB. Bernardo Hurault © 1988; *Christian Community Bible, 2nd Edition.* Bernardo Hurault. Madrid, Spain: San Pablo Internacional and Editorial Verbo Divino,

- **CEB – Common English Bible**
  Portions of scripture taken from the *Common English Bible* are marked CEB. Copyright © 2011 by Common English Bible. Retrieved from http://www.commonenglishbible.com.

- CEV – ***Contemporary English Version***
  Portions of scripture taken from the *Contemporary English Bible* are marked CEV. Copyright © 1995 by American Bible Society; *The Promise: Contemporary English Version.* Nashville, TN: Thomas Nelson Publishers, 1995.

- **CJB – Complete Jewish Bible**
  Portions of scripture taken from the *Complete Jewish Bible* are marked CEB. Copyright © 1998 by David H. Stern. Jewish New Testament Publications, Inc. Clarksville, MD.

- **CV – Confraternity Version of The Old Testament**
  Portions of scripture taken from the *Confraternity of Christian Doctrine Translation; The Old Testament of the Holy Bible: Confraternity Version* are marked CV. Copyright © 1964 by Joseph A. Grispino. New York, NY: Guild Press.

- **CW – The Clear Word**
  Portions of scripture taken from *The Clear Word* are marked CW. Paraphrased by Jack J. Blanco; Copyright © 2003 by Jack J. Blanco All rights reserved. Hagerstown, MD.

- **Dar – Darby Translation**
  Portions of scripture taken from the *Darby Translation* are marked Dar. This Bible is in the public domain.

- **DRB – Douay-Rheims 1899 American Edition.**
  Portions of scripture taken from the *Douay-Rheims © 1899 American Edition* are marked DRB. This Bible is in the public domain.

- **ERV – Holy Bible: Easy-to-Read Version™**
  Portions of scripture taken from the *Holy Bible: Easy to Read Version™* are marked ERV. Copyright © 2006 by World Bible Translation Center, Inc. and used by permission.

- **ESV – English Standard Version**
  Portions of scripture taken from the *English Standard Version* are marked ESV. Copyright © 2001 by Crossway Bibles, a division of Good News Publishers. Used by permission. All rights reserved.

- **EXB – The Expanded Bible**
  Portions of scripture taken from *The Expanded Bible* are marked EXB. Copyright © 2011 by Thomas Nelson, Inc. Used by permission. All rights reserved.

- **GNB – Good News Bible**
  (also known as Today's English Version – TEV)
  Portions of scripture taken from the *Good News Bible: The Bible in Today's English Version* are marked GNB. Copyright © 1976 by the American Bible Society. New York, NY.

- **GNT – Good News Translation**
  Portions of scripture taken from the *Good News Translation, Second Edition, Today's English Version* are marked GNT.

- **GOD'S WORD – God's Word Translation**
  Portions of scripture taken from *God's Word Translation* are marked GOD'S WORD. GOD'S WORD is a copyrighted work of God's Word to the Nations Bible Society. Quotations are used by permission.

- **HCSB – Holman Cristian Standard Bible**
  Portions of scripture taken from the *Holman Christian Standard Bible* are marked HCSB.

- **HNV – Hebrew Names Version**
  (also known as World English Bible – WEB)
  Portions of scripture taken from the *Hebrew Names Version* are marked HNV. This Bible is in the public domain.

- **ISR – The Scriptures**
  Portions of scripture taken from *The Scriptures* are marked ISR.

- **JB – The Jerusalem Bible**
  Portions of scripture taken from *The Jerusalem Bible* are marked JB. The Jerusalem Bible. Alexander Jones, General Editor.

- **KJV – King James Version**
  Portions of scripture taken from the *King James Version* are marked KJV. Originally published in 1611, this Bible is in the public domain.

- **Knox – Knox Bible: The Holy Bible, A Translation from the Latin Vulgate in the light of the Hebrew and Greek Originals**
  Portions of scripture taken from the *Knox Bible* are marked Knox. Monsignor Ronald Knox. Copyright © 1961 by Burns and Oates, London, England. Copyright pertains to all countries which are signatories to the Berne Convention.

- **LEB – Lexham® English Bible**
  Portions of scripture taken from the *Lexham English Bible* are marked LEB. Copyright © 2012 by Logos Bible Software. Lexham is a registered trademark of Logos Bible Software.

- **MLB – The Modern Language Bible**
  Portions of scripture taken from *The Modern Language Bible i*are marked MLB. The New Berkeley Version. Gerrit Verkuyl, Editor-in-Chief. Copyright © 1945, 1959, 1969, 1971 by Zondervan Publishing House. Grand Rapids, MI.

- **Mof – A New Translation of the Bible**
  Portions of scripture taken from *A New Translation of the Bible* are marked Mof. James A. Moffatt, Editor. Copyright © 1972 Harper & Row Publishers New York, NY.

- **MRB – The Modern Reader's Bible**
  Portions of scripture taken from *The Modern Reader's Bible* are marked MRB. Richard G. Moulton Copyright © 1895, 1896, 1897, 1898, 1899, 1907, 1923, 924, 1925, 1926, 1927, and 1935. by Macmillan Co. New York, NY.

- **MSG – The Message**
  Portions of scripture taken from the *THE MESSAGE* are marked MSG. by Eugene H. Peterson. Copyright © 1993, 1994, 1995, 1996, 2000, 2001, 2002. Used by permission of NavPress Publishing Group.

- **NAB – New American Bible**
  Portions of scripture taken from the *New American Bible* are marked NAB. The text of the *New American Bible* is reproduced by license of Confraternity of Christian Doctrine, Washington, D.C.; the owner of said Bible. Copyright © 1970 by P.J. Kenedy & Sons, New York, NY. All rights reserved.

- **NASB – New American Standard Bible**
  Portions of scripture taken from the *New American Standard Bible* are marked NASB. Copyright © 1960, 1962, 1963, 1968, 1971, 1972, 1973, 1975, 1977, 1995 by The Lockman Foundation. Used by permission.

- **NCV – New Century Version**
  Portions of scripture taken from the *The Holy Bible, New Century Version®* are marked NCV. Copyright © 1987, 1988, 1991, by Word Publishing, Dallas, TX. Used by permission.

- **NEB – The New English Bible**
  Portions of scripture taken from *The New English Bible* are marked NEB. Donald Ebor, Chairman. Copyright © 1974 by Cambridge University Press. Oxford, England.

- **NET – New English Translation**
  Portions of scripture taken from the *New English Translation (The NET Bible®)*are designated NET. Scripture quoted by permission. Copyright © 1996-2006 by Biblical Studies Press. All rights reserved.

- **NETS – New English Translation of the Septuagint**

- **NIRV – New International Reader's Version**

- **NIV – New International Version**

- **NIVUK – New International Version: UK**

- **NJB – New Jerusalem Bible**

- **NKJV – New King James Version**
  Portions of scripture taken from the *New King James Version* are marked NKJV. Copyright © 1979, 1980, 1982 by Thomas Nelson, Inc. Used by permission. All rights reserved.

- **NLT – New Living Translation**
  Portions of scripture taken from *The Holy Bible, New Living Translation* are marked NLT. Copyright © 1996. Used by permission by Tyndale House Publishers, Inc., Wheaton, IL. All rights reserved.

- **NLV – New Life Version**
  Portions of scripture taken from the *Holy Bible, New Life Version* are marked NLV. Copyright © 1969 – 2003 by Christian Literature International, Canby, OR. Used by permission.

- **NRSV – New Revised Standard Version**
  Portions of scripture taken from the *New Revised Version Bible* are marked NRSV. Copyright © 1989 the Division of Christian Education of the National Council of the Churches of Christ in the United States of America. Used by permission. All rights reserved.

- **NTPE – The New Testament: A New Translation in Plain English**
  Portions of scripture taken from *The New Testament: A New Translation in Plain English* are marked NTPE. Charles Kingsley Williams. Copyright © 1952 by Longman, Green & Co, University Press, Cambridge.

- **OJB – Orthodox Jewish Bible**
  Portions of scripture taken from the *Orthodox Jewish Bible* are marked OJB. Copyright © 2002, 2003, 2008, 2010 by Artists for Israel International. All rights reserved.

- **Phi – Four Prophets Amos, Hosea, First Isaiah, Micah: A Modern Translation from the Hebrew**
  Portions of scripture taken from the *Four Prophets Amos, Hosea, First Isaiah: Micah: A Modern Translation from Hebrew* are marked Phi. J. B. Phillips. Copyright © 1963 by The Macmillan Company. New York, NY.

- **REB – The Revised English Bible**
  Portions of scripture taken from *The Revised English Bible* are marked REB. Copyright © 1989. Revision of the New English Bible Oxford, Cambridge Press.

- **Rhm – The Emphasized Bible**
  Portions of scripture taken from *The Emphasized Bible* are marked Rhm. Joseph Bryant Rotherham. Copyright © 1959, 1994 by Kregel Publications. Grand Rapids, MI.

- **RSV – Revised Standard Version**
  Portions of scripture taken from the *Revised Standard Version* are marked RSV. Copyright © 1946, 1952, and 1971 by the Division of Christian Education of the National Council of the Churches of Christ in the United States of America. Used by permission All rights reserved;

- **Sept – The Holy Bible from the Greek (Septuagint)**
  Portions of scripture taken from *The Holy Bible from the Greek (Septuagint)* are marked Sept. Charles Thompson, J. Aitken, PA. Retrieved at: http://thetencommandmentsministry.us/ministry/charlesthompson_thompson.

- **TLB – The Living Bible**
  Portions of scripture taken from *The Living Bible* are marked TLB. Kenneth N. Taylor. Copyright © 1971. Used by permission of Tyndale House Publishers, Inc., Wheaton, IL. All rights reserved.

- **TNIV – Today's New International Version**
  Portions of scripture taken from *Today's New International Version®* are marked TNIV. Copyright © 2001, 2005 by International Bible Society®. All rights reserved.

- **Voice – The Voice Bible**
  Portions of scripture taken from *The Voice™ Bible* are marked Voice. Copyright © 2012 by Thomas Nelson, Inc. Ecclesia Bible Society.

- **WEB – World English Bible**
  Portions of scripture taken from the *World English Bible™* are marked WEB. This Bible is in the public domain.

- **Wuest – The New Testament an Expanded Version**
  Portions of scripture taken from *The New Testament an Expanded Version* are marked Wuest. Kenneth S. Wuest. Copyright © 2012 by William B. Eerdmans Publishing Company. Grand Rapids, MI.

- **WYC – Wycliff Bible**
  Portions of scripture taken from the *Wycliff Bible* are marked WYC. Copyright © 2001 by Terence P. Noble. Retrieved at http://www.ibiblio.org.

- **YLT – Young's Literal Translation**
  Portions of scripture taken from the *Young's Literal Translation* are marked YLT. This Bible is in the public domain.

APPENDIX B

List of the Burdens (Massa) of the Lord

Here is a list of the burdens of the Lord in the Bible that were given as prophetic words or songs to God's prophets. Most of the time the word is against a city or nation. But we look at these burdens with New Covenant eyes, because we know that our battle is not against flesh and blood. Instead, these words proclaim God's doom, defeat and destruction against the principalities and powers operating in the high places of that city or country.

1. **2 Kings 9:25:** Against Ahab, Jezebel, and their children. This is when Jehu kills Jehoram, the son of Ahab, and Jehu reminds his captain, *"remember how you and I were riding together in chariots behind Ahab his father when the Lord made this prophecy ('burden' in KJV) about him"* (NIV). He is referring to the prophecy of doom that Elijah gave years earlier in 1 Kings 21:17-29 against Ahab and his family. Jehu calls this prophecy a burden, a massa.

2. **1 Chronicles 15:22-27:** Chenaniah, the singing Priest, leading the people in the Prophetic Songs of God as they march into the city of Jerusalem bearing the Ark of God's Presence.
3. **2 Chronicles 24:27:** Against King Joash of Judah, *"and the greatness of the burdens* (*'curses'* in TLB) *laid upon him"* (KJV). He started off well; he helped restore the Temple. But just like King Solomon, Joash turned his back on God in his later days.
4. **Proverbs 30 (See KJV):** A series of prophecies (massa) given by Agur to warn and instruct Ithiel and Ucal, the waster (Prov. 30:1 Holy Bible in Modern English by Ferrar Fenton).
5. **Proverbs 31:** *"The prophecy (massa) that King Lemuel's mother taught him"* (Prov. 31:1 KJV). Warnings and instructions to King Lemuel by his mother. The focal point is to avoid Wine and the Whore, and find the Wise, Warrior Woman.
6. **Isaiah 13:1-14:23:** Against Babylon and the demonic power behind Babylon, lucifer.
7. **Isaiah 14:24-27:** Against Assyria.
8. **Isaiah 14:28-32:** Against Philistia.
9. **Isaiah 15:1-16:14:** Against Moab.
10. **Isaiah 17:1-18:7:** Against Damascus and Ethiopia.
11. **Isaiah 19:1-20:6:** Against Egypt and Ethiopia.
12. **Isaiah 21:1-10:** Against Babylon (vs. 9 is quoted twice in Revelation).
13. **Isaiah 21:11-12:** Against Edom.
14. **Isaiah 21:13-17:** Against Arabia.

15. **Isaiah 22:1-14:** Against Jerusalem (i.e. "the Valley of Vision").
16. **Isaiah 22:15-25:** This is a possible Messianic reference to Jesus when *"He became sin"* and bore all the wrath of God on the Cross.
17. **Isaiah 23:1-18:** Against Tyre.

    Note: the next 6 chapters in Isaiah are not burdens but they are all about songs and singing. This theme of songs and singing does not stop but still flows forward. It is like the War Songs of God's Wrath come against, overthrow, and silence the Songs of the World:

    - **Chapter 24:** Because of God's judgment there are no more songs or singing in the world (vs. 9), but we do hear "from the ends of the earth we hear singing, 'Glory to the Righteous One'" (vs. 16 TNIV).
    - **Chapter 25 Title:** Song of Praise for God's Favor (NASB).

      "The song of the ruthless is silenced" (vs. 5) but the people of God will celebrate and "sing the joys of His salvation" (vs. 9 MSG).

    - **Chapter 26 Title:** Song of Trust in God's Protection (NASB)

      "In that day this song will be sung in the land of Judah" (vs. 1 TNIV).

    - **Chapter 27:** God will slay the monster of the sea, the Leviathan, with His mighty sword (vs. 1 TNIV). As a result God's people will sing the song of God's Vineyard (vs. 2). They will destroy their idols and Asherah poles and worship the

Lord on the holy mountain in Jerusalem (vs. 9 & 13).

- **Chapter 28:** The prophet prophesies concerning God's gift of tongues to come, this is His rest for them but they refused it (vs. 11-12 with 1 Cor. 14:20-25). In spite of their rejection He stills the ballad-mongers, the mocking songs of the world against Him.
- **Chapter 29:** The deaf will hear and the blind eyes will see (vs. 18). *"The castoffs of society will be laughing and dancing in God, the down-and-o*uts shouting praise to the Holy One of Israel" (vs. 19 MSG).

So you see there is no break in the focus on songs and singing. We pick up where we left off with two more burdens in Isaiah chapter 30.]

18. **Isaiah 30:6-18:** Against the beasts of the Negev (lit. the South). This could refer to the Amalekites. The Negev was their homeland.
19. **Isaiah 30:27-32:** God's burden against Assyria.
20. **Isaiah 46:1-4:** Against Bel and Nebo, Babylon's false gods. They are unable to save themselves from the Wrath of God. Since Jeremiah is called the "Weeping Prophet," Isaiah needs to be called the "Singing Prophet!"
21. **Jeremiah 23: 25-40:** Warning: Don't mock God's Words (massa) of wrath. The word massa is used eight times in just four verses (Jer. 23:33, 34, 36 and 38). But it is used in a different context. Israel had turned their backs to the Lord and His Words of warning. Instead they listened to the words of the

false prophets, and made fun and mocked the true Words of God. Jeremiah concludes with, *"You shall never again mention 'the burden (massa) of the Lord;'* ***that is reserved for the man to whom He entrusts His message"*** (Jer. 23:36 TLB/NEB; emphasis mine).

22. **Ezekiel 12:8-16:** *"This burden concerns the prince of Jerusalem, and all the house of Israel"* (Ezek. 12:10 KJV). By his actions Ezekiel prophesies Israel's coming captivity to Babylon.

23. **Ezekiel 24:25-27:** To the parents of Israel, their children were *"the song (massa) of their soul"* (YLT). This is not a burden per se, but it's interesting to note that the Holy Ghost has Ezekiel use this word (massa) right before he begins to prophesy a series of Dirges (funeral songs) from God against the nations just like Isaiah. (See Ezekiel chapters 25-32 and compare them to Isaiah's list of burdens).

24. **Nahum:** Against the sorcery and seduction in Nineveh the capital of Assyria. Micah is not a burden, but his prophecy goes hand-in-hand with Nahum.

25. **Habakkuk:** Against the demonic spirit of violence in Babylon.

26. **Zechariah 9:1-11:17:** Against Damascus, Tyre, Philistia, and Greece. With Greece, the Lord is coming against their slave and sex trading.

27. **Zechariah 12:1–14:21:** For Israel to see Jesus their Messiah and soar as God's eagles.

28. **Malachi:** Against the 'Covenant–Breakers.' How Jesus, the Messenger of the Covenant, must come with all His tools to restore our broken covenants and return us to God's favor.

In the New Testament:

- Rev. 14:8 Quotes Isa. 21:9 against spiritual Babylon.
- Rev. 18:2 Quotes Isa. 21:9 against spiritual Babylon.

As you can, see there are nearly 30 War Songs in the Old Testament. Study these word weapons, ask God for the music to go with them. Let's proclaim and sing their doom. Let's sing of the victory we have in Jesus over the hordes of hell. Everybody dance now!

MEET THE AUTHOR

JAMES "MARK" MASSA

James M. Massa is a retired Lieutenant Colonel with thirty years in the military—a veteran of both the Vietnam War and the War on Terror. He served six years with the U.S. Marines and 24 years with the U.S. Air Force. His last five years in the Air Force (2008-2012) were spent serving as the Chief Nurse in the 118th Medical Group of the 118th Airlift Wing in Nashville, TN.

Massa's service in the Marines taught him the importance of knowing his weapons and how to fight. His service in the Air Force medical field taught him the importance of knowing how to heal those who were wounded in the fight.

This military background coupled with the Hebrew meaning of his last name (massa/burden) provoked this decades-long study—the result of which you hold in your hands. Mark passionately communicates how God's songs against His enemies are available for our warfare. He wants you to learn how to use these divine WMD's from God's arsenal.

Married to his wife, Sharon, for 34 years, together they have three sons: Mark-Aaron, Seth Josiah and Fredrick (Rick) James (married to Megan). They own a small ranch in Richardsville, KY, caring for four horses, three dogs and two cats.

James & Sharon Massa